The Israeli Third Sector

Between Welfare State and Civil Society

NONPROFIT AND CIVIL SOCIETY STUDIES
An International Multidisciplinary Series

Series Editor: Helmut K. Anheier
*University of California, Los Angeles, California; London School of
Economics and Political Science, London, United Kingdom*

A Continuation Order Plan is available for this series. A continuation order will bring delivery of each new volume immediately upon publication. Volumes are billed only upon actual shipment. For further information please contact the publisher.

The Israeli Third Sector

Between Welfare State and Civil Society

BENJAMIN GIDRON

Ben Gurion University of the Negev
Beer-Sheva, Israel

MICHAL BAR

Hebrew University of Jerusalem
Jerusalem, Israel

HAGAI KATZ

UCLA
Los Angeles, California

KLUWER ACADEMIC / PLENUM PUBLISHERS
NEW YORK, BOSTON, DORDRECHT, LONDON, MOSCOW

Library of Congress Cataloging-in-Publication Data

Gidron, Benjamin.
    The Israeli third sector: between welfare state and civil society / Benjamin Gidron,
    Michal Bar, and Hagai Katz.
        p.   cm. — (Nonprofit and civil society studies)
    Includes bibliographical references and index.
    ISBN 0-306-48028-X – ISBN 0-306-48029-8 (pbk.)

    1. Nonprofit organizations—Israel.   2. Welfare state—Israel.   3. Civil society—Israel.
    I. Bar, Mikhal.   II. Kats, Hagai.   III. Title.   IV. Series.

HD2769.2.175G54 2004
361.7′63′095694—dc22   2003061965

ISBN 0-306-48028-X (hardbound)
       0-306-48029-8 (paperback)

© 2004 by Kluwer Academic/Plenum Publishers, New York
233 Spring Street, New York, New York 10013

http://www.kluweronline.com

10 9 8 7 6 5 4 3 2 1

A C.I.P. record for this book is available from the Library of Congress.

Permissions for books published in Europe: permissions@wkap.nl
Permissions for books published in the United States of America: permissions@wkap.com

Printed in the United States of America

Foreword

The First Directory of Israeli Researchers published a few years ago revealed for the first time that there were 48 researchers from 11 disciplines in 14 different academic institutions in this small Middle Eastern country. It is not surprising, therefore, that with such intellectual resources, Israel can produce year after year social science research of the highest quality such as this first case study of its Third Sector. The three authors, each with an impressive record of highly regarded, sophisticated empirical research were selected to participate in the first of a series of international comparative studies of nonprofit organizations in the mid-1990', directed by Lester M. Salamon, Director of the Center for Civil Society at Johns Hopkins University in the US. This book is an outcome of the analysis of data collected from two main sources: The Hopkins Project and the Israeli Third Sector Database recently developed by the Israeli Center for Third Sector Research at Ben Gurion University of the Negev in Beer-Sheva.

Originally part of an international study involving 40 countries in Europe, Asia, Latin America, and the US, the first results were published in 1999 in *Global Civil Society: Dimensions of the Nonprofit Sector*, edited by Salamon and his associates. It was here that I learned for the first time the extent of the economic importance of the Israeli third sector, the subject of this book. It qualifies as a major industry whose expenditures in 1995 exceeded $11 billion amounting to almost 13% of the country's GDP. This made it one of the largest in the world, not only in relation to the Israeli economy, but also compared to its counterparts in other countries.

As one of the early researchers of the third sector in Israel, I began my initial study there in 1968 when I was on a sabbatical leave from the University of California in Berkeley. At that time, the third sector was usually called the voluntary, nonprofit, independent, or nongovernmental sector. I subsequently returned to Israel almost every year thereafter while I was engaged in what came to be called during the 1970's, third sector research.

During the next two decades, I continued to be impressed by the enormous expansion in the scope and content of the social services, health and education systems in Israel. Indeed, the 1970's and 1980's were often described as a "Golden Age", reflecting the evolution of the Israeli welfare state which, together with the increasing number of voluntary associations comprising the civil society is the subject of this book.

Described as "The Two Faces of the Israeli Third Sector," the authors develop an original, dual approach to the social welfare policy and organizational (bureaucratic and associational) aspects of the Israeli third sector. In the process, they share their extensive and sophisticated understanding of the unique organizational culture of Israel and the pluralism that characterizes it today. The reader will learn much about the socio-political context of the Israeli third sector, and can benefit from the scholarship and lifelong experience of the authors as perceptive insiders and observers of Israeli society.

Ralph M. Kramer
Professor Emeritus
University of California at Berkeley

Preface

This book provides the non-Hebrew reader with a look into the Israeli third/nonprofit sector for the first time. While voluntary, nonprofit organizations have a long history and deep roots within Israeli society and have played an important role in its development, knowledge about these organizations is sparse. This is clearly demonstrated in the many books and articles that deal with Israeli society and/or its political system, but ignore the third sector as a social, political, and economic factor. This situation can be explained by the lack, thus far, of appropriate conceptual tools to analyze the third sector and its components, a problem that many other countries and societies share. However, this issue has begun to change over the past decade as interest in the third sector worldwide has grown and a developing literature on the subject has emerged. These changes enabled us to undertake comprehensive and multi-faceted analyses of the Israeli third sector based on empirical data, which are the first ever to be collected on the Israeli third sector. These analyses provide the reader with a macro view of the sector, its key characteristics as they have developed throughout history, and the sector's relationship to other societal institutions.

This book is not merely a description of the Israeli third sector, however. It goes a step further and anchors the data in two major concepts that are very much in the public limelight worldwide—namely, the welfare state and civil society. In Israel, as in most countries, the development of the third sector coincided with a trend to cut public funding and the provision of social services within the welfare state system. It also intersected with the debate over the "space" between the public and the private arenas and the increased participation of various groups and populations in shaping and impacting that "space."

Finally, this book uses existing theoretical formulations on the third sector to test the Israeli case. While Israel clearly shares certain similarities with other countries (mostly those of continental Europe), its history, demography, links to the Jewish Diaspora, and politics have created unique features that make it impossible to fit the country neatly into existing third sector theories. This is particularly true of the social origins theory (Salamon and Anheier, 1998). Thus, we used a modified and enlarged version of the social origins theory to fit the Israeli case—an exercise that could be employed in analyzing other countries and thus strengthen the theory. Likewise, this approach shows how several theories that are currently used to examine Israeli society could be strengthened by the introduction of conceptual frameworks developed to analyze the third sector.

In practical terms, this book is a product of two processes that nearly coincided. The first was the *Comparative Project of the Nonprofit Sector* conducted by the Center for Civil Society at Johns Hopkins University, in which the nonprofit sectors of over 30 countries were analyzed during the 1990s; Israel joined the project in 1996. Through the course of the Hopkins Project, an international operational definition of nonprofit organizations was established that enabled the comparative measurement of nonprofit sectors and sparked public debate on the issue. The second was the establishment of *The Israeli Center for Third Sector Research (ICTR)* at Ben Gurion University of the Negev in 1997. ICTR, which also housed the Hopkins Project, established the infrastructure for this new and fascinating area of research in Israel and created a framework for researchers of all disciplines and academic institutions to obtain knowledge of the Israeli third sector. The development of the Israeli Third Sector Database within ICTR in 1998 enabled us to undertake many of the analyses presented in this book. The authors of this book were deeply involved in both of these processes; therefore, this book in a product of the insight on the Israeli third sector that we gained in structuring this new research area, which encompasses several academic disciplines.

Many people were involved in the writing of this book from conceptualizing, gathering, and analyzing the data; developing the organizational infrastructure for the data; and providing input into, translating, and editing the manuscript. We would like to thank them all. In particular, we offer thanks to Professors Lester Salamon and Helmut Anheier, directors of the Hopkins Project, who laid the intellectual infrastructure for the study on the third sector internationally and helped, each in his own way, in its implementation in Israel; Professor Joel Fleishman, who has worked and continues to work tirelessly to develop knowledge on the third sector in Israel and other countries; Dr. Hadara Bar-Mor, Rivka Duchin, Professor Joseph Katan, Dr. Alon Lazar, Dr. Ze'ev Rosenhek, Professor Shmuel Shye, Dr. Ilana Silber, and Motti Telias, who studied the different aspects of the Israeli third sector within the Hopkins Project; Ben Gurion University (BGU) President, Professor Avishay Braverman, and the former and current BGU Rectors, Professors Nahum Finger and Jimmy Weinblatt, for their continued support for the development of research on the third sector at BGU; the foundations that funded the Hopkins Project in Israel and their directors, Ariel Weiss of Yad Hanadiv Foundation and Shira Herzog of The Kaganoff Foundation, for their trust, interest, and support; the Fulbright Foundation that funded Professor Gidron's leave of absence in 2000–2001, which was used primarily for writing the manuscript, and

Professors Yeheskel (Zeke) Hasenfeld and Barbara Nelson of the UCLA School of Public Policy, who served as perfect hosts and supporters during that period; those who provided the data: Nava Brenner from the Central Bureau of Statistics, Amiram Bogat from the Registrar of Associations, and Beatrice Almog and Zvi Halamish from the Ministry of Finance; the translator of the book, Yaffa Murciano, and its editor, Rena Hasenfeld; and last, but not least, the very devoted ICTR administrative assistants: Smadar Kra-Moreno, Efrat Nativ-Ronen, Efrat Keynan, and Maggi Levy, who steered, directed (and if need be redirected), and pushed—always in good humor—all administrative matters and did not stop until the task was completed.

Contents

Chapter 1

Introduction

On an almost daily basis, readers of Israeli newspapers come across the concept of "Amutot" (associations or nonprofit organizations) in many different contexts. Sometimes the reporting is negative. For instance, the papers may describe the abuses, fraud, or scandals in which "political associations" are involved. On the other hand, the reporting can also be positive, as when entrepreneurs initiate new associations to deal with specific populations or problems. Examples of such Amutot include one that provides "bridging" services to immigrants from Ethiopia to help them navigate the social service system, or another that uses horses to rehabilitate handicapped persons. The newspapers also report on Amutot engaged in social and political change, such as pushing to initiate a constitution for Israel, advocating for a different policy towards the Palestinians, or protecting the environment. Finally Amutot are featured as an underlying concept in the discussion surrounding the funding of the ultra-religious educational system.

Israeli newspaper readers also read articles about the larger sector, as a whole, of which the Amutot are a part. Lately, more and more articles have been published on the implications of privatizing social services and the trend toward using for-profit and nonprofit organizations to provide such services, primarily in the fields of welfare, education, and health. Furthermore, in public disputes on the nature of Israeli democracy, issues regarding public participation in civil society and the exclusion of certain population groups have led many writers to probe into the patterns of associations among those populations. Thus, nonprofit organizations in Israel are active and involved in a wide variety of issues and use different strategies to pursue their objectives. Furthermore, a review of Israeli history shows that third sector organizations, designated by different terms and names, played a major role in society's development and, as we will show, changed their roles to accommodate the social and political changes that Israeli society was experiencing.

Despite this interest in what we have termed, "the third sector," and the many important and diverse roles that nonprofit organizations fill, thus far there has been little interest among researchers or policymakers in the sector as a distinct concept. The delineation of sectors has been rather ambiguous in Israel; therefore, the concept of a third sector, with clear-cut, distinct societal roles and functions, does not exist (Gidron, 1992). Indeed, most Israelis have difficulty grasping the idea of a single sector that encompasses very diverse organizations, including large service-provision bureaucracies (such as universities or hospitals), grassroots community-based voluntary organizations, and ultra-orthodox religious educational institutions. For most Israelis, each of these organizations is associated with different aspects of society that ostensibly do not "mesh" together.

The recent interest in nonprofit organizations and related issues (e.g., philanthropy, volunteering), on the one hand, and the lack of appropriate conceptual and empirical knowledge of the subject, on the other, is by no means unique to Israel. This situation can be found in most countries where the sector has grown significantly in size and importance without the relevant frameworks to understand and guide the research. Thus the developments in Israel are part of a global phenomenon, which Salamon (1994) terms, "the associational revolution." He identifies five factors that simultaneously have contributed to the increase in these organizations, their scope of activity, and the public interest in them. Some of these factors pertain to specific regions of the world, such as formerly Communist countries or Latin America, but two of them are clearly relevant to Israel. These are: (1) a diminishing confidence in the public sector's ability to direct welfare policy in Western countries, and (2) the growth of social movements in areas such as women's, environmental, and human rights that is manifested in thousands of third sector organizations. These two factors have brought about a very significant increase in the number of nonprofit organizations in Israel, especially in the past two decades.

The welfare state crisis and the privatization of public services, which began in Israel in the 1980s and accelerated significantly in the 1990s, brought about the establishment of thousands of new service-providing associations. At the same time, the older organizations expanded their activities. In many cases these associations replaced or complemented educational, welfare, and health services that the state previously provided. Though nonprofit organizations in Israel historically played a crucial role as service providers even prior to the welfare state crisis, over the past two decades the government has intentionally transferred the responsibility for certain services to private organizations, both for-profit and nonprofit, and has initiated new ones that are at least partially funded by the public purse. The reason for this change is the ostensibly higher efficiency of private organizations and their ability to attract funds from additional sources. Thus, for example, parents' associations have replaced public schools' informal education services; women's associations have opened shelters for abused women and rape victims; and health associations have come to care for cancer, AIDS, Alzheimer's, and MS patients and their families.

At the same time, the global increase in social movements has led to the establishment of hundreds of associations in Israel that are concerned with social change. These organizations attempt to bring about changes in their particular area of interest; usually this also involves a change in concept, often with political implications. These associations deal with numerous and diverse issues, such as changes in the electoral system, foreign workers' rights, the environment, social justice, equal rights for Arabs, etc. In addition, a third type of association has developed in Israel: members' associations. These organizations either focus on a particular area of interest, such as butterfly collections, triathlon races, or early music, or may be self-help groups that deal with life-experiences, such as obesity, alcoholism, parenting a disabled child, etc. Unlike many of the service-providing organizations in Israel, these groups are not established to replace or complement government or business sector activities. Additionally, these groups do not exist to criticize or challenge existing policies, rather they concentrate on a specific activity that is of interest to their members.

All of these organizations belong to one category, legally termed, "nonprofit organizations."[1] This category of organizations is different and separate from the business sector, which includes profit-making organizations, and from the public sector (on the national and municipal levels), which includes organizations established by laws or regulations. However, like the business and public sectors, which include all business or public organizations within a specific country, the nonprofit or third sector includes all nonprofit organizations within a single comprehensive framework.

DEFINING THE THIRD SECTOR

This definition of the third sector assumes that it is easy to distinguish between organizations from different sectors in Israel. This is perhaps the case for business or public organizations, which have distinctive characteristics, but the situation for third sector organizations is much more complex. As we shall see, for both historical and political reasons, nonprofit organizations in Israel developed primarily in conjunction with and in close proximity to the public sector. Thus, the third sector is considered a residual sector that includes those organizations that do not fall into the public or business sectors. Yet almost all democratic countries have laws that recognize and distinguish nonprofit organizations. These organizations have a defined status, which sometimes includes tax exemption, have a unique identity, and perform special social functions. This is the case in Israel, which actually has three separate laws for incorporating different types of nonprofit organizations (i.e., associations, nonprofit companies, and foundations) and has developed over the years an extensive system of public financial support for nonprofit organizations. Nevertheless, these laws do not clarify the blurred lines that exist between the sectors, particularly the public and third sectors. Certain institutions that were considered "national" institutions in the pre-state era did not disappear with the establishment of the state, but instead acquired new roles and changed their orientations. They continued to exist in that borderline area between the public and the third sectors, with a special legal status that accentuates this hybrid form. The Jewish Agency and the health funds (i.e., health insurance schemes) are primary examples of such cases.

While all democracies have a "third sector," they are not necessarily comprised of the same types of organizations, a fact that enables us to differentiate between countries. To overcome these differences, Salamon and Anheier (1997) developed an international definition of the types of organizations that comprise the third sector through their work on The Hopkins Project, an international study of nonprofit sectors. This definition includes the following five conditions: the organization must: (1) be a formal organization, (2) be separate from the state, (3) not distribute profits, (4) have independent governing mechanisms, and (5) have philanthropic and/or voluntary inputs. Since those Israeli organizations that are legally defined as "nonprofit" meet all five of these criteria, the Israeli third sector can be defined, by and large, as being composed of nonprofit organizations, which include those that are registered as associations, public-benefit organizations, and foundations.[2] This is the operational definition of the third sector that we use in this book and upon which we base our empirical analysis of the third sector in Israel.

Although it appears that this definition would enable us to easily examine different aspects of the third sector, as well as the organization of civil society in Israel, we encountered major obstacles obtaining appropriate data on these organizations because this information is not regularly collected.[3] Given that the major impetus for engaging in this endeavor was the authors' participation in The Johns Hopkins Comparative Nonprofit Sector Project, this was the first time that most of the economic and non-economic data (e.g., legal, historical, policy-oriented data) were comprehensively collected in Israel. This endeavor indirectly brought about the formation of the Israeli Third Sector Database within the Israeli Center for Third Sector Research (ICTR) at Ben Gurion University. The database, which collects data from different government agencies that deal with nonprofit organizations and enables users to combine data from different sources, provides an important source of data in addition to those collected for the Hopkins Project. Thus, major parts of the empirical data outlined in this book are actually presented for the first time.

Although we regard empirical data on the third sector's volume, composition, and funding sources as highly significant, this information alone does not provide a comprehensive picture of the entire sector. Like the business and public sectors, the third sector operates and grows within certain social, political, economic, legal, and cultural contexts. The sector is influenced not only by its history but also by the environment in which it operates and vice versa. The data need to be analyzed within all of these contexts in order to grasp the essence of the third sector in Israel, which is what we attempt to do in this book.

ORIENTATION OF THE BOOK

The recent attention given to the nonprofit sector has brought about interest in another, closely related concept: civil society. This concept dates back much further than the third sector and was first found in the philosophy of Aristotle. Although the two concepts do not overlap, there is of course a link between the third sector and civil society. While the third sector is defined as the sum total of formal nonprofit organizations in a given country—an absolute and quantifiable definition—civil society is usually defined as a sphere of activity that, in addition to formal organizations, includes social networks, informal organizations, and the unorganized activities of individuals.[4] Since the definition of this sphere of activity is even more context-dependent than the third sector (Foley and Edwards, 1998), civil society is all the more difficult to measure. This book does not address the issue of Israeli civil society, as a whole, but rather examines one of its facets—the formal organizations that comprise it.

The third sector and civil society also vary in that they are rooted in different disciplines and theoretical orientations. The third sector is based on an economic discipline and usually uses economic parameters as its measures; civil society has a political/sociological orientation and takes this as its focus. Therefore, although both concepts relate to a similar reality, they "see" a different picture. An economic orientation focuses on the third sector's volume, fields of activity, sources of income, work force, and unique components that are not present in other sectors, such as philanthropy and volunteering. In an era of privatization of public services, understanding these aspects of the third sector, particularly within the welfare state context, is crucial to policymaking processes. A socio-political approach, on the other hand, focuses on citizens' patterns of association and organization, factors that encourage or discourage those patterns, and the relationship and implications of those patterns to the political system and its democratic foundations. These types of data are relevant to the debate on the nature of Israeli democracy, civility, discrimination, and social involvement. Comprehending the differences between these two orientations is crucial to understanding Israeli nonprofit organizations and the character of the third sector, as a whole. Together, these orientations shed light on a fascinating aspect of Israeli society that heretofore has not been examined.

Both orientations serve as the basis for our analysis of the main functions of nonprofit organizations in Israel and in other welfare states: the third sector economic orientation refers first and foremost to the service provision function of third sector organizations and their links to the public service provision system, mostly within welfare states. As such, the focus is on areas in which third sector organizations are active (e.g., welfare, education, health, etc.), the volume of their activity in those fields compared to business and public organizations, their funding sources (e.g., donations, self-generated income, public funding), and the trends and historical developments of these systems (e.g., the process of privatization of public services). The civil society social-political orientation primarily relates to the associational aspects of the third sector. It examines associational patterns and characteristics in society as a whole and among specific population groups. It also examines patterns of relationships between these associations and government, which range from antagonistic to supportive, and the implications of those relationships on society and the polity.

Both of these orientations overlap, more or less, with the third sector's major historical functions in Israel, which include: (1) service provision that complements or replaces the public system in the welfare state context, and (2) a framework for the organization of independent (non-partisan) associations concerned with various issues that their members deem important, including those that challenge the government or the state. Many democratic countries use the nonprofit organizational framework to fill these two social roles. As such, this book is similar to previous studies that have examined this conceptualization of the third sector in other countries (Yamamoto, 1998; Archambault, 1997; Anheier and Seibel, 2001).However, while these two functions are by no means mutually exclusive and a specific organization can fill both, the reliance on third sector organizations in Israel is not a new phenomenon and was only accelerated by the ideology and process of privatization. In fact, for many years an elaborate system of contracts existed between nonprofit organizations and the government, which viewed these organizations as if they were an executive arm, filling the government's policies only using a different organizational framework.

When analyzed from this angle, it is clear that Israeli third sector organizations can be classified along two dimensions: (1) those nonprofit organizations that are integrated into the Israeli welfare state primarily through a system of contracts, function as the government's executive arm, and receive significant public funding; we have designated these organizations as being Integrated within the Welfare State System (IWSS); and (2) those organizations that do not receive government funding but have developed independent funding sources; we have labeled these as Civil Society Organizations (CSOs).[5] This distinction enables us to present empirical data on civil society organizations in Israel as a distinct component of the third sector for the first time and is especially significant for the debate on the role of the third sector in Israel. Thus, these two categories are the central themes along which this book evolves.

THEORETICAL FRAMEWORKS

As previously mentioned, this analysis of the third sector in Israel, affords us an opportunity to analyze Israeli society from a new angle. Since hundreds of publications and theories have been offered to explain Israeli society and its development, our analysis synthesizes theoretical and conceptual literature on both Israeli society, as a whole, and the Israeli third sector/civil society. This integration of knowledge should aid in our understanding of the changing roles of the third sector and its contributions to the evolution of Israeli society. As such, we present here conceptual frameworks that pertain both to the third sector/civil society and to Israeli society, in general. Given the focus of the book, the frameworks we provide are brief and contain references for further reading. The respective applicability of these frameworks is dealt with in the concluding chapter.

The Nonprofit Sector

The major economic theories regarding the nonprofit sector deal with the question: Why does the nonprofit sector exist in society and how can its specific characteristics be explained? Demand-side theories maintain that the failure of either the government (Weisbrod, 1977; 1988) or the market (Hansmann, 1980; 1987) to meet the demand for needed services among specific populations gives rise to the nonprofit organizational form. Supply-side theories argue that ideological entrepreneurs interested in attracting adherents to their ranks form nonprofit organizations that offer welfare or educational services at below market prices together with an ideological indoctrination (James, 1987; 1989). The welfare state and the interdependence theories (Salamon and Anheier, 1998) focus on the relationship between the state and the third sector in the context of welfare service provision. The former explains nonprofit organizations as a residual category, a remnant of the pre-welfare state era. As soon as a society moves into public service provision, these organizations are replaced by public agencies. The latter is based on the notion of voluntary failure and the need to replace voluntary organizations with public agencies. It focuses on modes of cooperation and collaboration between nonprofit organizations and the government as indicators of how government can counter such deficiencies in voluntary organizations. Finally, the theory of social origins of the nonprofit sector (Salamon and Anheier, 1998) suggests that the existence, the size, and the specific characteristics of the nonprofit sector in a given country are a function of that country's history. The complex relationships and power struggles that evolve between the landed elites, the labor unions, and organized religion result in a specific pattern of welfare service provision.

Based on Esping-Andersen's welfare regimes, Salamon and Anheier present four nonprofit regimes that can result from these struggles:

1. Liberal regime—there is hostility towards extensive government involvement in the provision of welfare services and a preference for voluntary frameworks in fulfilling that function. Under these circumstances, the third sector is sizable, primarily based on self-generated income and donations, with limited government involvement. The US and the UK exemplify this pattern.
2. Corporatist regime—the government is forced to form alliances with old elites (some of whom gained power in the pre-modern era) in order to maintain their loyalty and support. As such, the government has to leave certain areas of activity in the hands of third sector organizations that are controlled by those forces. Thus, as public welfare services expand, so too does the third sector, enjoying considerable public funding. France and Germany are examples of this pattern.
3. Social-democratic regime—the working class holds substantial political power and this is manifested in a preference for provision by the state. In these cases a comprehensive system of state welfare service provision is found, with a small third sector that is focused on social and political activity rather than service provision. The Scandinavian countries display this type of pattern.
4. Statist regime—the state holds considerable power, often corresponding to the interests of economic elites or the church, although the state does not control these elites. The working class has a relatively weak status. Consequently, the government adopts a conservative policy with essentially limited involvement in welfare service provision and the third sector due to the conflicts of interest between the state and the capitalists. Japan illustrates this pattern.

These categories help explain differences in size, characteristics, and patterns of funding among nonprofit sectors in different countries. While this theory uses political and historical data to justify its findings, its focus is solely on the welfare service provision function of the third sector, and it uses as its yardsticks the economic size of the third sector or its components, as well as data on the public sector's welfare expenditures.

Civil Society

Theoretical frameworks pertaining to civil society can be difficult to characterize given that the concept has a very long history, is hard to define, and has recently been used in a wide variety of contexts with many different meanings. Nonetheless, in the context of this book, we view civil society as a sphere of activity in society that is different and separate from both the state and the economy, as well as from primary familial relations; it entails the involvement of individuals and collectivities in non-coercive activities, pursuing their own interests or those of society (see Walzer, 1995; Kimmerling, 1995; Cohen, 1995; Dahrendorf, 1997; Anheier, 2000).

The underlying assumptions regarding the existence of civil society and the specific rules that govern such activity are far from universal; in fact, they differ greatly by time and place. As such, it is helpful to operationalize the definition of civil society to reflect changing circumstances. For example, Foley and Edwards (1996) make the distinction between civil society I and II. Civil society I involves activities that challenge the state or government. This type of civil society actually serves as a counterweight to the state, offering an alternative for collective action that is denied by the state. This notion of civil society evolved as a result of the developments in Eastern Europe that eventually led to the end of the Communist regime in the late 1980s. Citizens' groups challenged the regime (e.g., "Solidarity" in Poland), which in turn led to the development of an ideology explaining the roles of such groups in an oppressive regime. Civil society II associations are separate from the state; citizens can organize freely and independently around different issues that do not necessarily counter the state. Such a notion of civil society is obviously characteristic of democratic regimes, which safeguard the freedom of association. While this distinction is clearly useful for comparing civil societies among different countries, it can also serve to distinguish between different types of associations within a specific society: Organizations in civil society I would be those that take an antagonistic stance towards the state or government and are mostly engaged in advocacy or social change; organizations in civil society II would include those that evolve around issues important primarily to their members, such as membership associations, self-help groups, etc. (Foley and Edwards, 1998; Minkoff, 1997).

One of the most important theoretical contributions in the literature on civil society is the concept of social capital developed by Putnam (1993; 2000). Basing his work on De Tocqueville (1959) and Coleman (1990), Putnam emphasizes the indirect contribution of participation in voluntary organizations. He argues that associating in social organizations is the key to social cooperation, as well as the improved functioning of state and economic systems. Such participation creates social capital, which entails values such as trust and cooperation; these in turn are vital for a stable democratic regime. From the citizens' perspective, those who live in a society with deeper social involvement will aspire to create more efficient institutions and be more willing to participate in their establishment. Government, on the other hand, will act more efficiently since its actions are based on civil societies and democratic values, which both citizens and public officials share. Thus, using the concept of "social capital," Putnam links social associations to theories of democracy. When operationalized, this definition focuses not on the economic but the associational aspects of third sector organizations, such as their organizational and leadership patterns, their concentration among specific populations, the degree to which these organizations represent the populations for which they speak or for whom they serve, etc.

Israeli Society

Many social scientists have attempted to explain the evolution of Israeli society with its unique history that includes links to both the Jewish religion and the Jewish people in the Diaspora. Such theories build upon the dramatic events in Israel's history over the last century, including the settlement of the land by the first pioneers, the building of social and political institutions, the Holocaust, mass immigration, the wars and conflicts with neighboring Arab countries, and finally the inner tensions within Israeli society.

In reviewing the vast, mostly sociological literature on the subject, three major schools of thought can be identified. The first is the Jerusalem School, which dominated Israeli sociological literature for many years. S. N. Eisenstadt initiated the first studies on Israeli society at the Hebrew University in the 1950s (see Eisenstadt, 1954; and others) and is clearly the dominant figure among these theorists. Coming from a structural/functional/systemic school of thought, his early writings depict Israeli society as a system in which the state, driven by a dominant ideology of national Zionism, exists at the center. The state is the source of institutional authority, but also of society's values, norms, and symbols, and a focus around which consensus and solidarity are built. This model fits the evolution of Israeli society from a small number of pioneers to a society that integrates new immigrants into a "melting pot," while preserving its basic institutional and cultural structures. The focus is on the unifying elements in society, expressed in the national identity, while other identities (e.g., ethnic, political, or religious) are secondary. Thus, the central Israeli identity is capable of "absorbing" other changing and conflicting identities, without significantly changing the overall structure. In this model, culture (and acculturation) is seen as the major force for social change. Since the predominant culture during the early phase of the state was Jewish and secular, those of other populations (e.g., Arab, religious) were ignored.

The second major sociological school of thought regarding Israeli society is functionalism revisited, propounded primarily by Lissak and Horowitz (1989). This group, writing from the late 1970s onward, was no longer able to ignore the inner tensions and conflicts within Israeli society, but did not use a conflict model to analyze them. Their major model is a system model that went astray: The rifts and conflicts within society are offset by broad common denominators that enable society to exist and function despite the fact that it is simultaneously cohesive and divided. This is explained by the fact that the rifts are not dichotomous but graded. For example, a possible solution to the schism between Jews of European and Middle Eastern descent is indicated by the "inter-marriage" rates between them. The political center is the focus where these conflicts are handled and resolved through negotiation and coalitions.

The third major sociological school of thought in Israel is that of critical sociology (Ram, 1994), which primarily criticizes the functional school of thought that assumes culture and ideas are the driving forces in society. Critical sociology, on the other hand, considers the elite, class relations, group interests, and power to be the major influences on society and its evolution. Furthermore, while the functional school of thought regards the central Jewish state as functional and therefore necessary, the critical school perceives faults in this framework and attempts to change it. Since the second half of the 1980s, several other theories have been derived from the critical sociology school of thought. Elitism (Shapira, 1991; Etzioni-Halevy, 1977) views society as a power struggle between elites. Shapira primarily analyzes the Labor movement as an elite power interested in preserving its hegemony in society. Etzioni-Halevy considers society to be composed of different elites (i.e., economic, religious, political, military) and analyzes relationships among these various factions. Pluralism (Smooha, 1978) views Israeli society as being ethnically layered, with Ashkenazi Jews trying to maintain their dominance over other ethnic groups through paternalistic cooptation (e.g., "immigration absorption") and other socializing mechanisms (with regards to the Sepharadi population) or through military force and economic dependence (with regards to the Arab minority). Marxism (Swirski, 1989) and colonization (Kimmerling, 1983) regard the development of Israeli society in terms of a power struggle based on class or national domination, respectively. According to these frameworks, the closed nature of society for the first thirty years of Israel's existence enabled its leaders to shape institutions so as to preserve their advantages.

ORGANIZATION OF THIS BOOK

Chapter 2 presents extensive data on the Israeli third sector. The first part of the chapter includes general data on its volume, areas of activity, sources and patterns of funding, etc. These are presented in a comparative context that mainly emphasizes the integration of the third sector into the welfare state service system. The second part of the chapter examines the organizational/associational aspects of the sector, focusing on its patterns of association. Here we include data on registration patterns, organizational activities, areas of activity, functions, and connections to funding patterns, and consider the differences between organizations that receive public funding and those that do not. Together, these two parts present, for the first time, a comprehensive picture of the third sector in Israel based on empirical data.

Chapter 3 examines the legal foundations upon which the operation of nonprofit organizations is based and the related state policy exercised towards these organizations. Both of these systems create the main contextual frameworks in which third sector organizations operate. They limit or encourage their development in certain directions and therefore affect specific characteristics of the Israeli third sector. The discussion on policy includes data on goals, patterns, and the volume of state support to exemplify the principles addressed in the chapter.

Chapter 4 surveys the history of the Israeli third sector. It examines the question of how the third sector attained its current form by exploring its religious, social, and political sources, as well as its development processes.

Chapters 5 and 6 examine the contributions of the third sector to Israeli society. In chapter 5, we look at the involvement of third sector organizations in the welfare state, specifically in the areas of health, education, and personal welfare services. In chapter 6, we examine the contribution of third sector organizations to the development of civil society. In particular, we emphasize the development of third sector organizations among two specific population groups with unique characteristics and needs—the Orthodox/Haredi and the Arabs. In both cases, we consider the social-political framework that enabled the third sector to develop among these population groups.

Finally, Chapter 7 summarizes the data presented in the previous chapters and integrates the data into the theoretical formulations outlined in the book. It also suggests areas for future research.

NOTES

1   Although "voluntary organization" is a popular and more common concept, there is no formal definition for the term and therefore we do not use it.
2   The five conditions that the Hopkins Project identified as the defining characteristics of third sector organizations do not provide an entirely clear definition for some organizations in Israel. For borderline cases and other definitional issues, see Appendix 2.
3   For more on the methodological problems involved in researching the third sector in Israel and the specific methods we used in this study, see Appendix 1.
4   For a detailed definition of civil society, see Chapter 6.
5   For detailed information on how we distinguished between organizations that are Integrated within the Welfare State System and Civil Society Organizations, see Appendix 3.

Chapter 2

The Two Faces of the Israeli Third Sector

A Quantitative Profile

In Chapter 1, we delineated two main schools of thought for examining nonprofit voluntary activity: the third sector approach and the civil society approach. Each of these frameworks offers a different research focus; the former is concerned with the economic characteristics of nonprofit activity at the macro level, while the latter deals with its associational aspects. Examinations of the Israeli third sector using these two approaches do not produce a consistent and conclusive image. In fact, an analysis of the economic activity of third sector organizations yields a totally different picture than an examination of its organizational patterns. Any attempt to draw a quantitative profile of the third sector in Israel must consider each of these aspects separately. Thus, in this chapter, we present quantitative data on the Israeli third sector, first from the third sector approach including data on its characteristics and economic activity, and then from the civil society angle with data on the sector's volume and associational aspects.

THE THIRD SECTOR APPROACH: THE THIRD SECTOR IN ISRAEL'S ECONOMY

More than 30,000 third sector organizations are currently registered in Israel. These include all organizations that fit the operational definition of third sector organizations and are legally registered as associations, public benefit companies, or foundations.[6]

Table 1. The Economic Volume of Israel's Third Sector, 1995

Employment	FTE	Share of National Employment*
Paid	147,166	9.3%
Voluntary	25,544	1.4%
Total	172,710	10.7%
Current Expenditures NIS Millions		Share of National GDP
Total	34,371	13.0%
Added Value		Share of National Added Value
		7.3%

*Nonagricultural

Employment and Expenses

An analysis of both the labor volume and current expenses of the Israeli third sector shows that it contributes roughly one-tenth of Israel's economic activity. As indicated in Table 1, the number of paid, full-time employees in third sector organizations in 1995 equaled close to 147,000—more than 9.3% of the non-agricultural labor force. When third sector volunteer work is included, these numbers total more than 170,000 full-time positions or 10.7% of the non-agricultural labor force. Since many third sector employees hold part-time positions, the number increases to 197,000 when we count the overall number of people employed in the sector. In contrast, the number of employees in the financial business sector (including banks, insurance companies, credit, pension funds, etc.) in 1995 totaled 69,000 people,[7] and employment in the entire manufacturing and mining sector totaled 407,000. Thus, the number of employees in the third sector is three times that of the financial sector and roughly half of the entire labor force in all fields of production.

Present data on the third sector in Israel shows continued growth. Although the rate of growth was slower in the 1990s compared to the boom of the 1980s, it is still significant. During 1991–1995, third sector expenses rose by 13.5% and 18,760 full-time positions were added—a 14.6% increase in the employment rate (Gidron and Katz, 1999). A report by the Central Bureau of Statistics (CBS) for a project involving the development of a satellite account for the third sector in the UN system of national accounts (a follow-up endeavor of the Hopkins Project) showed that employment in the Israeli third sector in 1997 encompassed more then 206,000 full-time positions, a rise of 40% over the two-year period from 1995–1997 (Brenner, 2002). As Figure 1 shows, the third sector's share in the Israeli economy based on employment rose in the 1990s from 8.3% of total

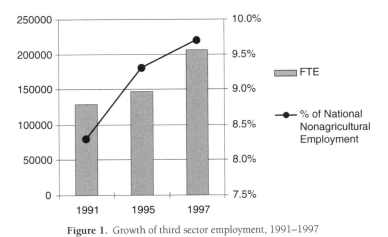

Figure 1. Growth of third sector employment, 1991–1997

nonagricultural employment in 1991 to 9.7% in 1997, with the number increasing to 11.5% when volunteers are included (Brenner, 2002).

When the third sector is examined by selected fields of activity, its economic volume is even more significant: As indicated in Figure 2, in 1995, 44% of full-time positions in health were in the third sector, 37% were in education, and close to 30% of the positions were in culture and recreation, religion, and social services, respectively, as indicated in Figure 2. These data show that employment in the Israeli third sector is significant, particularly in the areas of service provision, which are largely funded by the state.

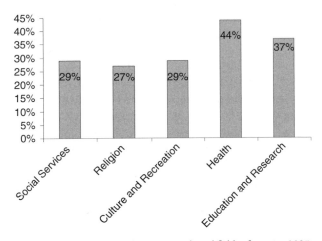

Figure 2. Third sector employment in selected fields of activity, 1995

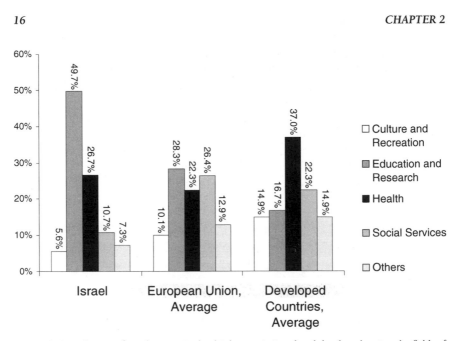

Figure 3. Distribution of employment in the third sector in Israel and developed nations by fields of activity, 1995

An analysis of the economic activity of the Israeli third sector by fields of activity reveals a skewed picture. More than 90% of all third sector employment is in the provision of human services in the fields of health, education, social services, and culture and recreation. As Figure 3 shows, this rate is similar to or even higher than those of other Western countries and, in particular, resembles patterns found in a number of Western European countries (especially Ireland and Belgium). This reflects the deep involvement of third sector organizations in the provision of social services, particularly education, welfare, culture, and health.

Data on salaries in third sector organizations indicate that the average monthly salary in such organizations is 5816 NIS (linked to the standard of living index of September 2001) and is 20% lower than the average salary in Israel (6984 NIS). Compared to other sectors in the Israeli economy, the gap between the salaries of those working in management versus other employees is larger in the third sector: the average salaries of those working in the highest tenth percentile of the third sector are 3.9 times higher than the salaries of other employees in the third sector; within the rest of the Israeli economy, those employed in management earn 3.5 times more than other employees (Gabay and Brik, 2002).

The expenses of third sector organizations in 1995 exceeded 33 billion shekels (the equivalent of approximately $11 billion dollars according to the 1995 average exchange rate), constituting 12.7% of the GDP that year. This figure also increased steadily during the 1990s, growing from 11.5% of Israel's GDP in 1991 to 14.3% in 1997 (Brenner, 2002). Likewise, the added value of the sector's activities (calculated as the sum of wages and the economic value of volunteer work, see Donoghue, Anheier and Salamon, 1999) reached 7.3% of the total added value of the Israeli economy in 1995. In fact, the Israeli third sector is one of the largest in the world relative to its national economy. Among the 22 countries compared in the Hopkins Project (Salamon, Anheier, et al., 1999), Israel ranked fourth in terms of the relative size of its third sector (after the Netherlands, Ireland, and Belgium). As indicated in Figure 4, the Israeli third sector's share of the entire (non-agricultural) labor

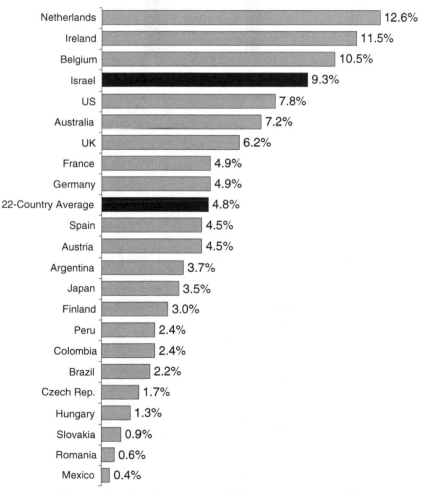

Figure 4. International comparison of third sector employment, 1995

market is almost double the average of these 22 countries combined and is higher than those of the U.S. and Britain, both of which are traditionally considered to be especially large.

Funding Patterns

The funding structure of the Israeli third sector also corresponds to those of Western European countries, as Figure 5 indicates. Public funding is the main source of financial support for the third sector in Israel, constituting 64% of the sector's total income and exceeding 21 billion shekels in 1995 and 29 billion in 1997 (Brenner, 2002). Over one-third (38%) of all active third sector organizations enjoyed public funding in 1998. Third sector organizations in Israel view public funding as an important and desirable source of income, with as many as 75% of all active organizations seeking government funding, according to data presented by the Associations' Registrar to the Knesset's finance committee. In fact, many more organizations seek funding from the government than actually receive it. Such high rates of public funding are characteristic of countries in which the third sector is relatively large compared to the economy and plays a major role in the provision of basic welfare services, such as education, health, personal social welfare, and

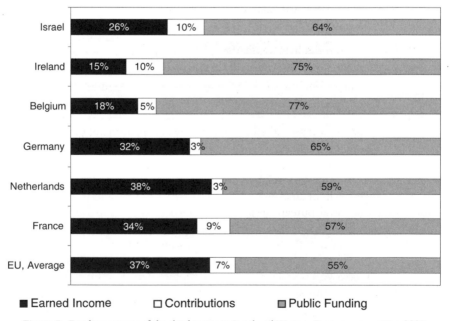

Figure 5. Funding sources of the third sector in Israel and Western European countries, 1995

culture. This pattern is indicative of the complementary role that the third sector plays with respect to the government in providing services that are considered to be part of the welfare state system.

Not all Israeli third sector organizations enjoy generous public funding, however. An examination of funding patterns by specific fields of activity reveals considerable differences. Public support for third sector organizations is primarily concentrated in three areas: health, education, and culture and recreation. The largest share of government support is directed to organizations in the field of education and research (10.2 billion shekels in 1998, mainly to higher, professional, agricultural, and religious educational institutions) and in the field of health (9.5 billion in 1998, mostly to "health funds" mandated by the Health Insurance Law to provide primary health care services). These two areas constitute more than 80% of the entire economic activity of the third sector. In seven[8] of the remaining nine fields of activity, self-generated income is the primary source of funding, while philanthropic inputs provide funding for the last two[9] fields of activity. The fact that the largest areas of the sector are funded primarily by the public purse stresses the important role that the Israeli government plays in the expansion and stabilization of the third sector and the specific areas that comprise it.

Philanthropy and Volunteerism

Funding patterns in Israel, as well as those in other countries, disprove one of the most common beliefs about the third sector—that it primarily relies on monetary donations. Data in Israel show that donations constitute only one-tenth of the sector's total funding. Yet, this rate is relatively high compared to those of other Western countries and is second only to the U.S., where donations constitute nearly 13% of all of the sector's sources of income (Salamon, Anheier, et al., 1999). An analysis of data gathered from surveys on patterns of giving and volunteering among the Israeli public shows that donations generated from private and household sources to third sector organizations total less than half a billion shekels a year (465 million shekels in 1997, Shye, et al., 2000). Earlier studies show that nearly half of all donations to third sector organizations in Israel come from abroad (Central Bureau of Statistics, 1996).[10] Thus, donations from individuals and households in Israel only constitute approximately one-seventh of all donations to the sector; the rest is received from foundations and, to a much smaller extent, business corporations.

In a survey we conducted among a representative sample of the adult Israeli population examining the philanthropic behavior of the Israeli public (see Shye, et al., 2000), we found that three out of every four Israelis donated money to third sector organizations in 1997. However, most gave small amounts and

Table 2. Targets of Individual Philanthropy in an International Context

	Country Year of Survey				
Field of Practice	Israel 1997	Netherlands 1995	UK 2000	Canada 2000	U.S. 1999
Culture and Recreation	–	5%	2%	5%	9%
Social Services	37%	6%	37%	10%	11%
Religion	24%	42%	14%	49%	60%
Education and Research	13%	1%	19%	3%	6%
Health	19%	20%	8%	20%	7%
Philanthropy	–	–	–	7%	2%
International Activity	–	18%	9%	2%	2%
Environment	–	8%	8%	2%	3%
Others	7%	–	4%	2%	–

Sources: Canada: Hall, McKeown, and Roberts (2001); Netherlands: Burger and Dekker (2001); UK: NCVO (2001); US: Kirsch, Hume, and Jalandoni (1999).

three-quarters gave less then 1% of their income. The median annual monetary donation per household was NIS 50 ($14.50). As Table 2 shows, almost all of the contributions made by individuals and households went to organizations involved in four fields of practice: social services, religion, health, and education. Thus, the organizational fields that receive the largest share of individual and household donations in Israel primarily correspond with those that receive the most public funding. Moreover, the specific organizations that interviewees mentioned in the survey as receiving large-scale donations also collect public funding. These include large, highly visible human service organizations with substantial contracts with the government, as well as organizations that are directly affiliated with the government, or other public agencies.

A comparative look at the distribution of individual philanthropy in Israel reveals that Israelis donate money to a much less diverse group of organizations than residents of other countries. This pattern of giving is somewhat similar to that of the UK in that most donations go to human service organizations and those fields that receive the most donations overlap with those that also receive substantial public funding. In the U.S., the Netherlands, and Canada, religious organizations receive most of the donations and these organizations generally are not publicly funded. Given the meager volume of contributions to the third sector in Israel and the fact that the same organizations receive the majority of both individual contributions and public funding, individual philanthropy cannot be viewed as a vital source of funding for the Israeli third sector. This situation further accentuates the government's dominance in the sector.

Volunteer patterns in Israel also resemble patterns of giving. Although our survey found that rates of volunteerism among the Israeli public are impressive, with every third Israeli doing some kind of volunteer work, only some of these people volunteer in third sector organizations and when they do most work only a few hours per month (Shye, et al., 2000). Volunteerism within third sector organizations constitutes only 78% of all volunteering performed by the Israeli public and totals 56 million hours a year. In addition, two-thirds of all the volunteer activity in the third sector is carried out by less than one-fifth of the total number of volunteers. Like philanthropy, volunteerism within the third sector occurs primarily among public agencies that deal with security (e.g., civil guards, fire-fighters), health, education, and welfare (e.g., public hospitals, schools, welfare bureaus). As with donations, most volunteers spend their time primarily in larger, better known service provision organizations in the areas of welfare and health that, in most cases, also enjoy substantial governmental support.

The financial value of volunteer work in third sector organizations was estimated in 1997 to be 840 million shekels. Considering that the economic volume of the third sector exceeded 33 billion shekels in 1995, the economic value of volunteerism is meager. This situation is further emphasized when we compare Israel to Western Europe where the rate of volunteerism in third sector organizations is much higher. Volunteer work in Israel constitutes roughly 15% of total employment in the sector, while in France and England it amounts to 53%, in Germany and the U.S. it equals 39%, and in the Netherlands it numbers 33% (Salamon, Anheier, et al., 1999).

Summary

Thus, an economic analysis of the Israeli third sector according to the third sector approach reveals a very clear image: the Israeli third sector strongly emphasizes the provision of human services, which are primarily financed through various public funding arrangements including the bureaucratic system of contracts and the purchase of services or the politically laden system of grants and gifts. Interestingly, individual philanthropy and volunteerism also correspond to this pattern, with most of these contributions going to large service provision organizations that also receive substantial public funding. It appears that the Israeli third sector is extremely dependent on the government, working closely with it to provide social services within the context of the welfare state. It should be noted that the vast economic volume of education and health organizations in the Israeli third sector mostly account for these findings; their dominance in the economic analyses overshadows smaller, pervasively distinct currents occurring in less economically visible fields of practice in the sector.

THE CIVIL SOCIETY APPROACH: THIRD SECTOR ORGANIZATIONS IN ISRAEL

An organizational analysis of the Israeli third sector according to the civil society approach yields a very different image from the third sector approach— one of plurality and autonomy. The associational patterns of Israeli third sector organizations reveal extensive, multi-faceted, and independent civic activity, as well as significant differences in the organizational patterns among various social groups.

Organizational Patterns

While most of the economic activity of the third sector takes place within a relatively small number of large organizations, the analysis of organizational patterns reveals a completely different picture. First, during the 1980s and 1990s more than 30,000 third sector organizations were established. By the end of 2001, there were 34,291 registered associations, foundations, and public benefit companies in Israel. During the 1990s, an average of 1,650 new third sector organizations was created every year, as indicated in Figure 6. Thus, compared to other countries, Israel falls somewhere in the middle in terms of the number of third sector organizations per population size. By the end of 1999, 502 organizations were registered in Israel per 100,000 citizens; this is similar to the U.S. rate of 458 organizations per 100,000 citizens in 1990, lower than Belgium's rate of 814 in 1995, higher than the Russia's rate of 109 in 1997, and substantially higher than Egypt's rate of 44 in 1998 (Salamon, Anheier, et al., 1999; Ibrahim, Adly, and Shehata, 2002).

It is important to note that not all of these registered organizations are still active in Israel.[11] During the 1990s, on average, only about 35% of all registered organizations were active, and this rate slowly declined over the decade due to the aging of organizations, a failure to monitor the reporting of organizations and the dismantling of inactive ones, and a trend during the 1990s of establishing short-term organizations oriented towards a single, specific goal (e.g., promoting a candidate for election, helping a patient to have surgery abroad, etc.). By the end of the 1990s, nearly 10,000 organizations were active in Israel, constituting a little over one-third of all those registered as third sector organizations (Gidron, Katz, and Bar, 2000).

Third sector organizations established by Israelis are active in a vast variety of areas. In contrast to the economic analysis that showed a concentrated pattern of activity around welfare issues, an associational examination reveals extensive heterogeneity in terms of the areas around which Israelis organize, reflecting the diverse nature of Israeli society. As indicated in Figure 7, categorizing the organizations according to their fields of activity shows that by 1999 there was no single dominant area of activity.[12] The highest number of organizations was concentrated

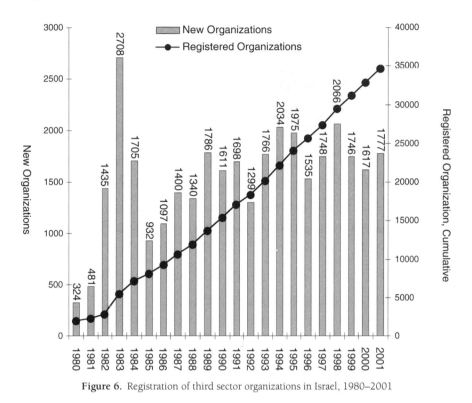

Figure 6. Registration of third sector organizations in Israel, 1980–2001

in the area of religion, constituting nearly a quarter of all third sector organizations. These include primarily worship institutions (synagogues, mosques, churches) but also organizations that attempt to encourage religious practices, proselytize, etc. The distribution of registered organizations by fields of practice did not change significantly during the 1990s despite the substantial increases in their numbers. Yet, it is clear that there are five dominant areas around which nonprofit activity occurs: religion, education and research, philanthropy, welfare, and culture and recreation. More than 80% of all third sector organizations in Israel were engaged in activities in these areas.

We also analyzed third sector organizations according to their main function: service provision, advocacy, and/or funding. For example, an organization involved in the field of education can promote its mission to enhance literacy by providing a tutoring service to students through the work of hired professionals or volunteers (service provision), it can bring about social/political change by bringing the issue of illiteracy to the public's awareness (through demonstrations, lobbying, media, etc.) and by convincing policymakers to make changes (advocacy), or it can achieve change through grant-making to individuals (e.g., scholarships, research

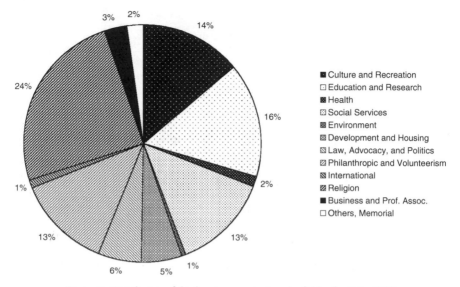

Culture and Recreation
Education and Research
Health
Social Services
Environment
Development and Housing
Law, Advocacy, and Politics
Philanthropic and Volunteerism
International
Religion
Business and Prof. Assoc.
Others, Memorial

Figure 7. Distribution of third sector organizations by fields of activity, 1999

grants) or to organizations fighting illiteracy (funding). Our analysis shows that approximately three-quarters of all third sector organizations are engaged in service provision, primarily in four areas: religion, education and research, welfare, and culture and recreation. The number of organizations advocating for different population groups or specific issues increased during the 1990s from 3% of all new organizations registered at the beginning of the 1990s to 9% by the end of the decade. Likewise, in the 1980s, on average, 3.4% of all new organizations each year were advocacy organizations, while this number grew to 5% in the 1990s. Most advocacy organizations are active in the legal, social change, political, welfare, and environmental areas. Third sector organizations that are primarily concerned with funding organizations or individuals (mostly foundations) constitute 14% of all registered organizations in Israel—half of them support individuals and only 9% support more than one organization.

Global Civil Society Networks

We analyzed the organizational patterns of Israeli third sector organizations in an international context by examining their participation in global civil society networks. In a recent book, Anheier (2001) suggests a detailed operational plan for conceptualizing and analyzing global civil society that can be adapted for use at the national and local levels, as well. One of the main elements of civil society included in this plan is the existence of an organizational infrastructure that can be divided into three components: the existence of civil society organizations, their links to local and global networks, and the purposes and activities in which they are engaged. While it is evident that civil society organizations exist in Israel in large numbers, networks are lacking at the local level. There is little cooperation between Israeli third sector organizations; only a few have organized into umbrella organizations, and membership in Israel's largest umbrella organization—the Voluntary and Nonprofit Sector (VNPS)—includes no more than a few hundred organizations. In terms of the purposes in which third sector organizations are engaged, there is contradictory evidence. On the one hand, advocacy organizations comprise a small minority of the total number of organizations in the sector. On the other hand, research shows an encouraging growth in the number of advocacy organizations, as well as large numbers of independent third sector organizations that do not provide welfare state services (see Gidron, Katz, and Bar, 2001).

At the global level, however, Israel demonstrates a high level of civil society. In 2000, there were 58 secretariats of international civil society organizations in Israel. This amounts to 9.4 secretariats per million people, a ratio similar to those found in middle-income countries (Anheier, Glasius, and Caldor, 2001, pp. 283–286). These figures are even higher for Israeli third sector organizational memberships in international civil society organizations: 3,139 Israeli organizations participated in international networks in 2000, the equivalent of 383 organizations per million people, and approximately one-third of all active Israeli third sector organizations. Thus, there is a high level of participation in global civil society networks among Israeli third sector organizations.

Specific Population Groups

One of the main characteristics of Israeli society is the dynamic use of third sector organizations among the Orthodox community, particularly the Haredi community. The Israeli Orthodox population is characterized by a pattern of extensive volunteer work that follows old organizational traditions typical of the Jewish community in the Diaspora. This pattern includes the existence of multiple service provision organizations, in addition to considerable volunteer and philanthropic activity. Thus, the Orthodox community has established a large number of third sector organizations that considerably exceeds its population rate in Israeli society. For instance, throughout the 1990s, third sector religious organizations constituted 43% of all organizations registered in Israel. Although half of these were religious service, and sacramental organizations, thousands of religious organizations were operating in other areas, such as education (particularly within the Haredi educational system), welfare (charity-funds), and culture. As Table 3 demonstrates, the distribution of Orthodox organizations by areas of activity is completely different from that of the third sector overall (see Figure 7). Interestingly, many organizations in this community are multi-purpose, with religious organizations, such as synagogues, also being active in other areas like education, welfare, health, etc.

Table 3. Registered Organizations by Population Groups, 2001

	Arab Organizations		Religious Organizations	
Culture and Recreation	458	28.4%	322	2.2%
Education and Research	159	9.9%	3,302	22.3%
Health	22	1.4%	21	0.1%
Social Services	224	13.9%	2,138	14.4%
Environment	11	0.7%	N/A	N/A
Development and Housing	219	13.6%	87	0.6%
Law, Advocacy, and Politics	112	6.9%	113	0.8%
Philanthropic and Volunteerism	60	3.7%	348	2.3%
International	8	0.5%	7	0.0%
Religion	299	18.5%	8444	56.9%
Business and Prof. Assoc.	29	1.8%	16	0.1%
Others, Memorial	12	0.7%	36	0.2%
Total	1,613	100.0%	14,384	100.0%

In contrast to the Orthodox community, the number of Arab third sector organizations is meager, comprising a little over 4.7% of the sector—1,613 organizations in 2001—a rate much smaller than the overall Arab population in Israeli society (19%). However, this number has been climbing steadily over the last two decades. It is also safe to assume that there are probably many informal organizations engaged in numerous activities that are not registered for various reasons (Ghanem, 2001 states this as one of the reasons that organizational analyses are not applicable to studying the third sector among the Arab population in Israel). The establishment of third sector organizations among the Arab population in Israel is a relatively new phenomenon: nearly two-thirds of all Arab organizations were registered during the 1990s (80% since 1988 following the outbreak of the first Intifada).

These organizations are active in a variety of areas; over 25% of all Arab organizations are involved in culture, close to 20% in religion, and nearly 15% each in welfare and in housing and development. Interestingly, there is a high rate of multi-purpose organizations in the field of housing and development that are also concerned with many social activities, such as education, culture, community development, health, religion, etc. This evidences a limited level of professionalization and specialization within Arab third sector organizations that is similar to the Haredi community and can be attributed to traditional patterns of association in both communities, and to the late development of a third sector among the Arab population.

A change in the organizational patterns of the Arab population group became evident in 1999. Whereas Arab organizations constituted 5% of the new organizations registered in 1998, this number climbed to 7.5% (131 organizations) in 1999. In 2000 and 2001, the rate of registered Arab organizations exceeded 7%, as well. The beginnings of this pattern were apparent in the early 1980s. Since then the rate of all Arab organizations registered every year has doubled, reaching a mean average of 5.3% of all yearly registered organizations, with significant increases following the first Intifada in 1988. Thus, in 1981 only 0.4% of the total number of registered third sector organizations was Arab, in 1990 this number grew to 3.1%, and in 1999 Arab organizations comprised 7.5% of all newly registered third sector organizations, amounting to 4.4% of the cumulative total of Israeli third sector organizations to date. The significant increases in 1999 can thus be regarded as a culmination of formal organizational activity among this minority group.

Finally, it is interesting to note that philanthropic contributions and volunteer work tend to remain primarily within the respective Orthodox and Arab minority communities in Israel. Therefore, religious Jewish Israelis primarily contribute to and volunteer in Jewish religious organizations, while Arab-Palestinian citizens perform these same activities within their own organizations (Shye, et al., 2000).

Summary

Thus, the organizational analysis engendered by the civil society approach reveals a very different image of the Israeli third sector than the economic analysis. The organizational dynamics and structure revealed here show the Israeli third sector to be an extremely diverse amalgam of organizations that represent various social groups and promote different objectives through diverse strategies. The large number of independent organizations, the growing number of advocacy organizations, and the increasing number of organizations among the Arab population contradict the findings from the economic analysis showing a dependency upon public funding among third sector organizations. However, the civil society analysis does support the dominance of service provision organizations that was apparent in the economic analysis. Finally, the large number of religious organizations evident in this analysis demonstrates the important role that religion plays in the Israeli third sector, and the strong culture of association that characterizes the religious communities in Israel.

CONCLUSION: THIRD SECTOR IN ISRAEL: TWO SIDES OF THE SAME COIN

The research literature usually emphasizes two main roles for the third sector: service provision (mostly welfare services) and the development of civil society. Both of these functions are intertwined, support each other, and can be considered two complementary aspects of the same phenomenon (Gidron, Katz, and Bar, 2000). The analysis of the economic activity of third sector organizations in Israel and the organizational patterns presented by the civil society approach are two sides of the same coin, and each reveals one of these two complementary roles.

The nature and volume of the economic activity of the Israeli third sector demonstrate its important and central role in the Israeli economy, in general, and in social service provision, in particular. In fact, this reflects the common perception among Israelis that the main role of the third sector is to complement the welfare system provided by the state or replace parts of it. This perception is also reflected in the associational patterns that show the clear and definite dominance of service provision organizations. Yet, the analysis of the associational patterns shows that the third sector plays another important role in the development of civil society in Israel. The extensive volume of third sector organizations and their considerable variety attest to the existence of dynamic and versatile civil activity in Israel. This activity is mostly characterized by a participative pattern in which social groups create and maintain organizations that are engaged in service provision to both their members and to others. The complexity of the Israeli third sector also is evident in the significant differences in associational patterns among various social groups in Israel. The systems of organizations within the Arab and Orthodox communities focus exclusively on their respective population groups, maintaining donations and volunteering solely within these boundaries.

Thus, these analyses reveal two primary characteristics of the Israeli third sector: the sector demonstrates: (1) a significant amount of economic activity within the Israeli economy, reflecting the central position of third sector organizations in different areas of service provision; and (2) a high number of associations in a variety of activity areas. Although from an economic viewpoint service providing organizations in the areas of health, education, religion, and culture appear to be dominant, the distribution of third sector organizations reveals a considerable variety of organizations in other areas. As such, the Israeli third sector functions both as a major service provider of substantial economic importance and as a means for promoting different civil activities and various group interests and identities. Although these latter activities may not necessarily carry major economic value, they are of highly significant social and political importance, as will be illustrated in Chapter 3.

NOTES

6   For the operational definition of Israeli third sector organizations used in this book, see Appendix 2.

7   According to Central Bureau of Statistics personnel surveys.

8   These seven fields of activity include: welfare and social services; environmental and animal protection; housing and development; philanthropy and the promotion of volunteering; religion; commercial organizations, trade unions, and professional associations; and other organizations (memorial organizations).

9   These two fields of activity include: law, advocacy and politics; and international activity.

10   These data include donations to the organizations' current budgets, but provide no information on international donations to the development budgets of such organizations.

11   An active organization is defined here as one that is legally registered in the associations and foundations registry, or as a public benefit company in the company registry and submits an annual IRS report as required by law.

12   We adapted the categorization of activity areas from the Hopkins Project, as outlined in Appendix 4.

Chapter 3

The Policy Environment of the Third Sector in Israel

In this chapter, we review the legal status of and the government's policy towards the third sector in Israel. We have chosen to link these two issues together for three reasons. First, the functions of the Israeli third sector—namely, to develop civil society and deliver welfare services—are defined both by the legal infrastructure in which the third sector operates and by the government's policies towards the sector. Second, the legal and governmental systems in Israel are closely intertwined since the government creates and enacts many of the laws affecting the third sector. Finally, the specific laws and regulations pertaining to the third sector are representative of the government's attitudes and policies toward the sector and the work in which it is engaged.

This chapter is divided into three parts. The first part examines within a historical context the primary laws pertaining to the third sector, outlines from a legal perspective the various types of third sector organizations that can be established in Israel, and delineates the restrictions Israeli law places on these organizations. The second part of the chapter focuses on public policy affecting the third sector by examining public allocations to, the external supervision of, and recent government policies towards the third sector. Finally, in the third part of the chapter, we discuss major issues confronting Israel's public policy towards the third sector today. Overall, it is apparent that the government's policies towards the third sector have been established in a haphazard manner in response to various circumstances and political considerations rather than any overriding guiding principles. As a result, third sector organizations in Israel carry out their work in a highly ambiguous and unpredictable environment.

THE LEGAL CONTEXT OF THIRD SECTOR ORGANIZATIONS

All third sector organizations operate within a specific sociopolitical context. In totalitarian regimes, for example, independent voluntary associations are usually banned or extremely restricted and subject to close supervision. In democratic regimes, on the other hand, the right of citizens to organize voluntarily is a fundamental element of the political system and is usually expressed in a state's constitution or basic laws. There is, however, always a danger that this freedom of association may be abused—to undermine the democratic regime, for example—and therefore the state must protect itself. This tension between the need to protect the basic right to freedom of association versus the need to guard against elements hostile to the state is clearly reflected in the set of laws governing third sector organizations in Israel. On the one hand, third sector organizations are voluntary and the management of their internal activities and affairs should be free from legislative intervention. On the other hand, these organizations rely on donations and public funds, exist to serve the public, and often provide welfare services on behalf of the state or are instrumental in developing civil society; therefore, regulations must be established to ensure that they conduct their affairs in an honest and respectable manner. The laws governing third sector organizations in Israel attempt to strike a balance between these two contradictory goals.

Legal Overview, Pre-State to Present

The laws affecting the third sector in Israel stem from the country's unique history and are primarily influenced by elements of the Ottoman and British legal systems that existed prior to the establishment of the state. In particular, two laws have significantly influenced the legal framework in which third sector organizations operate: the 1906 Ottoman Law of Associations (hereafter referred to as the Ottoman Associations' Law) and the 1921 British Companies Law. The Ottoman Associations' Law dealt with the formation and organization of nonprofit organizations and was the first of its kind regulating the association of individuals for the achievement of nonprofit goals. Pursuant to the French law on which it was modeled, the law stipulated that although a permit was not necessary for the establishment of an association, registration with the proper authorities was required. Further, the law forbade the establishment of associations that: (1) contravened the law or general morality; (2) undermined the country's security; (3) were subversive and aimed to change the current form of government or create divisions between ethnic groups for political ends; (4) held racist or ethnic objectives or designations; or (5) had secret objectives. Later, under British rule (1917–1948), the Mandatory Legislature imported the 1921 British Companies Law as a mandatory ordinance, which they termed the Companies Ordinance and adapted to local needs.

In addition, laws regulating the formation of public and religious endowments were first established in Israel during these periods. Under Turkish rule, religious endowments (Jewish, Christian, and Muslim) were set up according to Muslim *Shari'a* law A writ of endowment was drawn up before a religious judge and the endowment was registered in an endowments register, some of which still exist today. Shari'a law restricted endowments of real estate, which created problems for public institutions and for the beneficiaries of these types of endowments. In practice, however, endowments formed under Ottoman law could be set up as *waqf* property, a form of real estate that could be endowed both to private individuals and to the public. Later, under British Mandate, property could be endowed in two ways: (1) through a religious endowment, over which the Jewish, Christian, and Muslim courts were granted authority, according to the Order-in-Council of 1922; or (2) through a secular endowment, over which government officials were granted broad powers, as stipulated in the Charitable Endowments Ordinance of 1924, the Charitable Endowments Ordinance (Public Trustee) of 1947, and Regulations on Charitable Affairs (Public Trustee) of 1947.

In the second decade of its existence, the state began drawing up an independent legal code better suited to the country's needs.[13] Although there is no explicit constitutional provision for the right of association in Israel, the state has recognized this as a basic civil right. In 1980, the Ottoman Associations' Law was largely revoked in favor of the 1980 Nonprofit Associations Law, which sanctions the formation of nonprofit organizations according to the following conditions: the organization cannot (1) be established for illegal purposes or serve as a front for illegal activities; (2) deny the existence of the State of Israel; or (3) deny the democratic nature of the state. This law omitted the prohibition in the Ottoman Associations' Law against associations that contravene morality or public policy. Thus, the freedom of association is extremely broad in scope, precluding only illegal activities or activities that undermine democracy. Likewise, the Companies Ordinance was replaced by the Companies Law of 5759–1999, which provides for the establishment of public benefit companies (the only difference between a public benefit company and a commercial company is that the members of a public benefit company cannot share in the company's profits). Similarly, the Charitable Endowments Ordinance of 1924 pertaining to public endowments was amended in 1973 to enhance the supervision of endowments, and later the Trust Law was passed in 1979 regulating the establishment and management of religious and public endowments.

In addition, over the last decade, two basic laws affecting fundamental human rights have been introduced: (1) Basic Law: Freedom of Occupation, and (2) Basic Law: Human Dignity and Freedom. Although these laws do not explicitly address the right to association, they were designed to provide constitutional protection for a broad range of human rights and the Supreme Court has interpreted this to include the freedom of association. For instance, Israel's Chief Justice, Aharon

Barak, has interpreted the term "human dignity" in Basic Law: Human Dignity and Freedom to include the right of association. Thus, the Supreme Court will only limit the freedom of association when there is clear and convincing evidence that it could lead to serious violence.

In addition to the Supreme Court's ability to restrict the freedom of association under dangerous circumstances, specific laws have been developed prohibiting the establishment and operation of subversive or dangerous organizations. The justification for these restrictive laws is based upon the concept of a "self-protecting democracy"—namely, that a democracy recognizes society's right to defend itself against elements that threaten to undermine its foundations. These laws include the Penal Law of 5737–1977, the Defense [Emergency] Regulations 1945 (Regulations 84 and 85), and the 1948 Prevention of Terrorism Ordinance. The Penal Law of 5737–1977 (paragraphs 145–150) prohibits any organization from committing violence or inciting violence against the state and/or its agencies. A similar prohibition is incorporated in the Defense [Emergency] Regulations 1945 (Regulations 84 and 85). Organizations that violate these regulations incur extremely harsh penalties, such as the seizure and confiscation of their financial assets. The 1948 Prevention of Terrorism Ordinance restricts the freedom of association for state security reasons. This ordinance is intended to prevent the establishment and operation of terrorist organizations.

Finally, Israel is unique in that the separation between religion and state is not distinct. Therefore the freedom of association is often linked with the freedom of religion, the freedom to worship, and the freedom of conscience. Not surprisingly, these principles are reflected in the laws governing various third sector religious organizations and the services that they provide on behalf of the state. For instance, the Law of Jewish Religious Services [consolidated version] of 5731–1971 regulates the financing and supervision of the Jewish religious councils, which provide religious facilities and services, often through nonprofit organizations. In addition, laws have been developed to cover religious services that are offered to all citizens of Israel, such as burial services that are provided by nonprofit burial societies and are paid for by the National Insurance Institute (NII).

Types of Third Sector Organizations

In legislative terms, third sector organizations in Israel can be divided into two broad categories: associations and foundations. Associations are comprised of groups of people who work together to achieve a common objective without any profit-sharing intent and include *amutot* (nonprofit associations) and public benefit companies.[14] Foundations are institutions that use their capital to achieve philanthropic ends and include non-profit-distributing private trusts and public or religious endowments.[15] Below, we describe in detail these legal frameworks and the specific laws that pertain to each type of organization.

Amutot

The 1980 Nonprofit Associations Law provides for the establishment of amutot, which are the most common types of nonprofit organizations (NPOs) in Israel. The term "amuta" denotes an association of people gathered in the spirit of friendship, cooperation, and brotherhood to undertake an activity for the public good. To form an amuta, two or more people must submit an application to the Registrar of Associations. The Registrar can only reject the application if the objectives of the proposed organization deny the existence or the democratic nature of the State of Israel or if the Registrar believes that the organization is a front for illegal activities. In addition, the name of the proposed association may not mislead or offend the public, contradict public policy, or closely resemble the name of an existing organization. In order to encourage associations formed under Ottoman Law to re-register as amutot, an interim provision was introduced permitting the Registrar of Associations to disqualify any association that failed to do so. Although this prerogative has never been exercised, many associations have re-registered in order to benefit from the tax exemptions granted to amutot. The only organizations that have retained their status as Ottoman associations are trade unions and employers' unions registered prior to 1983.

Once an amuta has received a certificate of registration, it is considered an autonomous legal entity. The primary legal stipulation for an amuta is that it may not distribute profits to its members; any profits an amuta derives must be funneled back into the organization to further its activities. Membership in an amuta may include both adults and corporations, is subject to the approval of the amuta's general assembly and is considered personal and non-transferable. The law clearly distinguishes between the authority of the general assembly and the board of directors. The general assembly of the amuta has the authority to appoint and dismiss members of the board of directors;[16] can assume the board of director's administrative duties; and has the power to modify the association's articles, name, or objectives through a majority vote. The board of directors, on the other hand, is in charge of overseeing the association and fulfills any duties that have not been assigned to the general assembly or any other bodies within the amuta. The board of directors must be comprised of least two people and all board members must be selected from the general assembly.[17] Board members may not participate on any committees or hold any paid positions within the amuta and usually forego a salary, although the general assembly may decide to compensate them for their services. The board of directors may determine its own administrative policies (e.g., when to meet, how to conduct its meetings) and is expected to act in the best interests of the association.

Although it is not a legal requirement, larger amutot generally appoint an executive staff, including a director-general, who is responsible for the day-to-day operations of the association. In such cases, the executive staff is accountable to the board of directors, although in some instances the executive staff may be given special statutory powers over which the board of directors has no control. Every association must also appoint an audit committee to supervise its financial and economic affairs. Any association with an annual budget of over NIS 750,000 is also required to hire an accountant. The findings of the accountant and audit committee are open to public scrutiny and must be included in any reports of the general membership. In general, the association's documents (e.g., minutes of meetings, financial reports, auditors' reports, etc.) must be accessible to all members of the organization. In addition, an amuta cannot be held liable if it defaults on its contractual obligations (except in the case of unlawful behavior). Thus, an amuta's assets cannot be seized and compensation for damages cannot be filed against its directors. To alert potential contractors of this situation, an amuta is required to have the word "amuta" or "registered amuta" in its name.

Public Benefit Companies

The second type of non-profit association that can be established in Israel is a public benefit company. There are two laws under which public benefit companies can be registered: the 1983 Companies Ordinance [New Version] or the 1999 Companies Law. Public benefit companies have become increasingly popular in Israel because the laws regulating them provide extensive details on the day-to-day management of associations. To establish a public benefit company under the Companies Ordinance, a minimum of seven members is required. The company's name cannot resemble that of any existing organization, offend public policy or sentiment, or include the terms "cooperative," "state," "governmental," "municipal," or any other word that implies a connection with a government agency, unless approved by the Companies Registrar. The company's objectives must also be consistent with the law in order to prevent the formation of subversive organizations.

Once the company has been approved, the Companies Ordinance provides clear procedures for determining the status of the company's members; conducting general assemblies; managing the company; establishing the duties of its managers and directors; determining the company's accounting, auditing, and supervisory mechanisms; and liquidating the company. The general assembly of the company is granted most of the control of the organization: it can appoint and dismiss directors, modify the company's founding documents, and dissolve the company. The general assembly is required to meet at least once a year but may assemble at other times at the request of the shareholders or directors. Minutes from any meetings must be made accessible to all company members.

The board of directors, on the other hand, has the right to manage the company independently and the general assembly cannot override the board's decisions. The board of directors must convene at fixed intervals, may select their own chair, and may set their own procedures for running their meetings. In a large company, the board of directors usually determines the company's work plans, financial operations, and management strategies. Thus, the board is in charge of reporting to the general assembly, determining the organizational structure of the company, and establishing its salary policies. Officers of a public benefit company are also charged with the duty to act with care and skill and are expected to behave as an ordinarily prudent person in a like position would under similar circumstances. Thus, officers must disclose and avoid any activities that would cause any possible conflicts of interest. This provision enables shareholders to exercise some control over the company's directors, who incur penalties if they violate this stipulation. Generally, board members in public benefit companies receive no remuneration; those board members who are also professionals employed by the company on a permanent basis, however, are entitled to a salary and benefits.

The board is also responsible for appointing an executive (e.g., a director-general or chief executive officer) who must answer to both the board of directors and the general assembly. In addition, public benefit companies must appoint an accountant to monitor their annual financial reports. This role is considered so crucial that if an auditor leaves a company and no replacement has been found, the Companies Registrar must by law appoint another accountant. In addition to hiring an accountant, public benefit companies that are publicly owned are also required to appoint an auditing committee. Likewise, all public benefit companies must appoint an internal auditor to ensure that the company abides by the law and adheres to sound business practices.

Public benefit companies formed under the Companies Law (this law also governs the registration of commercial companies and is based on British Law) are organized according to the same hierarchical structure as those established under the Companies Ordinance. The criteria for their establishment are different, however. Under the Companies Law, a single individual may establish a public benefit company. The company must be established for public purposes, cannot distribute profits, and its objectives must comply with Israel's laws, morality, and public policies.[18] In addition, the Companies Registrar examines the company's proposed objectives to determine whether the organization is a non-commercial company. To qualify as a non-commercial company, an organization must promote the arts, science, religion, or charity; use its income solely for the promotion of these goals; and refrain from paying dividends to its members. Although the Companies Law requires that all companies include the word, "limited," in their name, this suffix is dropped if the company is determined to be a non-commercial company to inform anyone contracting with the company that its members have no personal stake in the company's profits. In addition, a company established under the Companies Law is considered a "public institution" (and therefore eligible for tax exemptions) if: (1) its objective is in the public interest; (2) it does not distribute dividends to its members; (3) it issues stocks (stocks from public benefit companies have no economic value) and (4) it confers equal voting rights among the members of its auditing committee.

Finally, according to the Trust Law of 1979, nonprofit companies formed under either the Companies Ordinance or the Companies Law may be granted the title of a "public benefit company" if they fulfill any one of the three following conditions: (1) the company has received permission to drop the word, "limited," from its name; (2) the company is exempt from paying income tax, property tax, or capital gains tax; or (3) a court has declared that the company is a "public benefit company" whose main objective is the public good (i.e., the promotion of education, culture, religion, science, art, welfare, health, or sports). If the company is a public benefit company, it is also required to enter itself in a special register of public benefit companies located in the Endowments Registrar (which serves as the registrar for both public benefit companies and endowments, as described below).

Trusts/Endowments

As mentioned previously, foundations consist of non-profit-distributing private trusts and public or religious endowments. Private trusts and endowments are essentially quite similar. An endowment is actually a trust fund established for a specific objective. The basic difference between a regular trust and an endowment trust lies in the purpose of the fund and the nature of the beneficiaries. In the case of private trusts, the owners endow their property to a specified individual for whom they are caring, such as relatives who are still minors. In the case of endowments, the owners endow their property for use towards a particular objective and dedicate it to a specific population group. Further distinctions can be drawn between public endowments (e.g., when owners dedicate property for the benefit of the inhabitants of the town in which they grew up) and religious endowments (e.g., when owners donate property for the purpose of building a synagogue). Again, the difference between these two types of endowments rests in their purposes: one is designed to promote public interests, while the other is established to promote religious concerns.

Those endowments established after 1979 are subject to the provision of the Trust Law, while those founded prior to 1979 remain under Ottoman and British Mandate legislation. The Trust Law distinguishes between public and religious endowments. It grants the rabbinical courts authority over the establishment of Jewish religious endowments and rabbis control over their internal management; jurisdiction over Christian and Muslim religious endowments is given to the religious courts of their respective communities. The Trust Law also provides specific regulations for the establishment, management, and supervision of all public secular endowments. A public endowment must be established in three stages: (1) the endowment must be formed, (2) a trustee must be appointed, and (3) the endowment must be registered with the Registrar of Endowments. The law further stipulates that public endowments are not separate legal entities and therefore cannot serve as centers for economic activity—that is, they cannot own property, incur liabilities, or employ workers.

In creating an endowment, the owner of the property is required to draw up a writ of endowment expressing his/her wish to establish an endowment and the objective(s) (e.g., the public interest), assets, and conditions of the endowment. In the absence of a writ of endowment, the court may define its objective(s), assets, and conditions. The conditions of the endowment can only be modified or rescinded if the writ of endowment allows for such changes, the beneficiaries give their consent, or the court grants approval. The endowment comes into existence when the endowed property is transferred to a trustee, who is appointed according to the writ of endowment. Minors, legal incompetents, bankrupts, or companies under liquidation cannot serve as trustees. By default, the court may appoint a trustee for a period of time and under specific conditions that it determines. In exceptional cases, the beneficiary of a public endowment may also serve as the trustee, even if this has not been sanctioned by the writ of endowment.

Trustees must discharge their duties in good faith and with the same care and diligence that an ordinarily prudent person in a like position would exercise under similar circumstances. The law uses the criterion of a "reasonable person" as a yardstick to measure a trustee's behavior. A trustee has restricted ownership rights over the endowed property, which means that a trustee cannot receive any profit accruing from the property or bequeath any part of the property to another party. Thus, unlike officers in other types of organizations, who are permitted and even expected to take steps and even risks to increase the company's wealth, a trustee is forbidden to do so. Furthermore, trustees cannot undertake any action that may create a conflict of interest between the trust and the trustee. Such actions are only allowed in rare instances, with the court's approval. Trustees may be dismissed if they fail to fulfill their required duties. A beneficiary or any other interested party may submit a request for dismissal to the court. The Registrar of Endowments must conduct an investigation to determine whether the trustee has failed to comply with the law or any provision of the writ of endowment. Through the course of the investigation, the Registrar may summon witnesses to testify. The findings of such investigations often serve as a basis for legal action.

Restrictions on Third Sector Organizations

Israeli citizens who wish to form a third sector organization are free to choose any one of the legal frameworks outlined above (i.e., an amuta, a public benefit company, or a trust/endowment). Regardless of the type of organization they decide to establish, they will be subject to a number of restrictions. First, in order to receive the full spectrum of government benefits granted to nonprofit associations, third sector organizations must incorporate. Although the law does not explicitly mandate incorporation and failure to do so is not penalized as long as the organization does not have a profit-seeking motive and meets the proper criteria for tax benefits, in practice, non-corporate organizations are ineligible for a variety of government benefits. For instance, in order to qualify for income tax exemptions, an organization must be defined as a "public institution" and register as a corporation. In other words, in the case of certain tax exemptions, Israeli law only recognizes organizations that have been awarded a certificate of incorporation and those that fail to incorporate are penalized by not qualifying for these benefits.

Israeli law also restricts a wide range of third sector activities. For instance, the Income Tax Ordinance prohibits tax-exempt organizations from incurring inappropriate expenses. Third sector organizations may not deduct expenditures for: (1) refreshments, foreign travel, per diem expenditures, gifts, hospitality costs, and telephone expenses; (2) benefits paid to employees, such as car allowances; and (3) severance pay exceeding the tax-deductible amount granted to a non-tax-exempt company. In addition, the law places a ceiling on certain types of expenditures (e.g., travel, dining). If a public institution exceeds this limit, it must pay an advance of 90% of the value of the excess expenditure. The law also regulates the compensation that third sector organizations pay to their employees and directors: if the organization pays unreasonably high salaries, it risks losing its status as a nonprofit association. According to the Value Added Tax (VAT) Law of 1975, nonprofit organizations must also pay an 8.5% tax on the salaries paid to their employees, except (1) if the salaries do not exceed a specified sum set by the Finance Minister (in 1997 this equaled NIS 63,503); or (2) if the NPO is a certain type of foundation. Likewise, the 1975 Employers' Tax Law requires NPOs to pay a 4% employers' tax on employees' salaries, which are narrowly defined and do not include bonuses, such as car allowances, telephone expenses, etc.

NPOs must also pay taxes on certain types of income. While NPOs are entitled by law to undertake commercial activities, any income derived from these pursuits is subject to income tax under the Value Added Tax Law. Therefore, although an NPO that has been classified as a public institution may be exempt from paying income tax under the Income Tax Ordinance, the company may still be subject to income tax under the Value Added Tax Law, which is based on profits. By taxing profits, Israeli law makes a clear distinction between an NPO's passive income, which is tax-exempt, and its commercial income, which is taxable. Thus, a public institution's income is taxable if it is derived from a business, interest, accrued interest, or dividends or the standard of living index from a company that the institution controls. In addition, nonprofit organizations are not allowed to deduct input tax (this is equivalent to the Value Added Tax); however, as a business, it may do so for the commercial part of its activity.

Israeli law also places certain restrictions on the political activities of third sector organizations. According to the 1992 Political Parties Law, third sector organizations are allowed to undertake activities of a political nature; however, they cannot put forth candidates to run for public positions in national or local elections since this would make them political parties. Officers of nonprofit associations, however, may accept political appointments since the law does not restrict the freedom of occupation. Thus, the law considers registered political parties to be separate legal entities that are not subject to the provisions of the Nonprofit Associations Law. This distinction can affect the tax status of third sector organizations: the law does not explicitly recognize third sector organizations engaged in political activity as public institutions; therefore, these organizations must appeal to the Finance Minister to obtain a tax-exempt status. This situation has resulted in a number of conflicts. For example, in the High Court case, *Constitution for Israel v. the Finance Minister, et al.*,[19] a nonprofit association established to lobby for a written constitution in Israel appealed to be recognized as a public institution. The association was financed primarily by donations and requested that its donors be awarded tax-exempt status. The High Court of Justice rejected this request stating that although the association had an educational/cultural purpose (i.e., educating people in the value of the constitution), its primary purpose was to bring about constitutional change, which could not be defined as a public objective. Therefore, tax-exempt status was not granted.

Gliksberg (1995, p. 211) argues that Israel's social, political, and economic circumstances make it hard to clearly distinguish between the party/political establishment and many third sector organizations because they are so closely intertwined. He argues that even if an organization has a political focus it cannot be separated from the public purpose it aims to achieve. In addition, disqualifying this type of organization from tax benefits undermines the basic right of freedom of expression under Basic Law: Human Dignity and Freedom 1992. In such cases, some compromise is necessary between the right to freedom of expression and the state's need to levy taxes. This has not yet been achieved in case law and is contingent upon a normative decision concerning the right of nonprofit organizations to participate in legislative procedures without losing their tax-exempt status. Glicksberg advocates for adopting a broader definition whereby "dual purpose" NPOs (those with both political and public purposes) would fall under the NPO tax system but be subject to various constraints. Since third sector organizations engaged in political activities are not politically neutral, they should not be entitled to government support for their party activities but should not lose their status as public institutions because of their political involvement. Based on the American model, Gliksberg believes that any government support for an NPO participating in political activity can be offset by taxing the money transferred from an NPO to a political party according to the highest tax rate on corporate income (Gliksberg, 1995, p. 213).

GOVERNMENT POLICY TOWARDS THE THIRD SECTOR

Despite the abundance of laws and regulations directly or indirectly affecting nonprofit organizations and the substantial sums of money they receive from the public sector every year, the Israeli government lacks a straightforward, established policy towards the third sector. This is evidenced on a number of different levels. For instance, the Israeli government has never set up a state or public committee to devise a national policy towards the sector; few members of the Knesset (MKs) or prominent politicians work on behalf of the third sector; there is no third sector lobby; no think tanks have ever been established in Israel to discuss various aspects of third sector activity; the third sector is largely absent from national and municipal elections in Israel; and none of the basic guidelines of the last four governments have given serious consideration to the sector. Given this ambiguity, we attempt to piece together in this section various elements that can be said to be representative of Israeli "policy" towards the third sector: existing government policies at the central and local levels, the system of public allocations to the third sector, government supervision of third sector organizations, and changes in policy over the last twenty years.

Government Policy at the Central and Local Levels

The central government's policy towards the third sector has evolved in a piecemeal fashion over the years in response to historical processes, constraints, and pressures rather than from a coherent view of the sector and its functions. Typically, the government's policy has stemmed from individual government or court interventions in response to problems pertaining to specific areas of activity (e.g., higher education, health), certain types of organizations (e.g., yeshiva), or particular organizations (e.g., the Wolf Foundation Law was passed for a specific fund). In none of these instances has any comprehensive government debate taken place regarding its overall policy toward the sector. Thus, although the government's policies reflect its position vis-à-vis the third sector, there are no documents outlining an ideological basis for this relationship.

Despite this ambiguity, the fact that government budgets have been increasingly diverted to third sector organizations over the years indicates the existence of a de facto policy. In fact, government ministries have allocated substantial sums of money to thousands of third sector organizations operating in various fields. Government ministries have even sponsored national and local nonprofit organizations such as *Eshel* (The Association for the Planning and Development of Services for the Elderly) and *Ashalim* (The Association for the Planning and Development of Services for Children). Likewise, a number of ministries have set up special units to deal with voluntary work at the national and local levels. The degree of cooperation between the ministries and third sector organizations varies—some ministries consult with representatives of the third sector regularly, others on an ad-hoc basis, and others not at all.

In their study, Telias, Katan, and Gidron (2000) clearly show the personal, improvised, and reactive pattern of decision-making characteristic of the Israeli government's policy towards third sector organizations over the years. This process has been influenced mainly by political interests and transient political considerations that serve the narrow interests of specific groups or individuals. Moreover, the study found that government officials and politicians are interested in preserving a vague policy towards the third sector since it allows them to continue using third sector organizations to consolidate their own political power and prevents these organizations from gaining greater financial and political legitimacy, importance, and prestige. On the other hand, some activists also fear that a clear government policy could lead to increased government intervention and supervision. Furthermore, both parties are interested in maintaining the status quo since it allows the unimpeded flow of government resources to third sector organizations, including those that advance the interests of political parties. Thus, a clear policy that defines priorities and determines criteria for allocating funds would obstruct the flow of funds to various organizations and hamper the use of this support mechanism as a means for furthering various political goals.

Telias, Katan, and Gidron also found that government support for third sector organizations is guided by three main considerations: 1) the government's wish to cut expenditures, lighten its administrative load, and circumvent restrictions that could impede the recruitment of manpower and the use of resources, as evidenced by decisions to contract work out to nongovernmental organizations; 2) a desire among government officials with party interests to support third sector organizations that further their political goals, as evidenced by those associations that have been established and funded by political parties; and 3) the government's wish to promote organizations that fulfill important functions the government is unwilling to address directly, as evidenced by organizations that provide services to populations with special needs, such as the handicapped, or those involved in education and culture. Government support of third sector organizations is thus largely motivated by expediency rather than principle.

In practice, the types of government funding provided to third sector organizations indicate that the government perceives the sector as complementing or, in certain circumstances, even replacing government services. This is evidenced by the government's funding priorities: those organizations that provide services, particularly in the fields of education and culture, are given generous funding while other types of organizations receive meager subsidies. This reflects a state ideology in which the government utilizes the service-provider functions of the third sector while it gives limited attention to or ignores other aspects of the sector (e.g., advocacy, entrepreneurship, the furtherance of civil society). In particular, the government tends to favor third sector organizations that provide welfare services, those that are large and labor-intensive organizations rather than those that are small and voluntary, and those that serve certain social groups (e.g., ultra-orthodox organizations).

These same trends are also evident at the local level. However, the situation is exacerbated at the local level due to a lack of coordination between the central and local governments. As a result, each local authority handles issues related to the third sector in a different manner. For those local authorities that have volunteer units, the range of services they provide varies greatly—some units have a director, auxiliary staff, and working budget, while most have only a part-time volunteer coordinator and an extremely limited budget or no budget at all—and do not reflect the importance that local authorities attach to volunteer work. In addition, no standard has been set for determining the level of budgetary support for third sector organizations at the local level. The attitudes of local authorities towards the issue of voluntarism vary and are influenced by a number of factors, including their degree of personal commitment, the extent of volunteer activity in the area, the number of organizations in the locality, and the ability of activists to persuade the local authorities that their issues deserve attention. Clearly, a key factor in the dynamics at this level is the ability to convince authorities that the activities of third sector organizations will enhance the well-being of the local population and contribute to the development of the locality.

Finally, since the central government views the local governments as its executive arm rather than elected governmental bodies with autonomy and broad discretionary powers, the government ministries do not consult local authorities when they fund third sector organizations operating at the local level. The worst example of this situation is the Bequests Fund, in which all applications (even those from local organizations) must be submitted to the appropriate government ministry without any input from the local authorities. This situation is further exacerbated by the fact that local authorities compete with third sector organizations for funds from the Bequests Fund. Although it is illegal, local authorities sometimes serve as "conduits" through which government resources are funneled to local organizations. For example, the Comptroller's Report found that the Ministry of the Interior was channeling funds to third sector organizations via local authorities (Comptroller's Report, 1991; see also Neeman Report, 1992) and took the case to court.

Although both the central and local governments lack a basic umbrella policy towards the third sector, the local authorities are more aware of, cooperate to a greater extent with, and have a more positive attitude towards the sector. This is due to the closer proximity and interdependence that exists between local authorities and third sector organizations. For instance, a large proportion of third sector organizations provide services to and deal with local populations and problems. In addition, as the gap has widened between the budgets of local authorities and the demands of citizens, authorities have become increasingly dependent on local third sector organizations to provide services. Finally, there is a growing perception among local authorities that citizens are "customers" whose opinions are important, as well as a greater demand among citizens to be consulted and heard. As a result of this growing cooperation, some local authorities have set up special units or appointed coordinators to liaise and coordinate with third sector organizations. Local authorities have also begun to recruit volunteers for their own agencies and other organizations. In addition, many local authority departments have developed direct working relationships with third sector organizations, consulting with them, jointly implementing projects, and entrusting them with the provision of services.

Public Allocations to the Third Sector

The lack of a clear government policy towards the third sector has given rise to a complex and diverse system of direct and indirect aid towards the sector. This system has also evolved in a piecemeal fashion and generally the regulations do not pertain to various types of third sector organizations uniformly. For example, those laws regulating third sector organizations in higher education (e.g., universities, colleges) are different from those regulating organizations that deal with culture (e.g., theaters, museums, dance companies) or religion. Likewise, even though many of the same laws govern third sector organizations involved in service-provision and those concerned with developing civil society, there is a perception among government officials that these organizations do not belong to the same sector and should be dealt with differently.

There are two types of financial support provided to third sector organizations—direct support and indirect support. Direct support accounts for almost two-thirds of the sector's total expenditures and entails the direct transfer of money from the public sector (e.g., government ministries, the NII—National Insurance Institute, local authorities) to third sector organizations via grant allocations, contracts, etc. Indirect support usually comes from government and municipal tax concessions and tax exemptions granted to third sector organizations and donors. We describe in detail below the various types of direct and indirect support available to third sector organizations in Israel.

Direct Support

Direct public funding of third sector organizations in Israel takes two major forms: contracts and grants. In addition, there are other forms of direct support made to third sector organizations.

A. Contracts. Contracts are the most common form of direct government support to the third sector. Contracts are usually drawn up between the state and a third sector organization (or occasionally a commercial organization) for

Table 4. Contractual Government Funding

Direct Funding—Contracts, 1998				
	Legislated Support		Payments for Services	
	NIS Millions	%	NIS Millions	%
Culture and Recreation	731	3.4	24	2.0
Education and Research	9,738	45.4	471	39.8
Health	9,400	43.9	48	4.0
Welfare	586	2.7	367	30.9
Environment	–	–	5	0.4
Housing and Development	–	–	64	5.4
Politics and Social Change	–	–	10	0.9
Foundations and Philanthropic Activity	–	–	115	9.7
International Activity	–	–	222	18.7
Religion	498	2.3	33	2.8
Business & Professional Associations	–	–	46	3.9
Miscellaneous	473	2.2	2	0.1
Total	21,426	100	1,185	100

the provision of services to the population in exchange for whole or partial state funding. The contract specifies the nature of the service to be provided, eligibility criteria, the fees to be charged for the service (if any), and the government control mechanisms for ensuring that the service is adequately provided. An organization contracting with the state may supply other services that are not covered by the contract and/or may undertake other activities with funding from other sources. The amount of government funding that is provided to third sector organizations in the form of contracts is extremely substantial, as is indicated in Table 4. However, most contracts are granted to a relatively small number of organizations.

Contracts between the government and third sector organizations may be made in the form of legislated support or payment for services. Legislated support is generally a long-term contract that is provided for in the state budget and is sometimes mandated by a specific law. In most cases, legislated support covers services that the government is obligated to provide to citizens for free or at a subsidized rate.[20] Thus, when third sector organizations receive legislated support, they are either complementing or replacing the government in providing the specified services. Such arrangements exist primarily in the fields of health and education. Most of the funding in the field of health goes to the health funds, which received NIS 9.4 billion in 1998 (over half of the Ministry of Health's total budget of NIS 17 billion). In the field of education, the majority of funding goes to higher education and ultra-orthodox educational institutions. To a lesser extent, legislated support provides funding to organizations involved in primary and secondary education, boarding schools, senior citizen homes, long-term care, research, and culture.

Some Israeli laws mandate the use of third sector organizations to provide government-funded services to the citizens of the state. Examples include the National Health Insurance Law of 1994 for the provision of primary health care services, the Long-Term Care Insurance Law of 1986 for the provision of long-term care services, the National Council of Higher Education Law of 1958 for the provision of higher education services, the State Education Law of 1953 for the provision of ultra-orthodox education services, the Jewish Religious Services Law of 1971 for the provision of various religious services, and the Adoption Services Law [Amendment 2] 1996 for the provision of international adoption services.

The 1994 National Health Insurance Law states that all citizens have the right to receive basic health care services and that these are to be provided by health funds. The health funds cannot arbitrarily refuse members and all citizens are legally entitled to select a sick fund of their choice. The funding of these services is derived from a variety of public sources, including a progressive health insurance tax levied by the NII, a parallel tax on employers and the self-employed (until 1997), a percentage of NII funds as specified by law, the government's health budget, and consumer fees to the health funds for services that are not included in the "basket of health services" that are covered by the health funds. Although the law stipulates that the health funds must register as NPOs, they may choose whether to register as nonprofit associations or public benefit companies.[21] The health funds exemplify a "contract regime" characteristic of many European welfare states wherein a service is almost entirely funded by the state but is provided by an NPO that is not part of the public system. In the case of the health funds, each is considered to be a separate legal entity run by autonomous bodies whose members are appointed independently. The Health Ministry is only allowed to appoint an observer to the health fund council (the health fund's chief body) to ensure that the fund is being properly managed.

With the passage of the Home Care Insurance Law of 1986, the NII has been granting allocations to third sector organizations for the provision of home care to elderly people who are dependent on others or who require supervision in carrying out their daily activities. These organizations are recognized by the Ministry of Labor and Social Affairs as licensed providers of home care services and their activities are regulated by a contract with the NII. The NII and local professional committees are responsible for funding these services, determining recipients' eligibility criteria, planning the range of services provided, and selecting and supervising the organization providing the service. Of the 150 organizations offering long-term care in 2000, 32% were nonprofit associations and the remaining organizations were for-profit companies or cooperatives. Over the years, tension and even rivalry have developed between the nonprofit and for-profit organizations providing long-term care services. The private companies claim that the NPOs receive preferential treatment (in the form of greater tax concessions and more patient referrals) leading to unfair competitive conditions. Although the authorities have largely rejected these arguments, tension and rancor still prevent coordination and cooperation between these two types of organizations.

The 1953 National Education Law stipulates that the Education Ministry must recognize any official institutions that provide state-run education or state-run religious education. Nevertheless, the law permits the establishment of unofficial educational institutions that are also recognized by the Education Ministry but do not belong to either of these two categories. This has led to the creation of an independent network of ultra-orthodox educational institutions that are funded by the state, according to the National Education Law, but are run by third sector organizations. When the National Education Regulations [Recognized Institutions] of 1953 brought all of the educational institutions in Israel under the aegis of the Education Ministry, these independent educational networks also became subject to the Ministry's supervision. Subsequent laws, however, have limited the supervisory powers of the Ministry: the School Inspection Law of 1969 allowed the Minister of Education and Culture to exempt a school from inspection subject to the approval of the Knesset Education and Culture Committee, while the School Inspection Regulations [Principles for Granting Exemptions] of 1970 went even further by including a blanket provision that enabled the Education Minister to dismiss a school from inspection. Thus, while the institutions of the independent ultra-orthodox educational system are funded by the Ministry of Education, they are not subject to its supervision and can determine their own curricula. Higher education institutions in Israel also maintain a high level of independence despite being funded by the state, as stipulated by the Council of Higher Education Law of 1958. According to the law, any academic institution that is an independent legal entity may manage its own academic and administrative affairs within budgetary constraints. According to the 1969 Schools Inspection Law, recognized higher education institutions are exempt from inspection by the Ministry of Education and Culture. The law only requires that these institutions base their budgets on principles of equity in order to continue to receive funding.

The Child Adoption Law [Amendment 2] of 1996 stipulates that the adoption of a child from another country must be carried out via a nonprofit association whose sole purpose is to facilitate international adoptions. Therefore, since 1998, only nonprofit associations have handled the international adoption of children. These associations must be recognized by the Minister of Labor and Social Affairs and the Minister of Justice, are supervised by the Ministry of Labor and Social Affairs, and are responsible for all procedures relating to international adoptions. Twenty-one nonprofit associations were licensed to work in the field of international adoptions in 2000, and, as of June 2000, four of the most highly recognized associations had processed 80% of the 357 children who had been granted entry visas to Israel for the purposes of adoption.

Payments for services, on the other hand, are short-term contracts between the government and third sector organizations. Payments for services are generally for the provision of specific services, such as classes for new immigrants, training courses for the unemployed, summer camps for handicapped children in community centers, professional refresher courses for civil servants at universities, etc. Compared to legislated support, payments for services account for a smaller portion of the public budget, although the funds provided are still quite substantial. While the sums allocated for legislated support have remained relatively constant over the years, the amounts for payments for services have grown, primarily due to increased privatization in the fields of education and social services. Over the last two decades, the government has increasingly ceded control of these areas to non-governmental agencies, and outsourcing to third sector organizations has intensified as a result (Gal, 1994; Doron, 1999; Katan, 1996). Indeed, 70% of government funding to third sector organizations in the form of payments for services is in the fields of education (39%) and social services (31%).

Thus, there are numerous opportunities in Israel for third sector organizations to receive contractual funding. The continuity of this type of funding arrangement throughout Israel's history is reflective of the third sector's traditional role as the state's executive arm. Over the years, however, this situation has made third sector organizations heavily dependent upon the state for funding. In fact, for certain institutions (e.g., the health funds, universities, and educational institutions), the term "third sector organization" is primarily a legal convention that does not necessarily reflect those features typical of a third sector organization, such as being involved in the development of civil society, voluntarism, entrepreneurship, etc. Moreover, organizations that receive contractual funding are obliged to meet certain conditions set by the government; this situation not only greatly restricts their autonomy, but also encourages them to emulate the government's priorities and modus operandi.

B. Grants. Grants are generally provided to an organization as a whole rather than to an organization for the provision of specific activities, although some grants may be given to develop certain programs or projects. Since grants are allocated from public funds, they always provide for supervisory and control mechanisms. However, unlike contracts, an organization has greater discretion over how the funding from a grant will be used. Grants are provided to organizations as support grants, Bequest Funds, support for special objectives, and National Insurance Institute support grants.

Support grants are given to organizations with the expectation that they will be used to "further the policy" of the government ministry that is providing the grant. During the 1990s, the size and number of support grants grew substantially. From 1991 to 1998, support grants more than quadrupled from NIS 600 million to almost NIS 2.6 billion. Although the amounts provided by support grants are far less than those offered by contracts, this type of funding supplies third sector organizations with a substantial source of income. Generally, support grants

Table 5. Government Subsidies to the Third Sector

| | Direct Funding—Grants, 1998 | | | |
| | Support Grants | | Grants from the Bequests Fund | |
	NIS Millions	%	NIS Millions	%
Culture and Recreation	425	16.4	3.2	4.4
Education and Research	1,393	53.6	5.0	6.9
Health	17	0.7	2.4	3.3
Welfare	98	3.8	40.3	55.4
Environment	26	1.0	0.5	0.7
Housing and Development	43	1.6	3.4	4.7
Politics and Social Change	10	0.4	0.5	0.7
Foundations and Philanthropic Activity	158	6.1	10.4	14.3
International Activity	2	0.1	0.2	0.3
Religion	338	13.0	1.2	1.7
Business & Professional Associations	71	2.7	4.1	5.6
Miscellaneous	16	0.6	1.4	1.9
Total	2,596	100	72.7	100

are intended to further professional activities, rather than finance an organization's current expenditures (e.g., salaries, overhead expenses, etc.) or infrastructure costs (e.g., building maintenance, office equipment, etc.), but an organization has more flexibility in how the funds from support grants may be used compared to contracts. Organizations that are eligible for support grants include public institutions operating in the fields of education, culture, religion, science, art, social affairs, health, sports, etc. As Table 5 indicates, the majority of support grants are allocated to educational and research organizations (53.4%), followed by cultural organizations (16%), and religious organizations (13%).

Since the system of support grants was designed to replace the previous arrangement of "special subsidies," which ministers exploited to finance third sector organizations that supported them,[22] the manner in which support grants are distributed is institutionalized and identical for all ministries so as to ensure equal opportunities for all applicants. The new system forces the government ministries to establish criteria for awarding support grants. The criteria must be approved by the Attorney General and publicized in the press. Government ministries are also required to set up "support grant committees" to consider each organization applying for a grant according to criteria recommended by the relevant department within each ministry. A committee cannot approve a request for funds that falls under the jurisdiction of another government ministry, and a list of the nonprofit associations whose requests are approved must be published in the Israeli government's official gazette. Government ministries award subsidies to third sector organizations via a signed document in which the ministry agrees to fund the organization while the latter agrees to use the funds for the purposes intended. The actual funds are transferred in stages. The organization must submit a report demonstrating that it has effectively met the objectives of the prior stage before funds for the next stage are provided.

Despite these complicated procedures, funding decisions for support grants often remain political in nature (DeHartog, 1999). This is due to problems inherent in the political decision-making process in Israel. The government does not have nor has it attempted to collect accurate data on the needs of third sector organizations or the government support that has been granted to these organizations. This situation has rendered statutory evaluations virtually meaningless and has made it much harder to devise equitable criteria for awarding support grants. Therefore, priorities are usually determined by the political considerations of the minister providing the support. As a result, government ministries continue to use support grants as political tools to further "preferred" associations in certain fields at the expense of others. Despite these problems, support grants still play a major role in promoting the growth and development of third sector organizations.

Another form of direct government funding comes through grants made from the Bequests Fund. Such bequests are divided into designated bequests, in which the donor designates the funds for a specific purpose, and undesignated bequests, in which the donor allows the state to decide the purpose for which the funds will be used. As indicated in Table 5 above, most grants from the Bequests Fund are allocated to organizations that provide social services (55%) and to foundations (14.3%). Like support grants, Bequest Funds are intended to be used to support an organization's activities rather than its running costs (e.g., salaries, overheads).

Money from the Bequest Fund for designated requests is allocated according to a written procedure that is published in the government's official gazette. This procedure mandates the establishment of a public committee (the Bequests Committee) that is presided over by a judge and meets periodically to discuss the objectives of the bequests relative to the government's national priorities. Applications for grants from the Bequests Fund are sent to the relevant government ministry. If the ministry approves the request, it must provide justification for its approval and determine the size of the grant. The recommendation is then sent to the Bequests Committee for further discussion. The committee, in turn, delivers its decisions to the Administrator-General in the Ministry of Justice, who ultimately awards the amounts approved by the Bequests Committee. The state allocates funds for undesignated requests via the Bequests Committee, as well.

In the decade since its establishment in 1990, the Bequests Committee has received roughly NIS 1 billion in funds from the Administrator-General to be distributed. In practice, only about half of this amount has been allocated due to: (1) a commitment to long-term projects, particularly those that are perceived to be high on the national agenda, such as the War on Drugs; (2) a desire to set money aside for areas not usually eligible for designated bequests; and (3) in the case of designated requests, a lack of organizations meeting the testators' requirements. On the other hand, of all of the applications sent to the Bequests Committee, only 15% have been approved due to an excess demand over supply. Thus, like support grants, this system of funding has the potential to promote growth and innovative projects; unfortunately, however, the sums are inadequate and their allocation is largely subject to the whims and political interests of the government ministries that approve the requests.

Another form of government funding is support for special objectives. These funds are allocated within the state budget and are granted to third sector organizations—such as universities, *yeshivot*, and institutions within the independent educational network (e.g., *Agudah*, *Shas*)—via the government ministries for specific purposes or to finance particular activities. Support for special objectives may not be used for services that the state is obligated to provide. Unlike support grants and Bequest Funds, applications for this type of support are not reviewed by specific committees within the government ministries. Instead, these funds are distributed in recognition of the importance and contribution of these organizations but also according to political agreements between parties in the government.

Finally, state-sponsored National Insurance Institute (NII) support grants are provided to various types of organizations via four different funds: the Fund for the Development of Services for the Handicapped, the Fund for the Development of Home Care Services, the Fund for Demonstration Projects, and the Manof Fund.[23] In 2000, the budgets of these funds (excluding the Manof Fund) totaled roughly NIS 194 million. While there is no precise data on the proportion of these funds that has been transferred to third sector organizations, many of these groups are supported by the NII, particularly those organizations that deal with disability, long-term care, and demonstration projects.

The Fund for the Development of Services for the Handicapped was set up after the passage of the General Disability Insurance Law in 1973. The fund's budget is derived from the statutory 5% tax collected from individuals and institutions by the NII. Grants from this fund are intended to cover infrastructure expenses only since the ministries are expected to fund direct services for the handicapped. Each year, the fund publishes a call for applications from all agencies for the handicapped. The fund does not support organizations that depend solely on donations, however, since these organizations are perceived to be unstable and are not subject to the intervention and control of the appropriate ministries. In 2000, the fund's budget totaled NIS 123 million.

The Fund for the Development of Home Care Services was established in 1986 as part of the Home Care Insurance Law. The purpose of the fund is to establish, broaden, and improve the infrastructure of services designed for handicapped elders and those eligible under the Home Care Law. Support from the fund is for infrastructure development only and is aimed at developing and improving the quality of community and institutionalized home care services, including the establishment of day care centers for the elderly, the purchase of equipment for special-needs populations, the training of manpower to care for the elderly, the upgrading of sheltered housing for the elderly, and the development of nursing homes. Many of the day care centers that, according to the law, currently provide services to the elderly were established with assistance from this fund. The fund is financed from the budget of the nursing unit in the NII. In 2000, the Fund for the Development of Home Care Services received NIS 32 million (the equivalent of 10% of the total budget allocated to this unit, which is the maximum stipulated by law (Stessman, 2000)).

The Fund for Demonstration Projects helps public institutions and voluntary organizations develop experimental and innovative social projects that serve as models for the development of vital social services. The idea is that successful experimental programs will be adopted by others in the community. The fund is not intended to finance services that the government is obligated to provide by law and does not offer grants in lieu of budgets that are to be provided for by government institutions. In 2000, the fund's budget totaled NIS 27 million. Finally, the Manof Fund is designed to promote work safety and hygiene and to finance activities aimed at the prevention of work accidents. The fund supports all types of organizations, including those in the third sector. In 2000, the fund's budget totaled NIS 12.2 million.

C. Other Forms of Direct Support.   In addition to contracts and grants, third sector organizations receive direct support from other public sources. While it is difficult to obtain exact data on the amounts of these allocations (particularly since most of the funds also support other types of organizations), it is estimated that this type of support to third sector organizations totals tens of millions of shekels, providing an important source of income particularly in light of recent cutbacks in the development budgets of many government ministries. In particular, the Jewish Agency provides an important source of direct support to third sector organizations, especially those working in the field of immigrant absorption. State support for third sector organizations is also funneled through 265 local authorities (through their own budgets or transfers from external funds or organizations, particularly the National Lottery), the religious councils, and other statutory bodies, totaling hundreds of millions of shekels per year (DeHartog, 1999). Likewise, the Knesset Speaker's Fund provides funds to nonprofit associations to complete specific projects. Applications for such grants are approved by the government ministry under whose jurisdiction the project falls. Of the 188 applications for grants from the Knesset Speaker's Fund in 2001, 34 were approved (equaling NIS 1.03 million or NIS 30,000 per association), 30 were rejected, while the remaining organizations are still waiting for a decision.

Indirect Support

Israel also has an extensive system of indirect aid that is comprised of: (1) tax exemptions to third sector organizations (on income, capital gains, property, municipal, local, and salary taxes), and (2) tax exemptions for donors to third sector organizations. The rationale behind this policy is that nonprofit organizations provide public services (frequently these are services that the state is responsible for providing); therefore, they are entitled to an economic "pay off." In other words, tax exemption is part of a policy that supports third sector organizations because of their public function. Underlying this policy is the belief that the government is not the sole provider of public services and that tax concessions should be used to encourage organizations to assume this role. This type of government subsidy is part of an approach known as tax expenditure, in which the reduction of state revenue resulting from tax exemptions to public institutions is equivalent to providing state allocations. As such, not all NPOs are entitled to tax concessions, only those whose activities the legislature wishes to promote.

This system of indirect support is primarily achieved through two laws to which all third sector organizations are subject: the Income Tax Ordinance [New Version] and the Value Added Tax (VAT) Law of 1975. According to the Income Tax Ordinance, which grants tax exemptions on specified income to public institutions,[24] an institution's objectives must be in the public interest in order to obtain a tax exemption. Thus, the income tax authority examines whether the source of an organization's profits is compatible with its objectives (i.e., with the public interest). Even if the source appears to be commercial in nature, as long as the income is an integral part of the organization's public objective, the organization is granted an income tax exemption. This also holds true for profits gained from returns on financial or physical assets.

On the other hand, the VAT Law, which taxes consumer expenditures, emphasizes the nature of a transaction—that is, whether or not a transaction is profit seeking—rather than the nature of the organization. This emphasis is designed to prevent discrimination. Thus, an organization may receive an income tax exemption according to the Income Tax Ordinance but have to pay VAT on certain transactions (or activities) it carries out. For example, an organization is obliged to pay VAT on profits accruing from a source that competes with the business sector. Similarly, tangential transactions, such as leasing out real estate or granting loans, are subject to VAT. In order to be exempt from paying VAT, an organization must:

(1) be an NPO (i.e., not a business organization), and (2) not carry out commercial transactions.

We describe in detail below the different types of tax exemptions granted to third sector organizations and their donors.

A. *Tax Exemptions to Third Sector Organizations.* Third sector organizations enjoy exemptions on income, capital gains, property, municipal, local, and salary taxes. To qualify for income tax exemptions an organization must meet a number of criteria. First, according to paragraph 9(2) of the Income Tax Ordinance, an organization must (1) be defined as a "public institution," and (2) have a pubic objective. In its definition of a public institution, the legislature lists the criteria that entitle an organization to an income tax exemption. The institution must be: (a) an association of at least seven people, the majority of whom are not related to each other (or an endowment, the majority of whose trustees are not related to each other); (b) that exists and operates exclusively for a public purpose, and whose assets and income serve to promote the public interest only, and which (c) files annual reports of assets, income and expenditure with the Income Tax Authorities, according to the regulations stipulated by the Minister of Finance.

"Public purposes" are defined as "religious, cultural, educational, scientific, health, welfare, and sports-related purposes, or any other purposes approved by the Minister of Finance as being in the public's interest." On various occasions, the Minister of Finance has added other "purposes" to this list, including: the promotion of savings in secondary and higher education; the Association for a Secure Israel and related objectives; the prevention of accidents; growth incentives to counteract unemployment; the Genesis Fund for the promotion and development of the Negev; help to disadvantaged localities; immigrant absorption; assistance to discharged soldiers; the promotion of sound government; the preservation of the environment; and the protection of civil rights in Israel. All of these categories, which are recognized in either case law, administrative dispositions, or ministerial decrees, share the following common denominators: (1) the objective is the public interest as a whole without discrimination; (2) the objective is achieved unconditionally without any correlation between the recipients of the service and their participation in its costs; and (3) the institution's activity continues over an extended period of time and focuses on a specific area rather than a particular case.

Once these criteria have been met and it is clear that an organization is a public institution, the question of whether or not income was derived from commercial activity is considered. The legislature's approach has been that a public institution is liable for taxes on income derived from business pursuits even if the institution's primary aim is to serve the public. However, the Minister of Finance published regulations in March 1997 stating that an activity is not considered to be commercial if it is congruent with the public institution's objectives. Thus, income derived from sales or from services that are an integral part of the institution's objectives is exempt from tax. For example, a public institution such as a museum is exempt from paying taxes on income derived from artistic activity linked to its objective, such as entrance fees for an exhibition. On the other hand, activities such as running a gift shop, reception hall, or parking lot are not an integral part of a museums' public objective and income derived from these activities is not tax-exempt.

According to the Capital Gains Tax on Real Estate Law of 1963, NPOs that qualify as public institutions according to the definition outlined in the Income Tax Ordinance are also exempt from paying capital gains taxes on sales of real estate, provided that the property was owned by a public institution for at least one year and was directly used for the institution's purposes at least 80% of the time. The law also exempts gifts of real estate to public institutions from capital gains tax, even if these gifts are defined as "sales," but only after the institution has held the land for at least five years. Likewise, in accordance with the 1961 Property Tax Law, a public institution is granted an exemption from paying property tax on: (1) real estate owned by (a) a public institution that uses the real estate for its intended purpose and from which the institution derives no income or, if income is derived, it is used to meet the institution's objectives, or (b) an endowment that is not used for profit but for educational purposes and, if any income is derived, it is used solely to maintain the school; and (2) land that is used for a public purpose, as determined by the Finance Minister with the approval of the Knesset Finance Committee.

Third sector organizations are also exempt from paying municipal and local taxes according to the provisions of the Municipal Taxes and Government Taxes [Exemptions] Ordinance. These provisions state that taxes will not be placed on any occupied building or land that is owned by a charitable organization, provided the building or land serves as a hospital, refuge, convalescent home, orphanage, nursery school, school, teachers' college, school for the blind, public library, etc. In addition, the occupied building or land may not be used to obtain financial profit. Unlike for-profit companies, third sector organizations are also granted exemptions from paying certain salary taxes.

Finally, third Sector organizations also derive an indirect benefit from the fact that their volunteers are insured under the NII against injury in the course of their duties. Also, third sector organizations are sometimes allowed to use public areas or public buildings and personnel (e.g., National Service volunteers) for free. There are no rules or formal regulations governing such benefits; they are contingent upon the decisions of the relevant authority.

B. *Tax Exemptions for Donors.* The state achieves two primary goals through tax exemptions for donors: (1) it encourages contributions to third sector organizations, thereby increasing private funding to public institutions the government is interested in promoting; and (2) it allows citizens to select those areas to which they would like to contribute some of their taxable income (over which they have no control), thereby forging ties between citizens and third sector organizations. Paragraph 46 of the Income Tax Ordinance grants a tax exemption to any person or corporation that donates money to an organization that has been recognized as a public institution by the Finance Ministry and approved by the Knesset Finance Committee. According to the Income Tax Ordinance, donors receive a 35% tax exemption on any contributions, provided the sum does not exceed 30% of a donor's taxable annual income. In 2001, an addendum was added to the regulations stating that a contribution must not be less than NIS 350 or exceed NIS 2,017,000 in any given tax year.[25] These limits are updated annually. In addition, the law allows these contributions to be made in monetary equivalents. For example, a gift to a public institution is exempt from capital gains tax according to the Income Tax Ordinance, and paragraph 61(a) of the Capital Gains Tax Law grants a tax exemption on the transfer of an estate to a public institution that is recognized as such according to paragraph 46 of the Income Tax Ordinance.

As Table 6 indicates, most indirect support of this kind is granted to educational and research organizations, religious organizations, foundations, and welfare organizations. This is primarily due to the criteria used to determine an organization's eligibility as a public institution and the political considerations that govern these criteria. For example, in early 1998 the Income Tax Commission decided not to renew the status of the Amitai Association for Sound Government

Table 6. Indirect Support of Third Sector Organizations, 1998

	Indirect Funding Tax Refunds to Donors	
	Eligible Organizations	%
Culture and Recreation	311	9.9
Education and Research	774	24.5
Health	79	2.5
Welfare	450	14.3
Environment	13	0.4
Housing and Development	35	1.1
Politics and Social Change	80	2.5
Foundations and Philanthropic Activity	469	14.9
International Activity	19	0.6
Religion	606	19.2
Business & Professional Associations	19	0.6
Miscellaneous	298	9.5
Total	2,596	100

as a public institution, even though the organization had an educational objective and had held a tax-exempt status for close to four years. The Income Tax Commissioner claimed that the association did not meet any of the seven criteria for tax exemption as defined by the Income Tax Ordinance. In response, opposition MKs rallied a majority for a draft bill permitting tax exemptions on contributions to such associations. When the Finance Ministry discovered that the bill was about to pass, it declared that the association's activity was covered by paragraph 9 (2) of the Income Tax Ordinance. Given these political factors, it is not surprising that the allocation of indirect funding closely resembles that of direct funding.

Supervision of Third Sector Organizations

Given the large amounts of money that the public sector invests in third sector organizations, it is not surprising that various external supervisory mechanisms have been created to prevent the misuse of funds. As we described in the first part of this chapter, third sector organizations are obligated by law to establish internal auditing mechanisms. In addition to these, the state has implemented a system of external supervisory mechanisms to oversee third sector organizations. These can be divided into: (1) administrative supervisory mechanisms, such as registrars and tax administrators, that inspect reports that the organizations are required to submit and, when necessary, perform investigations; and (2) operational supervisory mechanisms, such as the State Comptroller's Office and the government ministries, that determine whether third sector organizations are operating efficiently and effectively and that their administrations are sound. We describe both types of supervisory mechanisms in greater detail below.

Registrars and Tax Administrators

All third sector organizations are required by law to report periodically to an auditing body. The auditing body varies according to the type of third sector organization—that is, nonprofit associations, public benefit companies, and trusts/endowments are required to report to distinct oversight organizations. Nonprofit associations are accountable to the Registrar of Nonprofit Associations and the Tax Administrator. According to the Nonprofit Associations Law, nonprofit associations must provide the Registrar with legal documents dating back to the organizations' inception and continuing until the present, including the association's application for registration, the association's articles, the register with the names of the associations' members and board of directors; authorized signatories of the association; minutes of general meetings; financial statements; recommendations from the auditing committee or body; and notifications of any claims filed against the association or members of the board of governors in their capacity as board members.

By law, the Registrar of Associations is entitled to appoint an inspector to conduct an investigation into the way an association is being run, its compliance with legal provisions, and its financial activities.[26] During the course of an investigation, the Registrar has the authority to summon and interrogate witnesses. Once the investigation has been completed, the appointed inspector submits the findings to the Registrar. If any serious irregularities have been discovered, a claim may be filed against the officers of the association or a request for the liquidation of the association may be submitted. If the inspector finds that the association's activities have contravened the law, the association's objectives, or its articles, the Attorney General or the Registrar may submit a request for the compulsory liquidation of the association.

Any information submitted to the Registrar pertaining to the financial situation of nonprofit associations may also be used by the government ministries to help them allocate funds. Although nonprofit associations are required by law to submit annual financial reports to the Registrar, the Registrar is not required to liquidate any organizations that do not provide this information. In fact, in several cases, government funds were illegally awarded to organizations that failed to submit financial reports to the Registrar. Government agencies have failed to audit the activities of nonprofit associations effectively due to the enormity of the task—there are literally thousands of organizations receiving aid (approximately 4,500 in 1996). This lack of adequate supervision encourages corruption and the misuse of government funds.

Nonprofit associations are also subject to the authority of the Tax Administrator. According to the income tax regulations, any association in its capacity as a public institution is obligated to submit a detailed report on income and expenditures to the Tax Administrator. The report must specify the association's income and expenditures, its employees and their salaries, information on the bodies controlled by the association and any affiliated organizations, donations the association has given or received, and a report on the association's non-exempt income.

Like nonprofit associations, public benefit companies must answer to the Companies Registrar and the Endowments Registrar. According to the Companies Ordinance and Companies Law, a public benefit company must provide the Companies Registrar with all of the details of the company, including its application for registration, its founding documents, its goals, its assets, a registry of its directors, an audited balance sheet, an annual report, all of the company's mortgaged liabilities, and an annual account of the company's income and expenditures. The Companies Ordinance allows the Minister of Justice to appoint an investigator to examine a public benefit company.[27] If an investigation is undertaken, the officers and agents of the company must submit all of their pertinent documents for inspection. According to the Companies Ordinance, they may also be subject to interrogation, although this tactic has rarely been exercised and ultimately was rescinded by the Companies Law.

Upon request, a public benefit company must also submit a report on its affairs to the Endowments Registrar. According to the Trust Law, the Endowments Registrar may also carry out an investigation of a public benefit company if it has reason to believe that the company failed to observe a provision of the Trust Law, violated its stated objectives, or submitted incorrect documents the Registrar. The Registrar may invoke financial sanctions on the company if it violates any of its reporting requirements.

Like public benefit companies, public endowments are also accountable to the Endowments Registrar. According to the Trust Law, a trustee of a public trust must keep records of all matters pertaining to the trust and submit a report to the Endowments Registrar according to a schedule determined by the Minister of Justice. Furthermore, at any time, the Registrar may request to view relevant information pertaining to the trust, thus enabling the Registrar to be aware of problems that might lead to an investigation. If there is reason to believe that a provision of the Endowments Law or of the endowment writ has been violated, the Registrar may order an investigation. Although the law does not specify the course of action to be taken after an investigation, the Registrar may bring an action against any trustees who have defaulted on their required obligations or may advise the Attorney General to file a claim against such trustees (in the case of a religious endowment this would take place in a religious court).

Government Ministries and the State Comptroller's Office

Third sector organizations are also accountable to the government ministries that provide them with funding and to the State Comptroller. Unfortunately, neither of these mechanisms have been particularly effective at monitoring the activities of third sector organizations, primarily due to problems within their own institutions. While all government ministries are required to appoint an inspector to monitor and control recipient organizations on an ongoing basis, the ministries are responsible for determining their own auditing procedures when they allocate funds. Thus, the number of inspections that are conducted varies according to the size of the funds allocated, the number of recipient organizations, and the availability of inspectors. Reports show, however, that many government ministries fail to inspect the organizations they fund in an adequate manner. As a result, there are a number of organizations receiving sizable amounts of government funding that are dormant or semi-dormant (these organizations are dubbed "fictitious associations").

The State Comptroller is also charged with monitoring the activities of all state-funded organizations. In recent years, the Comptroller's Office has inspected only a handful of organizations. In such instances, however, it has discovered some serious violations. Often, these irregularities have stemmed from the government agencies charged with supervising the third sector organizations (e.g., the government ministries, the Bequests Committee). In particular, the State Comptroller's Office has found disparities between the amounts of funding available to be allocated to third sector organizations and the sums that actually have been disbursed. Over a several year period, only 76% of available funds had been distributed. In addition, the Comptroller's Office found that some organizations had submitted applications to more than one government ministry and that the absence of a centralized information center frequently led to the duplication of subsidies. The Comptroller's Office also found that in addition to government allocations, third sector organizations often received payments from other government budgets. Finally, it discovered that the methods the Accountant-General used to identify third sector organizations were inconsistent—some organizations were catalogued by their registration numbers, others by their tax filing numbers, and still others by a different identification number altogether. Unfortunately, these violations have made many Israelis mistrustful of third sector organizations and less willing to support them. As a result, these organizations have become even more dependent upon the government ministries for funding.

Government Policy since 1980

The social and political changes that occurred within Israeli society during the 1980s and 1990s have affected the government's current policy towards the sector. In particular, these dynamics have influenced: (1) the type of direct and indirect funding that third sector organizations receive; (2) the type of legislation that has been passed; (3) the types of public services that third sector and commercial organizations provide; and (4) the trend towards privatization. We describe each of these factors in detail below.

Funding Patterns

Over the last two decades, significant changes have occurred to improve the equitable distribution of government funds and increase government supervision of third sector organizations. For instance, the Bequests Committee was established in 1990 to ensure the equal allocation of Bequests Funds after it was discovered that the ministerial committees were using the funds to finance their current activities and promote their own political agendas. Indeed, today the distribution of funds is more transparent and open to public scrutiny, compelling the authorities to carefully consider the allocation of funds. This has been evidenced in a number of High Court rulings. For example, in a case where religious youth movements were receiving funds from both the Education and Religious Affairs Ministries, the High Court ruled that organizations could not receive duplicate funds. As a result, the number of third sector organizations eligible for government support has increased.

Likewise, after a decade of legal and political wrangling over the allocation of public funds (known as special funds) to political parties, an amendment was introduced to the Budget Law in 1992 to ensure a more equitable and efficient distribution of funds to third sector organizations. Unfortunately, as DeHartog (1998) points out, those aiming to promote specific political agendas have discovered loopholes to this law. For example, funding criteria have been "tailored" to match the characteristics of those third sector organizations that the government ministries are interested in promoting.

Another significant development has made it more difficult for organizations to qualify for tax exemptions (i.e., indirect support to third sector organizations), thereby increasing government supervision. In a Supreme Court case involving the nonprofit association, *Bi-Sh'arayikh Yerushalayim*, the VAT authorities argued that the association failed to meet two of the four qualifying criteria for an NPO: (1) the organization would be undertaking commercial activities or competing with other commercial organizations, and (2) the organization's classification as an NPO would not provide an advantage over commercial organizations in the same field. The High Court ruled in favor of the tax authorities, thereby allowing for stricter government supervision of third sector organizations. Despite these significant improvements, however, the government still adheres to a closed decision-making process and remains highly discriminatory in its approach to distributing funds to third sector organizations.

Legislation

The most important piece of legislation affecting third sector organizations over the last two decades is the Nonprofit Associations Law, which was enacted in 1980. This watershed piece of legislation granted government authorities greater supervisory powers over third sector organizations. The law replaced the 1906 Ottoman Law, and, as Yishai (1987) notes, differs from the old law in four distinct ways: (1) the Nonprofit Associations Law requires that new organization register with the Registrar of Associations, whereas the previous law required that new organizations simply notify the district governor of their existence; (2) the new law incorporates a restrictive clause prohibiting the establishment of an organization that threatens the existence of the State of Israel or the democratic nature of the state; (3) the new law stipulates that an association must establish internal structures (i.e., general assembly, board of directors, audit committee) and submit annual financial reports, while the old law did not intervene in an association's internal affairs or management; and (4) the new law allows the Registrar to close down an association.

In 1996, a number of amendments were introduced to the law increasing the powers of the Registrar of Associations (Tzahor, 1996), some of which further restricted the freedom of activity of third sector organizations. For example, the organizations were obliged to provide the Registrar with information on any litigation raised against them, clarify details of financial reports, submit any documents requested by the Registrar, and provide details of anonymous contributions as requested by the Registrar. On the other hand, some of the amendments worked in favor of the associations. Among these were: the board of directors' obligation to convene a meeting of the general assembly within 21 days of a request, even if the call came from a minority of members; the general assembly's right to submit a written vote; and the possibility of convening a "small" meeting of the general assembly composed of elected representatives if the general assembly has more than 200 members.

The debate leading up to the ratification of the Nonprofit Associations Law provided the Israeli legislature with a rare opportunity to discuss the role of the third sector in Israel. Unfortunately, it failed to rise to the occasion. Although the debate took place at a time when third sector organizations were proliferating, the main focus of the discussion was the issue of freedom of association and how this right would be affected by the new law. This is a good illustration of the political system's failure to devise a comprehensive policy toward the third sector, dealing instead with individual issues on a piecemeal basis and then only when required to do so. Nevertheless, the Nonprofit Associations Law constitutes one of the major legal safeguards for third sector activity in Israel today. Although some feel that the law (particularly recent amendments) intervenes too much in the activities of nonprofit organizations (Yishai, 1998), it undeniably constituted a turning point for the third sector and contributed to the rise in the number of such organizations in Israel.

The Provision of Public Services

A significant development over the last two decades has been the increased number of commercial organizations providing public services on behalf of the government (i.e., the outsourcing of government services to private companies). As mentioned previously, this trend has led to tensions between commercial and nonprofit organizations, especially within the home care industry for the disabled elderly. In particular, the private nursing care organizations claimed that they could not compete fairly with third sector organizations because the committee that chose those organizations that were eligible to receive government funding was headed by a local authority who was likely to favor local nonprofit associations over private companies and because third sector organizations received tax concessions from the government. In response to the first complaint, the government stipulated that no board members, owners, employees, or unsalaried workers of an association could become members of a local committee. Additionally, the NII issued instructions to local committees on how to choose providers in a fair and nondiscriminatory manner. Although the authorities have not altered the tax breaks that NPOs receive, all organizations must now undergo an inspection before being classified as NPOs or public institutions.

Clearly, the competition between business and third sector organizations has led to enormous friction and unfortunately has hampered any cooperation between these two types of organizations. Moreover, as a result of this struggle, many NPOs have been forced to adopt the business strategies of commercial companies or engage in new areas of activity (Katan and Loewenstein, 1999). As a result, the boundaries between the third and business sectors have become blurred and third sector organizations have lost some of their distinct features. It is not clear whether these developments have affected the quality of the services that nonprofit associations provide.

Trends toward Privatization

One of the most prominent features of Israel's socioeconomic policy over the last two decades has been the trend toward privatization—or the adaptation of market principles to the provision of public services. In the context of providing social services, privatization has meant that the state no longer assumes full responsibility for the funding, supervision, provision, or delivery of services (Doron, 1989; Gal, 1994). This policy of privatization, which has earned widespread support in Israel over the last two decades, is the result of neo-conservative ideologies that flourished in Israel during the 1980s (Doron, 1999). It was primarily prompted by the desire to reduce public expenditures, streamline the economy, and curtail government intervention. In addition, advocates of privatization argued that nongovernmental organizations are more efficient, provide a better quality of service, are more flexible and innovative, and offer customers a wider selection of services (Schmid and Borowsky, 2000). Furthermore, such proponents maintained that exploiting Israel's economic growth potential, which is predominantly dependent on the business sector, required less government intervention in the economy (Doron, 1999; p. 14)

In response to these pressures, a de facto policy of privatization has emerged in the fields of welfare, education, and health, with the outsourcing of various government services. In addition, elements of this policy can be seen in the legislation regulating the activities of non-governmental organizations. For example, the Home Care Law stipulates that non-governmental agencies are to provide home care services and the 1996 amendment to the Adoption Law explicitly states that only nonprofit associations can provide international adoption services in Israel. Moreover, the government's budget for 2000–2002 reflects a clear desire to decrease and optimize the public sector and increase competition within the economy. To date, privatization in Israel has been limited to the provision of services only. In most cases of outsourcing, the state continues to bear the cost of the service, determine the regulations and criteria governing its provision, and supervise its implementation (by choosing the service-provision organizations). This partial privatization allows the state to retain its control over social services while distancing and protecting itself from the demands of the recipients (Ajzenstadt and Rozenhek, 2000).

Nevertheless, this policy of privatization has significantly impacted the government's overall policy towards the third sector. Privatization has encouraged the establishment of many new third sector organizations, particularly within the home care industry after the Home Care Law was enacted in 1988. The policy of privatization has also created new funding options for third sector organizations as many services that the government formerly provided have been transferred to non-governmental agencies. As a result, third sector organizations have engaged in new activities or expanded their current services. To a large extent, the policy of privatization has also enhanced the prestige of third sector organizations within the government and has offered them opportunities to undertake new initiatives and develop innovative projects with government funding. In some instances, there was a sharp increase in the participation of third sector organizations in various projects and policy-making processes. In addition, privatization has emphasized the third sector's role as a provider of services in addition to a promoter of civil society.

On the other hand, privatization has presented third sector organizations with a new set of challenges. Partial privatization has intensified the third sector's dependence on the government, requiring that third sector organizations defer to the government's institutions, procedures, and bureaucracy. In some cases, this dependency has led to an erosion of autonomy and has threatened the unique features of third sector organizations, such as initiative, innovation, and advocacy on behalf of disadvantaged groups. In addition, privatization has created competition between third sector and business organizations operating in the same field. As we noted previously, this situation has generated friction between the two types of organizations and has caused some third sector organizations to abandon their previous policies and adopt business-style practices in order to become more economical and competitive.

CURRENT POLICY AND LEGISLATIVE ISSUES FACING THE THIRD SECTOR

The most pressing matter concerning the third sector in Israel today is undoubtedly the issue of public policy. Despite the impressive growth in the number of third sector organizations and their activities, as well as their growing social, political, and economic importance, the government has not made any attempt to devise a clear policy regarding the third sector. Furthermore, although there are laws, provisions, and procedures that regulate interactions between third sector organizations and the government, these provisions vary among the many government ministries and authorities. As a result, third sector organizations operate in a nebulous and potentially risky environment. Given the expanding roles of third sector organizations as service providers and developers of civil society, it is imperative that suitable legal and policy frameworks be established. In this part of the chapter, we present some of the main issues concerning public policy towards the third sector. In doing so, our aim is not to offer solutions to these problems but to discuss issues that often are overlooked.

Government Policy towards the Third Sector

The absence of a clear government policy towards the third sector creates problems for both parties involved. First, it hinders the development of a sound working relationship between the third sector and the government. Furthermore, it diminishes the autonomy of third sector organizations, making them subject to the various government authorities whose policies are hard to predict. This is particularly problematic for "civil society" organizations, which are usually smaller, less developed, and weaker than older and larger organizations (i.e., universities, health funds, yeshivot), which generally receive better treatment and whose relationship with the government is regulated by specific laws and arrangements.

In developing a comprehensive government policy towards the third sector, some questions must be considered: (1) What would be the boundaries of government intervention in the third sector? Would increased government intervention impinge on the activities and autonomy of third sector organizations? (2) Should government policy towards the third sector be comprised of a general framework or specific and detailed regulations? Should this policy be binding on all government institutions that interact with the third sector or should each institution be allowed to determine its own distinct policy towards the third sector?

Government Policy towards Different Types of Third Sector Organizations

Given that the third sector in Israel is comprised of different kinds of organizations with distinct characteristics, goals, and needs, it is worth considering whether the government should develop different policies for each type of organization. In particular, there is a significant distinction between those third sector organizations that provide services on behalf of the state versus those that promote civil society or have an advocacy orientation. It seems fairly logical that those organizations that are providing services for the state should receive a larger share of government funding than the other types of third sector organizations. Moreover, civil society or advocacy organizations are less inclined to accept government support on the grounds that it might impinge upon their autonomy. Given these distinctions, should the government develop separate policies for dealing with these distinct organizations? Should the government support third sector organizations working in specific fields of those that cater to specific populations? Is there reason to promote civil society organizations as a tool for strengthening democracy among specific population groups but not necessarily through direct government funding? Could a policy be created that favors the inclusion of advocacy groups in policy-making processes that affect the populations they represent? Could the relevant government ministries and bodies assume a consulting role vis-à-vis these different types of third sector organizations?

Government Funding of the Third Sector

The system of subsidies supporting third sector organizations in Israel suffers from bureaucratic problems, disorganization, and a lack of transparency. The system is based upon a mixture of protocols and agreements resulting from political pressures without any distinct ideological basis. This piecemeal system of support involving substantial sums of money has led many organizations to "tailor" their activities to conform to government eligibility criteria. It also has created expectations among third sector organizations that they will receive both direct and indirect funding from the government, which, in turn, has led to a situation of dependency, particularly since there are few, if any, alternative funding sources available to third sector organizations in Israel.

The system also fails to distinguish between different types of organizations in Israel (i.e., non-profit, public sector, or business). For instance, both business and nonprofit organizations are eligible to receive certain kinds of contracts (e.g., for managing homes for the elderly, long-term nursing care facilities) and both third and public sector organizations may receive particular types of grants (e.g., from the Bequests Fund). The failure to differentiate between the various types of organizations qualifying for public support in Israel reflects the fluidity of the boundaries between the sectors and the absence of a well thought-out policy towards the third sector and its unique contributions.

The political nature of the funding system also has a negative affect on both direct and indirect support. The grants system is plagued with political pressures at the national, ministerial, and local levels. While attempts have been made to develop a more consistent and fair system, particularly with regards to the Bequests Fund, new loopholes have been found. Likewise those organizations that wish to qualify as public institutions in order to obtain tax concessions must gain the approval of both a government minister and a Knesset committee. Even in the case of "in kind" funds (e.g., permission to use buildings or land, voluntary personnel, or various local tax concessions), no clear-cut policy exists and decisions are left to government authorities or other public figures.

In addition, the terms under which funds are granted to third sector organizations often are unclear, unnecessary, or discriminatory. Often, tax exemptions are granted reluctantly to third sector organizations, an indication of the lack of a clear policy on the issue. In addition, government ministries often specify that funds must be used for current activities only, without considering that organizations must pay infrastructure and overhead costs in order to provide services. As a result, organizations tend to inflate the costs of projects when applying for funds so that they will be able to cover infrastructure and overhead costs, as well. Finally, although third sector organizations are eligible for various tax exemptions, they are the only organizations in Israel that are required to pay "salary tax" and VAT for inputs purchased (that is, in addition to paying salaries to their employees, NPOs must pay taxes to the government on the basis of those salaries or the actual cost of all of those salaries; this is what is called the "input tax").

Lastly, the funding system suffers from a lack of clear eligibility criteria, agency coordination, and alternative funding sources. Without clearly defined standards, government ministries are more likely to tailor eligibility criteria to meet the characteristics of organizations they wish to promote. Likewise, the lack of coordination between the various allocating ministries raises doubts regarding the efficiency and equality of the system.[28] In addition, contractual funding tends to be restricted to a handful of large organizations (e.g., six universities, the four health funds, the three largest women's day care service-providing organizations, the major theaters and orchestras, large research centers, etc.) and there is little leeway for "newcomers." Other funding sources are necessary to promote entrepreneurship and the development of new organizations and activities. This need is especially urgent in light of the growing competition between third sector and commercial organizations operating in the same fields.

Supervision and Control of the Third Sector

There are a number of issues hindering the proper supervision of third sector organizations. The main problem common to all of the supervisory mechanisms overseeing third sector organizations in Israel is their lack of efficiency. For example, although nonprofit associations are inspected during the registration stage, the supervision of these organizations thereafter is virtually nonexistent with the exception of ensuring that various procedural mechanisms and arrangements (e.g., articles, audit committees, etc.) are in place. In addition, there is a lack of consistency in the policies of the various supervisory bodies, leading to a situation wherein some associations are subject to government supervision and control while others are not. Some of the methods that the supervisory bodies use to fulfill their oversight duties are also problematic, such as the subcontracting of external accountants and the manner in which these accountants are selected.

From the perspective of the third sector organizations, another concern is the considerable amount of authority vested in the supervisory bodies, enabling them to intervene in the associations' activities and apply various sanctions (e.g., the deferral or denial of permits). Despite these possible penalties, there have been a number of cases in recent years in which third sector organizations have misused funds. Although these cases have led to a strengthening of the supervisory mechanisms, unfortunately this has not resulted in greater efficiency. Moreover, there are lingering questions about the level of government intervention into third sector organizations that is acceptable and the way in which the government perceives third sector organizations and their activities. The current atmosphere seems to indicate that the government mistrusts third sector organizations. Given this situation, it seems worthwhile to examine ways of streamlining the various supervisory bodies to make them more effective. Given the concern among third sector organizations about the level of government intervention into their affairs, perhaps the supervisory bodies could consider acting in alternative roles, such as mentors or guides, rather than assuming a purely supervisory or punitive function. It may also be helpful to find ways to integrate third sector organizations into the supervisory system.

Government Policy towards Foundations and Philanthropy

Foundations and philanthropy are two of the primary sources of civil society activities within the third sector. The government provides a substantial amount of the funding that foundations receive and in many cases it is government rather than private financing that is critical to maintaining a foundation's existence (Gidron, Katz, and Bar, 2000). Despite the large number of registered foundations in Israel, however, only a small number of them support a specific cause or field of activity and as a result they are less likely to support more than one organization. In fact, the majority of foundations award grants to individuals (e.g., scholarships, payment of medical costs) or to a single organization (e.g., Associations or Friends of Universities, museums, theaters). Those foundations that do support a number of organizations, on the other hand, are eager to promote issues such as environmental quality or Jewish–Arab coexistence and can serve as an alternative funding source and as a catalyst for social change. These types of foundations, however, suffer from a lack of significant incentives that would promote their development. For instance, a capital tax policy that encourages citizens to transfer some of their property to charitable foundations could provide an alternate source of funding for these foundations.

Another serious shortcoming is the lack of coordination between the foundations and other third sector organizations. For example, no detailed information exists on the various foundations, their fields of activity, or their eligibility requirements. Similarly, other third sector organizations are not provided with any information on the financial options available to them from foundations or how to avail themselves of this source of funding. In addition, the foundations' policy of restricting funding to specific projects favors established organizations that have existing sources of funding for their current expenses. Ironically, therefore, the smaller, less established, and less financially secure organizations (many of which are advocacy groups) that are not eligible for government funding also have trouble qualifying for grants from foundations. This situation raises the question of whether the state, which has an interest in strengthening civil society, should support foundations and encourage philanthropy as a means of promoting civil society, and if so, how?

CONCLUSION

The basic principle underlying the legal provisions pertaining to third sector organizations in Israel is the attempt to strike a balance between the right to freedom of association in a democracy and the need to protect the state from any concomitant harm. Nevertheless, the government's policy toward the third sector has evolved in a haphazard way and remains extremely vague and unclear. Despite the existence of laws and provisions, there is no distinct government policy toward the third sector and in many cases the government's attitude toward the sector is ambiguous. On the one hand, the government clearly supports the freedom of association and promotes the third sector through direct and indirect support that amounts to large sums of money. On the other hand, the state is clearly interested in protecting itself from the activities of the third sector and restricts the freedom of association to a larger extent than many other countries in the world by grossly intervening in the associations' affairs through special supervisory mechanisms (Yishai, 1998). Moreover, the state directs most of its financial support to those organizations that provide services on behalf of the state and those that promote the state's political agendas. Therefore, this de facto government policy primarily maintains those organizations that provide welfare services and ignores other functions of the third sector, particularly the development of civil society. Those tools that are used to promote civil society in the rest of the world—i.e., direct subsidies and tax concessions—are primarily used to promote service-provision organizations in Israel.

Thus, despite the impressive growth in the number, scope, and range of activities of third sector organizations since the 1970s, there has been no significant corresponding development in the government's policy toward the sector. Clearly, Israeli policymakers have thus far failed to recognize the third sector as a separate entity with its own unique characteristics and functions. The various laws and protocols pertaining to the third sector lack a cohesive and unified vision and have not been founded on any predominant ideological or theoretical basis. Under these circumstances, irregularities are certain to arise. The various government bodies that interact with the third sector determine and apply policies differentially, without any attempts at coordination. In many cases, the policy of one institution differs from, clashes with, or even opposes the policy of another institution. Thus, the government's policy towards the third sector in Israel can be defined as obscure, muddled, inconsistent, and vacillating between conflicting goals.

NOTES

13 The legal code includes ordinary laws and basic laws. Basic laws are equivalent to constitutional laws. They have a higher status than ordinary laws and are intended to be transformed into a constitution in the future.

14 Cooperative societies, covered by the Cooperative Societies Ordinance 1933, are sometimes included in this category (see Bar-Mor, 1997). Despite the social nature of their activities, we chose not to include cooperative societies in the third sector because in Israel these organizations distribute profits to their members.

15 This type of incorporation includes sometimes statutory corporations, which are established by a special law. An example of this type of organization is the Higher Education Council, which was established by virtue of the 1958 Higher Education Council Law. Statutory corporations implement public objectives conferred by the state, may not distribute profits, and cannot be established by the public.

16 Although the general assembly usually elects the board of directors, the Nonprofit Associations Law also stipulates that any other body or person may select members of the board of directors. The general assembly can choose the method it prefers. If an association fails to appoint a board of directors, the Registrar of Associations may select board members from among the amuta's general assembly.

17 If a board member's term of office has expired and no replacement has been found, the member must continue in office until a suitable replacement is found.

18 This provision is in accord with the 1973 Contracts Law [general section], which places a similar obligation on all contractual commitments, and with the general policy of prohibiting the establishment of associations whose purposes undermine the basic principles of democracy.

19 High Court Petition, 647/89.

20 For example, the day-care centers that women's organizations (e.g., WIZO, Na'amat, and Emunah) provide.

21 In practice, the health funds are still incorporated as associations under Ottoman law and have no incentive to change their status to nonprofit associations.

22 Special subsidies were largely influenced by political considerations and were distributed in a highly inequitable manner. This was evident in a number of High Court cases. For example, in MK Ya'ir Tsaban v. the Minister of Finance, et al. (High Court Petition 59/88), the court determined that "for formal purposes, clear and transparent criteria for allocating financial support must be drawn up and suitable audit mechanisms set in place to ensure the money is serving its purpose." They further stated that "as far as the substance of the law is concerned, before the government authorities allocate funds, they must be convinced that the purpose for which the funds are assigned is one that the state has an interest in supporting." In a similar case, Yehuda Ressler v. Minister of Finance, et al. (High Court Petition 1593/90), the court stated that the manner in which special funds were distributed was cause for concern. Finally,

in 1992, following public pressure for reform, an amendment to the 1985 Budgetary Principles Law was introduced that forbid the funding of "special" institutions.

23   For further information on the various funds and their activities, see Y. Stessman, 2000.

24   The Income Tax Ordinance classifies third sector organizations as public institutions; the VAT law considers them to be nonprofit organizations.

25   This exemption is deducted from the amount of tax the taxpayer would have had to pay. This method is different from that used in the U.S., in which the amount of the contribution is deducted from the taxpayer's taxable income, allowing the taxpayer to be in a lower tax bracket.

26   An investigation is usually undertaken at the request of the public, the general assembly of an association (with the approval of one-quarter of all members), or an associations' auditing committee or body.

27   Members of the company may request an investigation if they have adequate justification and the support of at least one-fifth of the membership.

28   It should be noted that this problem is also evident in other public funding bodies, such as the Knesset, the local authorities, etc.

Chapter 4

Historical Development of the Third Sector
Continuity and Change

INTRODUCTION

Analyzing the Israeli third sector from an historical perspective entails several challenges. First, as we have described in previous chapters, the concept of a "third sector" is relatively new in Israel. Although these types of organizations have always existed in Israeli society fulfilling a variety of functions, the third sector has not received much attention from researchers. Of the hundreds of publications that have been written about Israeli society, most discussions have primarily focused on a particular organization or category of organizations, and no study has been undertaken to examine the contributions of the third sector as whole. Moreover, in attempting to analyze the history of the third sector in Israel, we are imposing a contemporary definition onto an earlier reality. This problem is not unique, however, and researchers who have studied the third sector in other countries have developed ways of overcoming this obstacle (Kendall and Knapp, 1996; Barbetta, 1997; Anheier and Seibel, 2001).

The system of government in Israel also presents challenges for an historical analysis. Unlike other countries where a clear-cut system of government has always existed, prior to 1948, Israel was governed by both an external system of government (Ottoman and British rule, respectively) and a communal system that represented an "internal" form of government. Although this "internal" government lacked formal sovereignty, for extended periods it was highly autonomous and held significant authority within the Jewish community in Palestine.[29] This type of "internal" government arrangement sprang from existing communal organizations, making the distinction between these two arenas vague and often indistinguishable.

Hence, throughout the pre-state era there was ambiguity over whether the Jewish communal institutions were part of the governmental or voluntary systems. Furthermore, these factors continued to influence the nature of the public and third sectors after the establishment of the state, making it very difficult to distinguish between the third and public sectors at various times throughout Israeli history.

Finally, a comprehensive analysis of the historical development of the Israeli third sector cannot be undertaken without considering the social, economic, and political developments affecting the environment in which the sector has operated. This situation is further complicated by the fact that third sector organizations often have been used as tools to generate changes within society. In other words, not only has the third sector been influenced by environmental factors, but the sector itself has served as a catalyst for transforming societal patterns. This point is especially apparent when we divide Israeli history into eras or subperiods. This type of division emphasizes structural changes within Israeli society and is generally accepted by researchers who analyze Israeli society and politics.

In our examination, we divide Israeli history according to the periodization approach, a generally accepted method of analysis (Eisenstadt, 1989) employed by earlier scholars of the third sector (Gidron, 1997; Silber and Rosenhek, 1999) that identifies important points in Israeli history, including both specific events and processes that have led to far-reaching ideological, social, and political changes. Thus, we analyze Israeli history according to the following time periods: (1) the "*Yishuv*" or pre-state period spanning from 1880–1948; (2) the "statehood period" extending from 1948 to the mid- to late-1970s; and (3) the "pluralistic period" ranging from the mid-1970s to the present. Unlike some other researchers, who have included the Diaspora period in their work,[30] we chose to omit this era because it extends over two millennia and involves populations on numerous continents. Moreover, information from this period is incomplete. Therefore, although this era was highly important and influential, we view it as a backdrop to the development of the Israeli third sector.

For each time period included in our periodical analysis, we present an overall picture of the third sector, outline the functions of the sector, and consider the extent to which third sector organizations served as precursors for impending societal changes. In particular, we consider: (1) the social, political, and ideological background of each era; (2) the central attributes of the existing third sector organizations, including the types of organizations, their activities, their funding arrangements, and their relationships within Israeli society; and (3) third sector organizations within the ultra-Orthodox (*Haredi*) Jewish and the Arab populations. Our discussion focuses primarily upon the conceptual framework we have presented throughout this book: the third sector's role in the provision of services within the welfare state and in the development of "civil society."

In conducting our analysis, we drew upon four types of publications: (1) publications dealing with the historical development of the third sector (Jaffe, 1992; Gidron, 1997; Silber and Rosenhek, 1999); (2) publications pertaining to a specific category of third sector organizations (Kramer, 1976; Yishai, 1990; Loewenberg, 1991; Hermann, 1995); (3) publications related to the development of Israeli society, politics, and economy that refer (even if remotely) to organizations that fit our criteria of the third sector; and (4) original empirical studies dealing with diverse aspects of the third sector, generally focusing on a specific organization. Overall, we found that although major changes have occurred within the third sector throughout the course of history, third sector organizations have remained a stable and continuous force within Israeli society.

HISTORICAL OVERVIEW OF JEWISH ORGANIZATIONAL TRADITIONS

Before undertaking a periodical analysis of the third sector in Israel, it is important to note significant, ongoing trends that have occurred throughout Jewish history (including the Diaspora) that have greatly influenced the development of third sector organizations. For instance, Eisenstadt (1989) suggests that the rise of ideological movements within Israeli society can be traced back to the social structures of the Jewish people. In particular, he believes that the monotheistic Jewish religion, which espouses direct (democratic) contact with God, has led to the development of institutional arrangements characterized by "structural heterogeneity, continuous differentiation, and conflictual situations between social groups ... [with] instability and heterogeneity at the center [and the existence of] numerous political, social, and religious elites." All of these factors have led to a "restructuring of the mutual ties between the leaders and the nation [that frequently has given] birth to different ideological movements" (p. 28). Elazar (1994, 1997) posits a similar thesis of continuity within the Jewish political tradition that has resulted in the creation of various ideological movements.

Another ideational basis for the development of the third sector in Israel has been the Jewish tradition of *tzedaka*—the giving of charity and mutual aid. Tzedaka is mentioned in the bible as being a cornerstone for the development of third sector organizations and has been reinforced in the rabbinical literature and throughout the Jewish communities in the Diaspora. In particular, the bible provides tenets on giving to the poor and the needy (e.g., Deuteronomy 15:7–10), as well as more detailed rules for establishing specific mechanisms for donating direct and indirect aid to the poor, such as *leket* (gleanings), *shikhekha* (the forgotten sheaf), and *pe'ah* (the poor man's tithe); over time, these traditions have led to the development of such institutions as the *kupat tzdaka* (charity fund) and *beit tamhoi* (the soup kitchen) (Silber and Rosenhek, 1999; Jaffe, 1992). Although it is difficult to estimate the extent to which these laws were actually implemented during ancient times, charity to the poor has been a central and basic religious obligation in Jewish communities throughout the ages (Bogen, 1917; Frisch, 1924; Bergman, 1944).

Many scholars consider the Middle Ages to be the golden age of the autonomous Jewish community (Katz, 1958), and the communal organizations developed during this period have served as models for future "Jewish" institutions. Four significant trends emerged during this time, often resulting from the repressive non-Jewish environment (Silber and Rosenhek, 1999). First, Jewish organizations became highly autonomous and developed a system that combined taxation and philanthropy to finance their activities. A variety of means of enforcement and constraint were employed to collect these funds, including social pressures and penalties such as restrictions on the freedom of movement and even flogging. Second, Jewish organizations established a communal system of fundraising and distribution, in which supervisors ran charitable institutions (e.g., soup kitchens, shelters for the poor, and hospitals) and oversaw the collection and distribution of funds. Third, in the late Middle Ages, voluntary enterprises and mutual aid organizations emerged that differed from and often clashed with existing communal organizations. Examples of these organizations include *hevra kadisha* (the burial society),[31] *bikur holim* (visiting the sick), *kolelim* (yeshivas), *kupot gemach* (benevolent funds), *hachnasat kalah* (bridal funds), and *pidyon shvuyim* (funds for the redemption of prisoners). Finally, funds (often referred to as "distribution" monies) were established to support the Jewish community living in The Holy Land. This was part of a long-standing tradition among Diaspora Jews dating back to the Babylonian Exile and continuing to this day. In addition, during the Middle Ages, Jewish society began to make little distinction between individual voluntary activity and coercion by the community to participate in such activity.[32] This trend would have a significant impact on the development of third sector organizations in Israel.

During the Age of Enlightenment at the end of the 17th century, the cohesiveness of the traditional Jewish communities was weakened due to the advent of the Jewish reform movement and a general change towards secularism among the Jewish people. At the same time, however, particularist voluntary organizations, mutual aid organizations, and sodalities grew stronger, gradually assuming the functions of the traditional organizations. Eisenstadt (1989) argues that instead of incorporating the trend towards modernization that was sweeping through Western Europe, Jews continued to perpetuate earlier patterns of behavior. Thus, Jewish religious, philanthropic, and academic organizations continued to be socially segregated, involved in multiple activities, and concerned with the provision of mutual aid. At times, these organizations helped strengthen each other, even when their activities clashed (Eisenstadt, 1989, pp. 80–81).

In the nineteenth and twentieth centuries, modern, mostly local, Jewish institutions were established in Eastern Europe that reflected a rich community life.

These included educational institutions (e.g., kindergartens, vocational training institutions, high schools, higher education institutions), a pluralistic press, political parties, ideological movements, trade unions, and labor organizations. These institutions strongly resembled those that were established during the Second Temple period in that each embraced strong ideologies that often led to internal and external conflicts, had difficulty acquiescing to their own respective leaderships, and stood united when faced with a crisis despite their conflictive inter-organizational relations (Eisenstadt, 1989, p. 85).

During the nineteenth century, in particular, Jewish international coordination organizations were established as Jews continued to become more secularized and integrated into the broader society and the professionalization of welfare activity increased. These organizations further contributed to the Jewish fundraising systems that channeled money to needy communities throughout the world, including Zionist organizations in the pre-state period. Of note were internationally active organizations that upheld and defended civil rights, aided emigrants, assisted the victims of war, promoted education and modernization, and offered training in manual labor. Such organizations included the *Alliance Israélite Universelle*, established in Paris in 1860, the Anglo-Jewish Committee, established in London in 1871, the Ezra Organization, founded in Berlin in 1893, and others that were founded by philanthropists such as Sir Moses Montefiore, Baron Rothschild, and Baron Hirsch. Many of these organizations sought to establish Jewish frameworks for agricultural and vocational training that would help integrate Jews emerging from the ghettos into the modern economic environment.

In Palestine, the Old Yishuv (the Jewish community living in Palestine) was concentrated primarily in four cities—Jerusalem, Hebron, Tiberias, and Safed. The Yishuv was poorer, older, and lacked the general communal structure evident in the communities of the Diaspora, upon which the Yishuv relied for financial support. This financial arrangement, in which specific Diaspora communities would send funds to a particular Diaspora Jewish community, in the Holy Land led to further fragmentation among the Yishuv community. These funds generally sufficed to cover living expenses, while the *kolelim* (yeshivas) provided additional funds to pay for educational expenses, medical treatments, and taxes (Karagila, 1981; Salamon, 1985). The philanthropic activity of Barons Rothschild and Hirsch at the end of the nineteenth century was intended to provide a more productive and self-sustaining arrangement for the Jewish populations in Palestine by developing agricultural communities. It should be noted that there had been earlier attempts at the local level to promote this type of agricultural activity (Avissar, 1970; Gat, 1974; Eliav, 1978; Elkayam, 1990).

Another force that impacted the activities of the Jewish community in Palestine was Ottoman rule. In particular, Jews were forced to contend with the *waqf*, a religious endowment regulated by Islamic law. Thus, in keeping with Ottoman law, Jewish religious trusts (such as synagogues) had to be registered and monitored by the Moslem waqf. According to Islamic tradition, a person may donate property or money for public purposes to the waqf, but the waqf must be managed by parties independent of the state. However, during the Ottoman era, the government assumed the management of these resources, thereby assuming control of the administration of Jewish public institutions and property that had been registered in this manner.

THE PRE-STATE PERIOD (THE YISHUV), 1880–1948

Background

In Israeli historiography, 1882 is considered the year in which the Zionist settlement in Palestine began. In contrast to earlier Jewish migrations, which were religious in nature, those who immigrated to Israel in 1882—the first *aliya*—embraced a political agenda aimed at a Jewish national revival. Rather than settling in the four holy cities (Jerusalem, Hebron, Tiberias, and Safed) in which the traditional religious communities resided, these immigrants created new settlements that would lay the foundations for the new Jewish Yishuv in Palestine. Through the establishment of these Zionist communities, the gradual process of state building began, providing the institutional and ideological underpinnings for the formation of the State of Israel in 1948. Since this organizational complex lacked sovereignty, many scholars have defined it as a voluntary system (Lissak, 1988; Eisenstadt, 1989; Tzahor, 1994; Loewenberg, 1991; Jaffe, 1992; Gidron, 1997).[33]

The Zionists who settled in Palestine during this time period rejected the type of Jewish philanthropic organizations originated earlier in the 19th century that did not espouse a national/political agenda but instead were established to help fellow Jews by developing educational projects that would disseminate modern Western culture and instill new social living patterns within the traditional Jewish community. Likewise, the Zionist settlers distanced themselves from the system of donations from Jews in the Diaspora, which they considered parasitic, and from those Jews who received philanthropic contributions from Barons Rothschild and Hirsch to develop self-sustaining agricultural communities in Palestine. As the Zionist settlements increased in strength during the early 20th century, these non-Zionist philanthropic frameworks gradually declined.

The key objectives of the Zionist philanthropic institutions were the founding of a national Jewish community in Palestine and the development of an autonomous political system. As a result, these organizations preferred to support Zionist settlers who were instrumental in developing this national framework. Their activities included the promotion of immigration, settlement, and economic development. Since it was necessary to care for arriving immigrants, they also provided social services. Despite the fact that various streams of Zionism were highly ambivalent towards charity and philanthropy, the Zionist community continued to rely upon financial resources raised from Diaspora Jewry to support most of its activities. These fundraising activities were instrumental in the nation-building process and also served an important ideological purpose in that they provided a means for enlisting the help of Western Jews in realizing the Zionist goals and aroused a national Jewish consciousness that sustained the fulfillment of the Zionist vision. All of this activity helped to advance the economic, social, and political objectives of the Zionist settlers. Moreover, it enabled the World Zionist Organization to become involved in broader spheres of activity. For example, in 1914 it formed the Educational Committee of Jewish Schools in Palestine, which assumed responsibility for developing new schools and supervising existing ones.

The British conquest of Palestine and the start of the British Mandate was an important turning point in the fulfillment of the Zionist vision. Unlike the Ottoman rulers, the British Mandate in its early stages supported the Zionist settlement movement. The Balfour Declaration of 1917 laid the political foundations for the central Zionist goal of establishing a national home for the Jewish people in the land of Israel. This generated momentum in the Zionist movement in both Palestine and abroad and considerably accelerated the establishment of a governmental infrastructure within the Jewish/Zionist community. One of the most important developments during this period was formation of the Jewish Foundation Fund (*Keren Hayesod*) in 1921 and the Jewish Agency for Israel in 1929.

The Jewish Foundation Fund (JFF) was a major fundraising tool for the establishment of the State of Israel. The Zionist leadership created the perception that providing donations to the JFF was akin to a "voluntary annual tax" that every Jew should pay in order to develop a Jewish homeland in Palestine (Elitzur, 1947). This tactic resembles those used throughout Jewish history in which donations have been likened to a kind of tax. Since the British Mandatory government offered very little in the way of social services, the JFF also helped the Zionist institutions provide educational, health, and social services; public works; and housing. These services were a key element in the social and economic absorption of new immigrants. This system was also an important factor in the growth and coalescence of the Zionist population—it simultaneously strengthened the Zionist institutions while making the new settlers increasingly dependent upon them.

The Jewish Agency was established as a partnership between the World Zionist Organization and non-Zionist Jews, and was instrumental in bolstering the Jewish people's commitment to and identification with the Zionist movement (Berkowitz, 1996). In Palestine, the Jewish Agency served as an organizational framework for the Zionist nation-building process. In the international arena, the agency acted as the primary representative of Zionist interests, and the British Mandatory government and the League of Nations recognized the Jewish Agency as being responsible for developing the national home in Palestine. Although it was never officially acknowledged as a sovereign body, the Jewish Agency became a strong, centralist, political organization during the 1930s, with features of a governmental system. In later years, in fact, the agency would serve as the primary institution around which the state mechanism was formed.

The next wave of Jewish immigration to Palestine in 1904—the second aliya—led to the development of a sectoral system (i.e., separate sectors based upon political/ideological orientations) that characterized Israeli society during much of the Yishuv period. Most of the new immigrants who came to Palestine were young people with a strong sense of national and political awareness. Their influence would have far-reaching effects on the Jewish community in Palestine, particularly in terms of improving its organizational abilities. Thus, from 1904 until the beginning of World War I, numerous professional and political organizations were established, as well as trade unions and district federations of rural settlements. As part of this process, two politically-based workers' parties were founded in 1906—*Poalei Zion* and *Hapoel Hatzair*—that, in the absence of other available systems, undertook a wide range of functions, including the provision of health, housing, and employment services for their members. Tzahor (1994) describes this process, in which idealistic but destitute immigrants imbued with motivation built for themselves mutual aid frameworks, as being "experimental," that is, such activities as establishing a fund to help the jobless, a club, or a library became incorporated into the immigrants' ideological activities (pp. 11–28). Over time, these frameworks became more sophisticated. Thus, the blending of political interests, economic activity, and the provision of services served as a tool for recruiting and integrating members into the Zionist movement during the Yishuv period and, to a certain extent, during the first years after the establishment of the State of Israel.

The provision of services by various parties marked the beginning of the development of a sectoral system in the Yishuv period, in which separate sectors within the Jewish community that were based on political/ideological orientations served dual purposes: on the one hand, they represented their members at the central level (which was evolving at the time) and, on the other hand, they provided their members with a broad range of services.[34] Thus, a sectoral system evolved that consisted of different ideological movements each of which built separate settlement, credit, financing, and marketing institutions for their members and allocated resources for a broad range of programs, such as housing and health services, which they offered to their members via the welfare organizations they had established. These activities were financed by money received from the "national institutions," (e.g., JEF) which, in turn, had raised these funds from the Jewish communities in the Diaspora. The institutions that the ideological movements established also served as an important source of employment, and those in managerial positions were able to allocate resources according to their membership's needs. In exchange, the sectors expected a deep commitment from their members, including political involvement, mobilization during election periods, and participation in organizational and educational activities (Eisenstadt, 1989, p. 127).

According to Horowitz and Lissak (1977), the Jewish settlement in Palestine began to coalesce through the establishment and growth of these various sectors. Together, the sectors gradually created a national center that worked towards achieving shared goals. In this sense, it was mainly out of necessity (e.g., the workers had to earn a living, needed health care services, etc.) that the workers' parties preceded other ideological movements in their organizational consolidation. In the absence of other frameworks, the workers developed their own organizational structures, particularly since they expected the same level of services that they had received in Europe. Given the socialist component of their ideological outlook, the workers tended towards a collectivistic approach, which facilitated the process of institutionalizing the frameworks they established. Thus, it was the workers who created the dominant model of a Jewish political party in Palestine. Horowitz and Lissak (1977) argue that this model was characterized by role expansion: "[The parties] did not confine themselves to clear-cut political functions, but sought to organize their members' lives in various spheres, first and foremost in the sphere of the provision of cultural, economic, and welfare services. As a result, economic organizations and welfare services came into being that were affiliated with the political parties, of which a substantial proportion was later transferred to the Histadrut Labor Federation [an umbrella framework of organizations that provided services to members of the Labor party] upon its establishment" (p. 90). They further emphasize the scope of the party's role: the parties strove to be involved in a broad range of activities that were not distinctly political in nature. This was an adaptive measure: "Immigrants without means arrived in a country without services, so that only political organization was able to secure them educational, health, and welfare services" (p. 104). On the other hand, Silber and Rosenhek consider the party phenomenon to be a result of the struggle between cheap Arab laborers and more expensive Jewish workers, who the Zionist institutions subsidized via an extended system of services. Thus, the purpose of developing industrial projects was to establish a separate Zionist economy that would be protected from cheap Arab labor (Silber and Rosenhek, 1999, pp. 17–18).

The two workers' parties, *Achdut Ha'avoda-Poalei Zion* (these were two groups that eventually united into one party) and *Hapoel Hatza'ir*, that first created this model eventually transferred most of their service functions to the Histadrut, a system of service-providing organizations for Labor party members that was formed in 1920. In addition to the "workers'" sector, parallel developments in the "civil" (middle class) and "religious" sectors eventually occurred.[35] Horowitz and Lissak (1977) refer to each sector that emerged during the Yishuv period as a "sub-center" that included nonprofit, economic, settlement, and security organizations. Thus, for example, among the organizations included in the "workers'" "sub-center" were the workers councils, *Bank Hapoalim, Tnuva,* the National/United Kibbutz movement, the workers' stream in education, the *Noar Ha'oved* (youth movement), and the *Haganah*. The "civil" (middle class) sector included such organizations as the Tradesmen's Association, the Craftsmen's Association, the Farmers' Association, *Maccabi, Beitar* (sports clubs), the Association of Sephardic Jews, *Etzel*, and *Lechi* (defense organizations); and the "religious" sector included, for example, Elitzur (sports clubs) and Mizrahi Women. The sub-center of "Haredi" (Ultra-Orthodox) sector included the yeshivot, the Council of Torah Sages, *kolelim*, and the *Eda Haredi* community of Jerusalem.

The Jewish population of Palestine was also geographically distributed according to the sectors: the workers sector encompassed most of the *kibbutzim* and *moshavim*, as well as the urban population employed in cooperative Histadrut plants and service organizations (e.g., *Kupat Holim*, the health fund). The civil sector, which was less organized, covered parts of the urban population, the settlements of the first and second aliyas, and the private agricultural settlements. The Zionist religious sector included parts of the urban groups under *Mizrahi* and *Hapoel Hamizrahi* leadership and the religious kibbutzim. The sectors could also be divided by their educational systems, which included the workers', the general, and the religious streams of education. The worker's sector was distinct from and ultimately more powerful than the other sectors with the establishment of the Histadrut, which increased the sector's organizational abilities. In contrast, as Segev (1999) notes: "The people of the 'civil camp' . . . were devoid of all ideological fervor. Their 'camp' also did not succeed in translating its interests into political clout: There was something colorless, pale, individualistic about it. They were unable to articulate an alternative patriotism to that dictated by the Labor movement" (p. 211) (See also Yatziv, 1999; Ben-Porat, 1999).

Since the various sectors that developed in Palestine during the British Mandate were distinguished by differing ideologies, the system that was formed falls into a consociational federative model, in which access to the centers of power and most public assets, including publicly-distributed private funds, was largely achieved through representatives from large consociational segments comprised of either religious, political, or local groups (Eisenstadt, 1989, p. 126). Dowty (1995) notes that the Yishuv period, in particular, was characterized by a consociational democratic culture, in which persuasion and general consensus were employed in making political decisions.[36] He adds that the existence of a non-sovereign Jewish governmental system was a decisive factor in the development of a consociational model. Since there was no existing framework to impose tax collection and law enforcement, an inclusive, voluntary approach was required. Those who did not agree with certain decisions could opt to leave the system; however, given the hostile environment in which the settlers of the Yishuv existed, most groups preferred to stay. Thus, all parties of the Yishuv accepted a proportional method for distributing power and benefits (i.e., the party key, in which positions and funds were distributed on the basis of each party's relative strength) as the only means of managing the community (Dowty, 1995, p. 33). Under this system, secondary frameworks (i.e., political parties) served as intermediaries between individuals and the national center, and basic rules were established to regulate these relationships (Horowitz and Lissak, 1977, p. 91). As a result, however, there were few voluntary organizations during the Yishuv period that were politically neutral and did not represent defined interest groups (Horowitz and Lissak, 1977, p. 93).

The Third Sector in the Pre-State Period

One of the most influential factors in the development of the third sector during the Yishuv period was the establishment of the Histadrut Federation of Labor Unions in 1920. The Histadrut significantly affected not only the scope of third sector organizations but also their interactions within the governmental environment. These patterns persisted many years after the Yishuv period, shaping both the Israeli social/political system and the third sector. Shortly after its establishment, the Histadrut rapidly became a central force in the economic and social development of the Jewish immigrant community in Palestine. By the mid-1930s, the Histadrut was actively involved in the defense arena, as well. By fulfilling a broad range of services and needs, the Histadrut enabled the Labor movement to become extremely powerful and influential with the Zionist organizational system.

According to Tzahor (1994), the Histadrut was first created in response to the profound economic crisis following the third aliya. Many of these new, idealistic immigrants had participated in the Bolshevik Revolution and were aware of the potential strengths that could be gained from organized groups. Given the large number of immigrants who arrived, it became necessary to establish a system to deal with their various needs. Thus, the Histadrut was formed to "assume responsibility for the entire constructive creation of the workers' movement: settlement, defense, trade unions, education, housing, health, banking, cooperation, welfare, and culture" (Tzahor, 1994, p. 32). Difficulties arose in fulfilling this broad mission, however. To meet the employment needs of its members, the Histadrut established contracting companies (the Public Works Department and later *Solel Boneh*) to build a physical infrastructure in Palestine. The Histadrut received contracts from both the British Mandate and the World Zionist Organization. To resolve the conflict between the need to provide work for the unemployed and keep costs down, the Histadrut created budgetary deficits ("for the sake of [the] absorption of immigrants") that it subsequently transferred to the World Zionist Organization, which covered these deficits so as not to appear to be interfering with the immigration absorption effort. For example, Tzahor notes that when the Public Works Department and later *Solel Boneh* collapsed, their managers escaped sanctions because they had favored the good of the movement over that of the economy; in fact, they were subsequently offered managerial positions in the new companies that were formed.

Thus, a pattern of close, almost symbiotic, relations developed between the Histadrut and the World Zionist Organization (and later the formal government of Israel). According to this arrangement, the government would assign the Histadrut "national" tasks, which it would fulfill though not necessarily in an economically sound manner. Inevitably, the governmental system would cover the deficits that arose. This pattern also applied to the financial management of the service organizations of the Histadrut (e.g., Kupat Holim, *Amal*). Tzahor believes that the cooperation between the Histadrut and the national institutions was contingent upon a delicate balance between the Diaspora Jews' desire to contribute to the creation of a Jewish homeland in Palestine and the willingness of the workers' organization to fulfill this vision. This tension was evident, for example, when the *Hadassah* organization negotiated with the workers' parties to become involved in the Histadrut's health fund, Kupat Holim:

> [The] Americans wondered at the impudence of the workers' demand and the manner of its presentation. In particular, they were disgruntled at the irresponsibility apparent in the negligent management, which, in their opinion, bordered on illogical and was a grievous waste of money. Whereas the Histadrut representatives were convinced that the Americans were indifferent to their enterprise, did not understand it, and were seeking to restrict it. Despite these deep differences of opinion, a mutual dependence was formed here between the Americans, who were sincerely determined to support the *halutzim* (pioneers), and the Histadrut, which was in desperate need of aid. Thus, in spite of the disagreement, Hadassah's support was formalized and a contract was signed. Hadassah built hospitals and clinics on behalf of the members of the Histadrut and bore a large proportion of the financing of the medical service (Tzahor, 1994, p. 48).

In fulfilling its many functions—including health services, pensions, services for the elderly, help for the unemployed, employment exchange bureaus, and housing services—the Histadrut, as well as many of the dominant Zionist organizations, developed strong, centralized bureaucratic frameworks that enabled them to mobilize external resources and distribute them among select population groups. Thus, the Histadrut was able to obtain most of the national resources earmarked for the services that they provided, and in the process they accumulated substantial power. According to Silber and Rosenhek (1999), the Histadrut served as a tool through which the Zionist Labor movement was able to gain authority and legitimize its ideological agenda by allocating resources to its proponents. For example, the social services that the Histadrut provided came to be defined as "mutual aid" and "pioneering programs," while aid extended to other social groups was considered "charity."[37] As a result, the Labor movement assumed a dominant position within the Jewish community. However, as Tzahor (1994) maintains, the Histadrut's primary—and sometimes only—considerations were development and expansion. Thus, economic feasibility, financial responsibility, and the economy's needs were rejected in favor of growing at the fastest rate possible.

As the Histadrut became the predominant employer in the Yishuv, more members of the Jewish community joined the organization. Although it remained voluntary, the fact that the Histadrut provided work and was an agricultural settlement institution that also granted medical and educational services created a situation of dependency among its members. In addition, as a dominant force in immigration absorption, agricultural settlement, defense, and the introduction of new professional fields, the Histadrut became a sort of "executive arm" of the Zionist movement. This type of dual dependency, in which the members became dependent upon the Histadrut for their subsistence and the Zionist movement relied upon it as a tool for realizing its vision, afforded the leadership of the Histadrut substantial power and authority. This organizational pattern—the organization's strong political ties, strong bureaucratic structure, clientelistic relations with its members, and disregard to the rules of economic responsibility in the name of ideological fervor—overshadowed all of the third sector's activity during the Yishuv period and would continue to influence organizational relations between the third sector and the national government after the establishment of the State of Israel.

In addition to the creation of the Histadrut, the sectoral model that developed in the Yishuv led to the establishment of numerous and diverse organizations within the different ideological sectors. Forming an organization within one of the sectors was a way of assuring that there would be an adequate supply of resources. In an attempt to express the Jewish community's emancipation, most of the other organizations that were established during this period fell within the umbrella framework of the Zionist vision. Once the organizations took hold, they were usually absorbed into the larger framework of the World Zionist Organization; however, a number of organizations were formed with varying degrees of ideological and institutional autonomy from the Zionist organizations. For example, following the end of the Ottoman rule, various women's associations arose that concentrated on rebuilding the community by establishing orphanages, soup kitchens, sewing shops for girls, and evening classes (Segev, 1999, p. 175). In addition, various professional, commercial, educational, and cultural organizations were created. For instance, Pevsner (1926) lists 21 professional associations (including two pharmacists' associations for certified pharmacists and clerks, a musicians' association, and an economists' association), 13 political associations, 5 women's organizations, and 23 philanthropic associations.

During the Yishuv period, several large, significant organizations were also established that remain in existence today, including the Teachers Association (1903), the Bar Association (1921), the Medical Association, the Engineers and Architects Association, the Writers Association (1921), the Chamber of Commerce (1919), the Industrialists Association (1921), the Language Committee, the Hebrew

University, the Technion, and the Chief Rabbinate. Several foreign organizations also developed institutional activity in Israel during this time, such as Alliance Israélite Universelle and Hadassah. In addition, the Society for the Prevention of Cruelty to Animals was established in 1908, discontinued its activities during the World War I, and renewed its work in 1921 under the sponsorship of the High Commissioner, Sir Herbert Samuel (Andrews, 1931, p. 82). None of these organizations was formed under the auspices of a particular sector, although some later forged ties with and received resources from the Zionist movement.

In 1928, the Jewish Social Research Institute conducted a survey of the existing (third sector) institutions in three major cities in Palestine. The survey included 186 organizations (10 of these refused to cooperate with the researchers and 16 ceased to exist) of the new Yishuv (i.e., the Zionist pioneers) and the old Yishuv (i.e., the religious Jews residing in the four sacred cities), but excluded the Zionist organizations affiliated with the World Zionist Organization, the Histadrut, Hadassah, and other "institutionalized" organizations. The survey identified the following eight categories of organizations: (1) kolelim and religious; (2) educational; (3) philanthropic; (4) benevolent; (5) healthcare; (6) orphanages (and those organizations providing aid to orphans); (7) infant care; and (8) elder care (i.e., old-age homes). The survey indicates that a multitude of organizations had been established in Palestine during the Yishuv period:

> It is highly doubtful whether there is anywhere in the world a country as small as Eretz Yisrael, with a Jewish population as small as ours, having as many philanthropic institutions of all kinds. It is enough to pass through the streets of Jerusalem and to observe the many signs of these institutions in order to understand that we have before us a sort of "jungle" of religious and secular institutions, philanthropic and benevolent associations, institutions for education, credit, mutual aid and just plain help, etc., etc. We use the term "jungle," because it appears to us that an outsider has never set foot in the "thicket" of these institutions. Most do not publish reports concerning their activities. Most will not allow an outsider inside to observe their work. Some perhaps cannot permit themselves such a thing (Divshoni, 1928, p. 3).

The survey also points to the large amounts of money that were funneled to organizations in Palestine from the United States:

> About a million dollars reach Palestine every year from America for philanthropic purposes. And if we add to this the portion of the money that remains in the hands of the emissaries, or in the institutions' offices across the ocean, it appears that the Jews of the United States give Eretz Yisrael—apart from their donations to the JFF, the JNF, Hadassah, etc.—another two million dollars or more. It would be good, therefore, if they knew where this money goes, and [the present survey] may perhaps be a first step towards a thorough and comprehensive inquiry into the activities of the institutions of the old Yishuv (Divshoni, 1928, p. 3).

Among the many organizations that gave large sums of money to Israel via the United States, Hadassah was one of the most influential. Zionist women in the United States formed Hadassah, which began working in Palestine during the first decade of the 20th century. Hadassah focused on providing health services to the Jewish community in Palestine and included training and guidance on hygiene and general health. In 1913, it established a nurses' visiting service in Jerusalem and in 1916 it opened a nurses' training school and a clinic for women and children. Its activities were greatly expanded following World War I when it developed the American Zionist Medical Unit, which eventually led to the establishment of the Hadassah Medical School at the Hebrew University (Levin, 1973).

Although Hadassah defined itself as a Zionist organization, it differed from its counterparts in many regards. First, it focused less on nation-building and adhered to the more scientific model of social work characteristic of American voluntary associations (Silber and Rosenhek, 1999). In addition, Hadassah's activities were more inclusive—the organization provided services to the Zionist settlers, the non-Zionist settlers of the old Yishuv, and the Palestinian Arab population, whereas the Zionist organizations almost completely ignored those communities since they did not participate in building the Zionist nation. The Hadassah leadership also fought fiercely to maintain autonomy from the World Zionist Organization. In 1927, for example, Hadassah refused an offer to be recognized as the "Health Department of the Jewish Agency" because this distinction would have incorporated the organization into the Zionist executive framework. These circumstances led to somewhat tense relations between Hadassah and the Zionist institutions as Hadassah fought to maintain its independence while the Zionist movement became increasingly dominant among the Jewish community in Palestine.

Ultra-Orthodox and Arab Third Sector Organizations in the Pre-State Period

Prior to the British Mandate, the Arab population was subject to the waqf system that was implemented by Ottoman rule. When the British came to power, the waqf system became independent from the governmental system. Thus, the British Mandate established the Supreme Moslem Council in 1921 and granted the Moslem community full autonomy in conducting its religious affairs, including management of the waqf system. As a result of its struggle against Zionism and its connection with the Palestinian National movement, the Moslem Council used the resources of the waqf as a tool to promote political objectives, including the mobilization of the population by offering services and allocations and attempting to prevent the sale of land to the Zionists. Thus, as in the Jewish community, third sector organizations among the Palestinian Arab population served as a tool for recruiting supporters to the national cause. After the Arab rebellion of 1936–1939, however, in which the Moslem Council played an active role, the British revoked the waqf's standing as an autonomous body in 1937 and imposed restrictions on public trusts, including a government-appointed committee. In this manner, the waqf became integrated into the state system and ceased to function as an independent national political tool (Reiter, 1997).

In addition to the waqf system, the Arab community formed other third sector organizations that were primarily characterized by a religious orientation, such as the Christian Association and the Islamic Association. These institutions chiefly undertook social, educational, and cultural activities and were most active in cities, such as Haifa (Zeidan and Ghanem, 2000, p. 8). The failure of the Arab rebellion, however, engendered confusion in the Palestinian community. As became evident in later years, this crisis—in combination with other factors— significantly affected the development of third sector organizations among the Arab population in Palestine.

The ultra-Orthodox society (i.e., the old Yishuv), on the other hand, was characterized by a duality during this period: on the one hand, it strove to maintain a traditional lifestyle characterized by a system of primarily communal service organizations financed chiefly from foreign donations,[38] and, on the other hand, it could not ignore the drastic changes engendered by the Zionist immigrants, whose ideology the ultra-Orthodox community opposed. It is important to note that during the Yishuv period the ultra-Orthodox society was comprised of various communities, with different orientations towards the environment in which they existed. For instance, Pond (1999) notes that when the ultra-Orthodox movement, Agudat Yisrael, was formed, one faction took a pragmatic approach and sought ways to cooperate with the Zionists, particularly once it became apparent that the State of Israel was close to being established and the ultra-Orthodox community saw the necessity of promoting issues it considered important. Thus, for example, following the Nazis' rise to power, Agudat Yisrael representatives cooperated with the Jewish Agency to bring Jews from Europe to Palestine. Another part of Agudat Yisrael, however, regarded the Zionist movement as having blasphemously profaned the name of God (hilul hashem) and called for total severance of all contacts. Thus, as Friedman (1995) demonstrates, during the Yishuv period, Haredi politics were based on "political extortion" that continued and even increased following the establishment of the state. Even after the Holocaust, the Haredim threatened to come to an agreement with the anti-Zionist British Foreign Minister, Ernest Bevin, that would prevent the establishment of the state, unless Ben Gurion promised to maintain the status quo on religious issues in the newly formed state (1995, p. 52).

Gradually, however, the ultra-Orthodox population found ways to cooperate with the Zionist institutions due to shared interests; this process greatly accelerated the establishment of statehood. In a 1945 meeting with Ben Gurion, leaders of Agudat Yisrael expressed their belief that the Torah should serve as the constitution for the Jewish state. However, since they could not realize this aspiration, they wanted to "find a way of guaranteeing in the constitution that we will be able to lead a religious life in Eretz Yisrael, in accordance with our aspiration and in keeping with Jewish tradition down the generations. We are prepared to cooperate in the political sphere in Eretz Yisrael in all areas of protection of Jewish rights and in the event it is decided to expand the Jewish Agency, we are prepared, under certain conditions, to join it, and ask that we be given the possibility of negotiating the terms of Agudat Yisrael's joining the Jewish Agency" (Friedman, 1995, p. 187). The ultra-Orthodox community made a clear distinction between "cooperation with the Zionist movement" and "participation in political institutions in a state from which it is impossible to secede." They did not consider their alignment with the Zionists in this matter as an "association, consent, aid, or capitulation," but as "girding ourselves to salvage whatever we can of the nation's inheritance" (Pond, 1999, p. 215). Thus, integration into the state was done out of compulsion, and Agudat Yisrael's role was to defend the religious camp against abuse from the Zionist leadership.

In a letter dated June 19, 1947 Ben Gurion promised Agudat Yisrael that the principles of Shabbat, *kashrut*, religious marriage, and religious education would be guaranteed. This letter preserved the existence of the Jewish religion in the state of Israel, and this policy still remains in effect today. This development led to the establishment of an independent system of services to the religious community that was and continues to be financed by the state. Nevertheless, this agreement caused great ambivalence among the ultra-Orthodox community, as expressed by Rabbi Wolf: "To see redemption in the state is a mistake in the understanding of redemption. However, on the other hand, there is no need to ostracize its technical means—it is possible that our institutions should be supported by the state but not controlled by it. The state is solely a monetary source, but one must beware the influence and method of its leaders. For the same reason, Haredi Jews may serve as members of the Knesset, because in his position a member of Knesset will be better able to act for the preservation of the Torah and education than would a private individual" (Pond, 1999, p. 214).

THE STATEHOOD PERIOD, 1948 TO MID- TO LATE-1970S

Background

The sharp transition from the Yishuv period to independent sovereign statehood required that the existing frameworks and institutions be adapted to fit the new circumstances. This could not happen spontaneously, and many aspects of the previous systems developed in the Yishuv period remained in place for many years. In fact, some elements are still in existence today. According to Horowitz and Lissak (1977), there were six primary traits of the political system established during the Yishuv period that continued after the formation of the state: (1) the existence of a large number of parties; (2) multi-dimensionality in the roles of the political parties (that is, they remained involved in a variety of fields including economics, culture, and social services); (3) the role of political entities as secondary centers of power; (4) a coalitionary political structure; (5) the existence of the "party key" principle, in which positions and funds are distributed on the basis of each party's relative strength; and (6) the tradition of political tolerance (pp. 274–275). Among these characteristics, the most relevant in terms of studying the third sector is the political parties' continued involvement in service provision. Thus, even after the state was founded, the parties tended to maintain specific frameworks for handling social service problems (e.g., housing, welfare, etc.) (Lissak, 1998, pp. 129–130).

During this period, Akzin defines Israel as a "party state," in which "a person can subscribe to a political party's newspaper, receive health care at a party's clinic, hospital, or retirement home, he spends his leisure time at a party club, takes part in sports activities of a party's team, receives books from a party's publishing house, and lives in a neighborhood in a city where most neighbors are members of that party. He is also accustomed to considering the party as the entity that can solve many of his everyday problems" (quoted in Lissak, 1998, p. 130). Thus, individuals in the newly established state remained very dependent upon the parties. Those parties that possessed broader political powers and were able to oversee the allocation of state resources were better able to broaden their activities than parties with more limited political influence (Horowitz and Lissak, 1977, p. 300). This situation, as well as the system in which the newly formed government provided public funds to the parties, created a close relationship between third sector service provision organizations and the public sector.

Despite these holdovers from the previous era, there were considerable attempts to shift from a sectoral to a statutory system when the State of Israel was established in 1948. In addition, there were systematic efforts to bring together all of the various sectoral, ethnic, economic, and ideological/political interests into the burgeoning state's new structures and to carry out what was defined as collective-national goals. Contributing to these collectivist and etatist perceptions, was the ideological trend of "statism"—an idea espousing the commitment of oneself to the benefit of all and the favoring of institutions that are managed collectively. Further influences included the prestige of the Zionist pioneering values, the perception of a strong state characterized by autonomy and influence (this originated largely from Continental Europe), and the charismatic personality of David Ben-Gurion, whose name is linked with the concept of "statism" (Galnoor, 1982). According to the ideology of "statism," the state is not only a framework that supplies citizens with services but also provides them with and mobilizes them towards a vision, imbues their lives with goals and meaning, and unites them under a single banner.

The state is perceived as possessing a quality that allows it to transform the mass of citizens into a moral community. Under this model, the consensual methods utilized in the Yishuv period to make decisions were no longer valid. Indeed, Ben-Gurion felt this approach from the voluntarist era had no place in a sovereign state. In other words, the lack of sovereignty during the Yishuv period had brought about the need to develop political coalitions and several political centers; once sovereignty was accomplished, there was no longer room for several centers, only a single one (Don-Yihyah, 1995, pp. 174–175).

In response to these predominant ideological perceptions, the political atmosphere in Israel became antithetical to voluntary organizations and initiatives and promoted a state mechanism that was substantively different from the previous period. This change resulted in ideological arguments and power clashes. Yanai (1987) maintains that Ben-Gurion viewed "statism" as an ideology of transition from the Diaspora and the Yishuv to the state. This new political situation required a different system of principles to uphold the state; however, this did not entirely exclude the existence of voluntary organizing, which Ben-Gurion considered to be a bulwark of a democratic country. Still, "more than the state wanted to consciously restrict the steps of the voluntary organizations, it saw itself as defending its own sovereignty against an unlawful erosion by sectoral organizations" (Yanai, 1987, p. 169). According to this perspective, the state was obligated to provide all citizens with basic services and spare them inter-party confrontations. In practical terms, Ben-Gurion wanted to distinguish between state and private institutions to ensure that those organizations providing vital services would fall within the state's domain.

It should be noted that Ben-Gurion's statism approach was anchored in socialist ideology. Ben-Gurion was trying to use "governed voluntarism" (Lissak, 1998) or "state-based pioneering" (Bar-Eli, 1999) to settle the contradiction between enlisting participants into the state's new coercive frameworks and the voluntary mobilization of the sectoral organizations. Ben-Gurion held that there was no conflict between the state's new initiatives and those of the "pioneering voluntary" institutions. In his view, the government frameworks would recruit volunteers for tasks that the state defined. In a 1955 letter to the secretary of *Noar Ha'oved* (a youth movement) regarding the possibility of transforming the *Gadna* (pre-military youth framework) into "a state youth movement," Ben-Gurion stated: "Fear of the state also contains, I believe, Diaspora habits as well as lack of a socialist awareness and foresight. This state is a state of the working people . . . in your fear of the state and your reliance on the voluntary framework you are alienated from the fundamental socialist assumptions. Every teacher of the socialist thought, of all kinds, has relied on the state, which will realize the socialist rule" (cited in Bar-Eli, 1999, p. 30). According to Bar-Eli, these arguments over the limits of state intervention served only to conceal the disputes over control and power, particularly between the bureaucracies of the consolidating government, on the one hand, and the ideological movements and the Histadrut Labor Federation, on the other. Specifically, since the *Mapam* socialist party was not part of the first coalition government, the party was primarily interested in preserving the autonomy of its own institutions, which *Mapai*'s rule of the state threatened (Bar-Eli, 1999, p. 35).

In practical terms, arguments over transforming the sectoral system into a statutory one focused principally on the educational, employment, and health systems.[39] Ben-Gurion's position was that these services should be part of the state framework. He was particularly insistent that education should not be entrusted to the political bodies. The new political leadership believed that the various political streams (e.g., the workers' stream, the religious stream) involved in education may have been compatible with pre-statehood needs, but they were antithetical to the new reality (Adler and Balas, 2000, p. 140). Ben-Gurion and his supporters aimed to institute a national education system, but eventually consented to a separate curriculum for the national-religious school system. No agreement, however, was reached with the ultra-Orthodox, Agudat Israel, and this group did not receive any state funds. Later, when its votes were needed in the Knesset, Agudat Israel was granted funds even though the Ministry of Education did not have the power to supervise the ultra-Orthodox Independent Education Network.

Ben-Gurion was also successful in transforming the sectoral employment bureaus, which were primarily linked to the Histadrut during the Yishuv period, into a single statutory employment bureau. However, he encountered difficulties when he tried to form a government-controlled health care system. Since there was no substitute for the Histadrut's Kupot Holim (health fund) in many communities, Mapai party officials believed that dismantling it would threaten the party's power-base, which was primarily comprised of members of the Histadrut (Yanai, 1987, pp. 178–179). Moreover, the Mapam party, which opposed Ben-Gurion, not only urged that the Kupot Holim be kept intact but that the government should pay for some of its funding: "The splendid service of Kupat Holim will continue to be at the disposal of the (working) class ... but that class, which constitutes the vast majority of the Knesset and the vast majority of the people, has the right to determine that a third of the expenses will be covered by the government: We are entitled to demand this from the state" (Greenberg, 1991, pp. 229–230). The Mapam party argued that covering part of the health funds' budget was the state's obligation, as was the case in other advanced nations . Eventually, Ben-Gurion capitulated and abandoned the idea of creating a national healthcare service at that time. Nevertheless, over time a statutory service system, anchored in laws (e.g., the Law of Compulsory Education, a Law of National Insurance—Social Security), gradually replaced the previous sectoral social service system.

Another aspect of the Yishuv period that did not wane with the formation of the state was the continued dominance of the Labor party and the organizations to which it was linked (whose status often became monopolistic), particularly the Histadrut. Thus, despite the statist ideology, many organizations continued to exist and even thrived under the aegis of the Histadrut. This was especially noticeable in the Kupat Holim, which became the principal provider of healthcare services to most of the country's population. The Histadrut, which also remained a major employer via its industrial and commercial enterprises, received government funding and subsidies and was considered the "service-contractor" for the state in a number of spheres, including housing where, for example, its construction company, *Shikun Ovdim*, received large-scale projects (Horowitz and Lissak, 1977, p. 284). Thus, the Labor movement gained social and economic power and the third sector organizations connected with it (e.g., *Mishan*, Amal, and the trade associations affiliated with the Histadrut) provided an important source of infrastructure for the movement.

It is important to note that the trend towards marginalizing less developed or new voluntary organizations occurred within the broader context of the huge tasks that policymakers faced in forming a new statehood, especially in the areas of security and immigrant absorption. Thus, the idea of abandoning well-experienced institutions, such as the Histadrut, that had functioned efficiently and provided services to the population became unfeasible and their services fulfilled the needs of the governing leadership. As a result, the idea of allocating roles of national importance to voluntary organizations was considered unconscionable. Within the framework of a central government steered by a single political and administrative center, voluntary organizations could only assume a helping role.

The Third Sector in the Statehood Period

For purposes of analyzing the development of the third sector during the statehood period, it is helpful to divide the time frame into two phases: (1) the 1950s, in which statist ideology was at its peak, and (2) the 1960s and 1970s, when statist ideology and practices showed signs of weakening. During the 1950s, the relationship between the government and third sector organizations was close. Third sector organizations were considered helpful to the government in that they operated in areas in which the government was unable or unwilling to act. At that time, third sector organizations were not regarded as independent institutions that could determine their own modes of operation. These organizations—even those that provided services—were also dependent upon resources derived from Diaspora Jews. The Jewish Agency, which no longer played a diplomatic role now that the Israeli State had been established and assumed the task of immigrant passage, absorption, and settlement, became a crucial medium for obtaining donations from Diaspora Jews. To achieve this task, the agency was granted the status of a "non-governmental organization" that was permitted to raise tax-exempt donations in the United States. To assure coordination, legislation was enacted that defined a clear division of labor between the agency and the government, and established the Institution for Coordination between the two entities (Horowitz and Lissak,

1977, p. 285). The Jewish Agency's political structure was very similar to that of the government in Israel, and the agency operated in full agreement with the government and the Mapai majority. Accordingly, an organizational framework was established in which donations from Diaspora Jews were earmarked for goals and assignments that the government dictated.

In addition to the Jewish Agency, other Jewish philanthropic organizations became active in raising funds for the newly established state. The most notable of these organizations were the Joint Distribution Committee (JDC), Hadassah, and the Hebrew Immigrant Aid Society (HIAS). Although each of these groups had its own distinct tradition and modus operandi, they were forced to change their patterns of activity to comply with the newly established state frameworks (Stock, 1995). In this way, the government mobilized external agents to help with the major tasks of establishing service infrastructures, which were created concurrently with the immigration of the 1950s. JDC's activity in absorbing Yemenite Jews, for example, led to the founding of the *Malben* organization and to the establishment of institutional and community service infrastructures for the elderly (Ofer, 1995).

The resource constraints of the 1950s, in conjunction with the increasing range of Israeli citizens' needs, led to the establishment of several voluntary organizations. Although these organizations were established outside of the public system, they became at least partially dependent upon government funds. Occasionally, these types of organizations were either established by the state, acted under its auspices, or were assisted by government funding. In such cases, the organization would undertake a government project that would pay for half of the organization's expenses, while the other half was derived from foreign philanthropic organizations. For example, Ben-Gurion urged the Jewish Agency to establish the Education Foundation in 1954, which opened hundreds of daycare centers and nurseries, especially in development towns. In the beginning, some of these service provision systems were started by the government ministries; later, the responsibility for providing services was transferred to third sector organizations while the ministries continued to fund a large proportion of the organizations' expenses. For instance, the *Matav* organization, which was founded in 1958 to provide homecare services to patients with chronic illness, obtained funds from the Ministry of Welfare, the Ministry of Health, Kupat Holim, and the Jewish Agency.

Additionally, citizens groups created organizations to address issues important to them. Most of these organizations quickly realized that in order to continue functioning, they needed to forge an alliance with the public sector. Notable examples of such organizations are *Akim* and *Ilan*, established by parents of handicapped children in the 1950s because no suitable frameworks were available to care for their children. Over the years, these organizations were able to obtain a variety of public funds (Kramer, 1976). Nevertheless, the government's financial involvement in voluntary organizations that provided services, even in the welfare arena, was still relatively low: in 1957–1958 the Ministry of Welfare's budget was IL 12,283,000 (including IL 1,500,000 for the Jewish Agency); the total budgets for 162 (voluntary) social welfare organizations and institutions was four times greater than this amount at IL 48,676,000 (Yefet, 1957).[40]

Given the political structure of the Yishuv period, it is not surprising that the parties also set up organizations or tried to find footholds in existing organizations after statehood. Lissak (1999) notes that the immigrants who came to Israel in the 1950s were dependent upon bureaucratic mechanisms characterized by strong partisan overtones; in fact, some relevant services were provided by organizations that were clearly under party control. For instance, the Mapai party held an absolute majority in Kupat Holim, which in itself had a monopoly in the provision of health services among immigrant communities (Lissak, 1999, pp. 127–128). Immigrant organizations or associations, which Lissak describes as "buffer institutions" between the social-political system and the new immigrants, were established primarily by the parties and chiefly served as instruments for political mobilization: on one hand, these organizations attracted ethnic groups by offering financial support to the needy, licenses for opening businesses, and help in finding permanent work; on the other hand, they served as a pipeline for enlisting ethnic activists to engage in party work via cooptation (Lissak, 1999, p. 129).

However, there were some attempts at this time to establish independent organizations that were less reliant on the state for support. These organizations tried to remain distant from the institutional framework in order to maintain their professional or ideological autonomy. Such organizations included Hadassah, the Israel Cancer Society, which was founded in 1952 and has since financed its operations solely on donations, and some autonomous immigrant associations. In addition, in the first decade following statehood some protest organizations were formed that existed outside of the party system, fought for social change, and exercised pressure on the government. Their activities included mass protests, street actions, and demonstrations on diverse issues such as the rights of new immigrants, the seamen's strike, keeping the Sabbath, the military government in Arab towns and villages, and German reparations for the Holocaust survivors (Hermann, 1995).

There were also "extra-parliamentary groups" (Hermann, 1995) or "marginal political groups" (Eisenstadt, 1989, p. 187) that were characterized by more stable organizational frameworks and focused their protest activities around a variety of issues, including nuclear disarmament (e.g., The Israeli Peace Committee), relations between Jews and Arabs (e.g., *Ihud*), support for a Jordanian-Jewish-Palestinian federation (e.g., *Hashemite* Action), objections to religious coercion (e.g., the League against Religious Coercion), and reform of government institutions (e.g., The New Regime). A very prominent example of this type of organization was *Shurat Ha'Mitnadvim* (A Line of Volunteers), which was organized in 1951 by students at the Hebrew University who volunteered to help new immigrants in the *ma'abarot* (immigrant transit camps) by teaching Hebrew. These students became involved in some of the most renowned legal struggles of the time when they exposed the establishment's problems, failures, and corruption.

Unlike the participants in street demonstrations, who were mostly new immigrants, these extra-paramilitary groups were composed of veteran Israelis who were well-acquainted with the political and organizational system and were not subject to alienation or discrimination; on the contrary, they were well-established and respected individuals, such as intellectuals, journalists, writers, and professionals. By leveling criticism at the government, they believed that they were serving the collective interest, even though their opponents deemed them to be subversives who had "gone astray." The government's response to these organizations was inevitably negative and severe, de-legitimizing the groups and their leaders, and the results of their endeavors were ultimately marginal and negligible (Hermann, 1995, pp. 110–112). Even so, the fact that these types of organizations existed at all is significant; in the face of wide-ranging support for the state system, they were able to present an alternate point of view and served as harbingers of the broader and better organized protest groups that dominated in the 1970s.

The second phase of the statehood period began in the mid-1960s following the Six Day War and lasted throughout the 1970s. During this time, widespread support for the statist ideology began to wane and with it came greater liberalization towards third sector organizations and their roles within Israeli society. This period, during which the seeds of the following pluralistic period were planted, was marked by the first signs of organizations with a private-particularist or sectorist approach rather than a collectivist-public one (Silber and Rosenhek, 1999). In addition, in the late 1960s and early 1970s, social movements flourished and were aided in their work by voluntary organizations. Likewise, there was increased activity among autonomous organizations with a clear ideology, primarily among service-providing, rather than advocacy, organizations that were in conflict with the state. Additionally, many "self-help" organizations were established to deal with such issues as parenting a large family (*Zehavi*), community and neighborhood development (*Ha'Ohel*), and support for homosexuals (the Organization for Protecting Individuals Rights). Other organizations with a broad public awareness were founded to deal with several social, political, and cultural issues, such as the Citizen's Rights movement, the Association to Advance Health Services to the Public, as well as organizations that encouraged tolerance and mutual understanding between different ethnic and religious groups (*Gesher*). Thus, there was a growing trend in Israel that would continue into the next era of establishing both general and population-specific third sector organizations.

Interestingly, the government's response to these developments was to further encourage volunteer activities. As early as the 1960s, systematic attempts were made to include volunteers in the work of local governments, particularly within the welfare arena. As a result, institutionalized relationships were developed with organizations like the Rotary Club, the Lions Club, and *B'nai Brith* around such issues as forming a Big Brothers program, old-age homes, or institutions for mentally handicapped children (Report by Welfare Minister Dr. Yossef Burg, 1965, pp. 20–22; Harman, 1970; Ministry of Social Welfare, 1966). In 1972, on the basis of recommendations from the Committee on Children and Youth in Distress (known as the Katz Committee), the Center for Voluntary Services was established in the Prime Minister's Office with the fundamental role of encouraging and coordinating volunteer work in Israel. Following its establishment, voluntary units were formed within the government ministries, the Jewish Agency, and the local authorities. All of these developments led to a significant enlarging of the third sector, particularly within the spheres of education and culture where there was a rapid increase and expansion of the high school and university educational systems, and among those organizations working with handicapped people.

Despite this growth, the third sector remained less powerful than the government and had not yet found ways of influencing public policy. Part of this situation stemmed from the third sector's funding sources. Throughout the whole statehood period, contributions from abroad continued to fund both statutory and non-governmental institutions; however, most foreign donations to organizations in Israel were channeled through the Jewish Agency, thus preserving and reinforcing the state's control of those funds. Political parties shared in these resources, as did most of the large cultural, educational, and medical institutions. Money raised in the Diaspora was used to build and finance museums, universities, theaters, orchestras, dance companies, and hospitals. In the very early stages of statehood, these institutions systematically mobilized funds from overseas, often employing the fundraising technique of "Friends" of the institution. The America-Israel Culture Fund, which was founded in 1939 by an American foundation for establishing institutions in Palestine, was particularly active during the 1960s. Some organizations were also founded to fundraise for local issues, such as the Jerusalem Foundation and the Tel-Aviv Foundation.

In contrast to the major donations from abroad, monetary contributions from Israeli citizens to third sector organizations were marginal. One reason for this situation was the "division of labor," in which Diaspora Jews were encouraged to finance the Zionist endeavor while Israelis risked their lives and endured harsh living conditions to realize the Zionist dream. In addition, there was the influence of the mindset that promoted the severing of ties with the venerable Jewish tradition of charity and philanthropy to be replaced by an atheist-socialist perspective that demanded a high level of taxation and left Israeli citizens with very little disposable income. Furthermore, the pioneering ethos of those years deemed such practices as donating to charity to be *galuti* (Diaspora) behavior that recalled grave situations in Jewish history that the Zionists did not want to repeat in the sovereign, independent State of Israel.

Surprisingly, even though the state began to promote and fund third sector organizations, it did not always attempt to supervise and control them. In fact, most of the organizations enjoyed a great deal of autonomy in determining their management and policies, as has been reported in studies of voluntary organizations during the latter half of the statist period (Kramer, 1976; Salzberger and Rosenfeld, 1974). Thus, in the absence of a uniform policy or coordination, relations between the state and third sector organizations were typified by convenience and pragmatic collaboration. As long as the organizations operated in spheres that the state authorized, did not challenge the state mechanism, and did not require major investments in supervision and control, they were considered legitimate and acceptable and received funding, support, and encouragement from the state. Moreover, this relationship did not require that any of the existing laws be modified. The 1906 Ottoman Law of Associations, which had never been amended and was still valid, provided a minimal legal structure that did not involve substantial intervention into the internal matters of the organizations or require government accountability or responsibility for them.[41]

According to Kramer (1976), the government's increasing interest in promoting voluntary organizations was a way of addressing the social divide that was occurring within Israeli society.[42] Thus, programs dealing with poverty, the absorption of new immigrants, and working with delinquents were created to manage social issues. However, this type of activity was occurring in a society that lacked a proper basis for encouraging the productive growth of autonomous organizations. Kramer argues that Israel was a centralized state with little tradition of independent local activity and an underlying belief that the government was responsible for dealing with and able to handle almost every problem. Due to the structure of the economy and security issues, taxation levels were high, which enabled very few people with available free time and income to support voluntary organizations. Nevertheless, paradoxically, there were many such organizations within Israeli society, whose numbers and variety were actually increasing during this period.

Kramer distinguishes between voluntarism based upon collective responsibility, in which individual volunteers are responsible for a collective framework and the collective is responsible for all its members, and voluntarism based upon individuals who are responsible for each other. This distinction coincides with the dominant attitudes of the Labor movement and the Jewish tradition, on the one hand, and that of Anglo-Saxon traditions, on the other. Unlike Anglo-Saxon practices, Israelis did not place any particular value on the idea of voluntarism, per se. Therefore, there was nothing to prevent the state from encouraging volunteering efforts, an idea that would have been regarded as paradoxical or with distrust in the U.S. or the UK, for instance. Kramer stresses that Israelis did not view the central government's widening role with suspicion; on the contrary, the government's intervention was seen as something desirable and the prevailing view was that "the government will take care of things." Thus, there was no tension between the government and voluntary efforts—the two sectors were considered a single entity. This led to an overlap between the sectors, blurring the traditional division between public and voluntary activity. The result was a system that Kramer calls "holistic," in which all issues were dealt with within the same broad framework without precise distinction between the various components.[43]

The relationship that developed between the Israeli government and those organizations dealing with various types of handicapped persons, which Kramer studied, typifies the situation for many third sector organizations at that time. These organizations—such as Akim, which was established by parents of mentally disabled children, Ilan, which was founded by parents of physically disabled children, and *Shema*, which was created for deaf children, and *Ha'aguda lma'an haiver*, which was originated to help the blind—were developed by populations whose needs were not being adequately addressed by the welfare state. Although they were founded by citizens, these organizations gradually created a relationship with the relevant government ministries in order to finance their services. Funding was generally given in the form of grants, without any kind of comprehensive examinations or planning and often to cover deficits. As a result, no accountability standards or methods of enforcement were drawn up. Generally, the relations between government officials and executives or managers were "warm," with attempts on both sides to gain advantages. For the government, this type of arrangement assured the public that the state did not hold a monopoly in any one sphere. In addition, the services that voluntary organizations offered were less expensive and could be financed by operational budgets rather than "rigid" budget items. Moreover, the voluntary organizations reinforced the work of the relevant government ministries, which in turn put pressure on the treasury to increase the ministries' allowances. For the organizations, on the other hand, government funding was vital not only to financing their operations, but also for obtaining public legitimacy and status in fulfilling important public goals.

Kramer also found that the organizations he studied were small in scale, with low levels of bureaucratization and tenuous links to their clients. There were considerable differences in terms of their internal structures and decision-making patterns, particularly with regards to how they allocated power and made policy-related decisions. In all of the organizations that Kramer investigated (with the exception of the Israel Cancer Association), there was a tendency to rely upon public funding. In most cases, the organizations raised donations through schoolchildren and members of youth movements who went door-to-door to collect money.

Lastly, in his study Kramer distinguishes between three roles that he believes voluntary organizations should fulfill: that of value guardians, societal vanguards, and societal improvers. Israeli third sector organizations during the end of the statist period only partially fulfilled these roles. As value guardians, third sector organizations are responsible for reinforcing voluntarism, which is manifested in the recruitment and deployment of volunteers. The organizations that Kramer researched fulfilled these duties in a limited manner, without any strong commitment. He suggests that this was due to the constrained space for social involvement within Israeli society that was mostly confined to political, societal, or religious rather than voluntary endeavors, as well as the lack of prestige for volunteers; although he did note that there were signs that this situation was changing. The role of societal vanguard entails developing innovative experimental programs with the intention that they eventually will be adopted by the public sector. Kramer found this to be a minimal role among voluntary organizations in Israel due to the government's preference for promoting and financing existing programs. Adopting such a role would also require attitudinal changes towards voluntary organizations, as well as the development of independent funding sources. Finally, the role of societal improver is evidenced by an organization's ability to impact policy so as to amend legislation or modes of operation. This was a relatively new role among the Israeli organizations that Kramer studied. Their involvement in advocacy generally involved attempts to obtain financial benefits for their members. One exception was the Akim organization, which as early as the 1950s advocated for the rights of mentally impaired children through lobbying efforts and press releases. Unused to this type of strategy, the government accused the parents who founded the organization of representing an Ashkenazi minority, promoting their own personal interests, and using an "over-emotional" approach that lacked "professionalism." Nevertheless, these struggles led to the creation in 1962 of a separate department within the Welfare Ministry for dealing with mentally disabled people and to legislation in 1969 that protected this population.

Ultra-Orthodox and Arab Third Sector Organizations in the Statehood Period

With the establishment of the State of Israel, the Haredi population faced a tough dilemma: if they utilized the universal service system that gradually developed they could become intertwined with and perhaps dependent upon the Zionist frameworks; however, forsaking those services could be a serious mistake, especially in those fields, such as income maintenance, which were anchored in the law and did not require complex interactions with public institutions. This predicament was further heightened when Haredi parties began to run for government election, relying on the perception that doing so was a legitimate use of the state's "technical means." Accordingly, a fine and fragile line developed between the state service system and the Haredi population. In this relationship, third sector organizations played a key role.

Eventually, the entire Haredi educational system came to be serviced by third sector organizations; moreover, as the Haredi population became increasingly important in terms of maintaining a coalition government, the public funding for ultra-Orthodox third sector organizations grew. Furthermore, thousands of Haredi organizations were established in the areas of health, welfare, and culture. These organizations complemented the public service system and allowed the Haredi population to receive services within their own communities in a fashion that was familiar and acceptable to them. In contrast to the educational organizations, almost all of these organizations were supported by private donations from both within Israel and overseas (foreign donations also supported yeshivot, gifted scholars, and institutions for religious research and publishing), and the patterns of traditional Jewish community charity organizations were transferred into new areas of specialization. Thus, in addition to the regular *gmach* (interest-free loans to the needy) organizations, special gmach funds were created to buy such items as children's toys, clothes, and household items (Landau, 1993). The development of these community organizations enabled the ultra-Orthodox Jews to maintain a safe distance from the secular population, although they were still willing to accept resources from the larger society. This resulted in an ambivalent collective identity towards the state, in which the Haredi demonstrated an unflinching stand for their rights and interests.

Among the Arab citizens of Israel, on the other hand, there was almost a complete lack of autonomous third sector organizations during the statehood period. As part of the disintegration of Palestinian society following the 1948 war, the structure of community and voluntary organizations that existed during the Mandate period completely disappeared, the waqf method ceased to operate, and health and welfare organizations closed down. Moreover, most of the political leadership or middle-class elite among the Arab population fled during the war, leaving a population that was rural, some of them refugees who had lost of their property, social and economic status, and livelihood. The Arab community was in a state of deep crisis and disorganization (Kamen, 1987). This situation was further exacerbated by the Israeli government's policy towards the Arab population. In the first years of statehood, the Arab population was subject to a military government and supervision, which severely limited the development of autonomous organizations since they were considered a danger to the state (Lustick, 1980). Furthermore, the government expropriated some of the Arab community's economic resources, particularly land, thus denying the residents of a means for establishing effective third sector organizations. Under the Law of Absentees' Property passed in 1950, the government even confiscated part of the waqf's assets out of fear that they may be used to develop autonomous organizations that might defy the state.

In 1965, reforms were passed that ended the military government of Arab citizens and the waqf funds were released on the condition that they would be used solely to develop organizations that provided education, welfare, and religious services with administrators who represented the interests of the Arab communities.

This change did not, however, reduce the government's control over the money and how it was to be used. According to the state's guidelines, the government was responsible for appointing waqf managers who were in charge of ensuring that the funds were used properly. The government, in turn, appointed members of prominent families to these positions and thus expected to control the process. In this manner, the government attempted to co-opt the Arab population. Nevertheless, after the Six Day War, a societal and political awakening was incepted among the Arab population, and various forms of autonomous organizing became discernible. This trend presaged the strong rise in the number of third sector organizations from the 1980s onwards (Zeidan and Ghanem, 2000).

THE PLURALISTIC PERIOD, MID- TO LATE-1970S UNTIL THE PRESENT

Background

Many of the developments that have occurred in the third sector during the pluralistic period are very similar and related to the major changes that took place at the political and social arenas during the same period. A fundamental change has been the way in which large segments of the population have begun to view the state. The etatist/statist ideology that dominated the first thirty years of statehood began to wane as a result of several interconnected processes: (1) Israel's isolation and siege mentality began to change after the negotiation of a peace process with Egypt; (2) demographic changes occurred within the Israeli population, including the arrival of immigrants from Western countries, who were used to living in a democratic society, and the maturation of the second generation of immigrants from North Africa and Asia, who had grown up in Israel and experienced the deprivations of the first generation; (3) technological developments increased, particularly in the area of mass communications, exposing Israelis to information on global events, ideas about an individual's place in society, and customs and conventions of other countries; and (4) the economy became stabilized, standards of living improved, and citizens became focused on the "self" rather than the collective. All of these factors led to a crisis of faith in the state's institutions and the methods used to mobilize the population's support. Deep ideological rifts opened up over the definition of the general will and general good, with citizens of all groups demanding greater input. As a result, voluntary organizing around particularist issues and interests, as well as new topics outside of the Zionist ideological framework gained broader legitimacy.

Within the Zionist movement, Roniger (1994) notes two distinct periods in which the relationship between the individual and broader society was altered. From the 1880s until the middle of the twentieth century, there was a dominant communitarian ideology that encouraged individuals to enlist for voluntary work and contribute their resources on behalf of the collective effort. The "pioneers" represented this ethos and, despite their low numbers, they served as the symbol for and definition of society as a whole. With statehood, this ideology was replaced by values emphasizing individuality according to Western models, particularly American philosophies. This change, in turn, has led to the advent of two significant cultural/political processes within Israeli society during the pluralist era. First, there has been a renewed trend towards sectoralization, reminiscent of the Yishuv period, in which different sectors of society have tried to create distinct, independent "estates" for themselves. In particular, the Haredi (both Ashkenazi and Mizrahi), Arab, and new immigrant (from the former Soviet Union) populations have engaged in extensive third sector advocacy and service provision activities that have been linked in different ways to party activities and financed directly or indirectly by public funds. These new organizations have served to maintain and reinforce each population's unique identity. Second, in response to government inactivity, there has been a movement towards establishing citizens' organizations. These groups have used various strategies to tackle a number of diverse issues, ranging from environmental quality, the rights of the disabled to the quality of government. Hastening these two processes has been a trend towards increased privatization of public services, in which sectoral organizations have begun to fulfill societal needs that the government has been unwilling or unable to meet. As a result, advocacy and social change organizations have assumed the government's role for initiating new social interventions.

The Third Sector in the Pluralist Period

The pluralist period has been characterized by a quantitative growth and expansion of the third sector. Whereas third sector organizations were closely linked to the public sector in the statehood period, they have developed new attitudes regarding state supervision and control in the pluralist era. These changes were preceded by a period of social protest around a variety of issues during the 1970s, although these demonstrations did not necessarily lead to the establishment of stable third sector organizational frameworks (Lehman-Wilzig, 1992). One of the most significant changes during the pluralist period has been the increased economic activity of third sector organizations. The third sector's share of the GDP grew from 6% between 1955 and 1975, to approximately 8% from 1975 to 1984, and reached 11.6% by 1991. Likewise, the number of employees in third sector organizations increased from 11% of the labor force in 1982 to 13.3% in 1991 (Central Bureau of Statistics, 1998). A second important development has been the growth in the number of new third sector organizations. On average, roughly 1,500 new organizations have been founded per year since 1980, bringing the sum total of registered third sector organizations to 30,000 by the end of the 1990s.

These changes have been the result of various, interrelated factors, including: (1) the privatization and sectoralization of third sector organizations; (2) the growth of civil society; (3) the advent of new funding sources for third sector organizations; and (4) the establishment of new training and coordination frameworks for third sector organizations.

Much of the growth of the third sector in the pluralist period can be attributed to the trend towards privatization. Like other welfare states in the 1980s, the Israeli government transferred a large portion of its service-providing functions to both third and private sector organizations. As a result, third sector organizations have increasingly been used as "subcontractors," offering services on behalf of the government and local authorities, often with state funding (Doron, 1999; Katan, 1997; Katan, 2000). This policy of partial privatization has limited the government's responsibilities as a service-provider and key employer, thereby insulating the state from increased pressure from the recipients and employees of service-providing organizations. Despite these measures, however, the state has not relinquished its control over the third sector, nor have the organizations themselves become more powerful. For example, while nonprofit organizations have served as subcontractors for the state under the Home Care Law, the government has retained a supervisory role with the authority to define eligibility criteria, determine the scope and quality of services, and choose those organizations that will deliver the services (Rosenhek, 1998). Likewise, the new policy that was developed to deal with the massive influx of immigrants from the former Soviet Union in the early 1990s decentralized and liberalized the process of immigrant absorption, giving immigrants greater autonomy in making decisions (regarding housing and employment, for example) and local authorities and third sector organizations greater responsibility for aiding the immigrants. Despite the state's reduced role, it has retained the right to supervise and manage these operations. Thus, although the state has encouraged and funded the work of third sector organizations, it has also developed various mechanisms to monitor them; the result has been a pattern of supervision resembling that of the statehood period.

Nevertheless, privatization has led to diversification and growth in the third sector. Third sector organizations have enlarged their areas of operation, incorporated new strategies, expanded their interactions with the state, and broadened the population groups they serve from those defined by a specific problem (e.g., a handicap, chronic illness, mental disorder) to those of a specific ethnicity (e.g., Haredi, Ashkenazi, Mizrahi) or nationality (e.g., Arabs, new immigrants from the former Soviet Union (Katan, 2000). These changes, however, have led to new problems. Although the government has claimed that its motivation in transferring its service provision function to third sector organizations has been to improve efficiency, cut costs, and provide services that are close to the populations they are serving, the sectoral systems that have been developed are not necessarily required to provide services in a completely professional and effective way; often the services are delivered in conjunction with ideological and cultural messages that are intended to strengthen politically the sectoral format in which they are offered. In addition, the fact that some of the services provided to the Haredi population via third sector organizations are state-funded has raised skepticism among the secular population who consider this arrangement to be an abuse of the system. This has led to a profound conflict between the religious and secular populations.

Concomitant with these changes in privatization and secularization has been the collapse of the service provision system linked to the Histadrut. A number of factors have led to this decline, including the Labor Party's fall from power, Israelis' exposure to other societies via mass communications, the need to develop a market economy, the emphasis on an individualist ideology, as well as the Histadrut's own corrupt, burdensome, and complex system that was rife with interior inconsistencies. However, the Histadrut's network of service organizations—such as the Kupat Holim health fund, the Mishan chain of old-age homes, the Amal group of vocational training schools, the pension funds, etc.—were deployed throughout the country and could not be immediately replaced. In order to settle the Histadrut's financial debts stemming from its failed economic endeavors, these enterprises were sold; the Histadrut's nonprofit systems became privatized and were separated from the Labor union system (one of the only aspects of the Histadrut that has remained intact). Thus, under the National Health Insurance Law of 1994, it is no longer necessary to be a member of the Histadrut in order to join the *Clalit* HMO; Mishan and its chain of old-age homes have been sold to a private entrepreneur; and the Amal network is in the process of establishing a new organizational system that is separate from the Histadrut.

The increase in the number of civil society organizations during the pluralist period has also affected the growth of the Israeli third sector. Usually established in response to discrimination, these types of organizations have focused on populations with special needs by creating an alternative structure in which a problem is addressed through self-help or advocacy. Thus, there has been a noticeable increase in civil society organizations that promote women's, children's, Arabs', and human rights; environmental quality; neighborhood and community activism; and religious freedom. Among the religious civil society organizations, many have been developed to promote different manners of practicing Judaism (e.g., Reform Judaism, Conservative Judaism) or approaching Judaism (e.g., emphasizing the humanistic aspects of Judaism). In addition, a number of organizations have been established to deal with political issues, such as improving the nation's democratic infrastructure (e.g., *Huka le'Israel*, A Constitution for Israel), public ethics (e.g., *Hatnua Le'Eichut Ha'Shilton*, the Movement for Quality Government Rule), pluralism and tolerance (e.g., *Sovlanut*, Tolerance), peace with the Palestinians (e.g., *Shalom Achshav*, Peace Now), or settling the territories captured in the 1967 war (e.g., *Gush Emunim*, Bloc of the Faithful).

One significant characteristic of most of these organizations has been their financial and institutional independence, which has enabled them to challenge the state (Gidron, 1997; Gidron and Bargal, 1986; Yishai, 1998). In contrast to other third sector organizations, civil society groups have not been connected to or dependent upon the state; on the contrary, they have regarded themselves as political campaigners or watchdogs, whose role has been to promote the rights of and draw attention to any government abuses against the populations they represent. In this respect, these organizations have been very unique within Israeli society. For the first time in Israel's history, the social, political, and ideological climate has permitted the formation of legitimate organizations that can criticize the government without being regarded as "state-haters." Thus, for example, the newer women's organizations that were founded in the 1980s (e.g., *Shdulat Hanashim* (the Women's Network), shelters for battered women, and rape crisis centers) have been much more militant and confrontational towards the state and less dependent upon the government than the older women's organizations that were established within the service-provision framework of the statehood period (e.g., *WIZO, Na'amat, Emunah*) (Atzmon, 1990; Fogel-Bijaoui, 1992; Yishai, 1998).

Nevertheless, these groups have not always "spoken the same language" and have often been in direct conflict with one another. This has been particularly noticeable among those organizations that have been created to improve conditions in distressed neighborhoods and development towns. Groups such as *Ha'Keshet Ha'Mizrahit* (Mizrahi Rainbow) have adopted a critical, confrontational approach that presents their demands as part of an ethnic conflict between Mizrahi and Ashkenazi Jews. Likewise, environmental groups established in the 1980s and 1990s, such as *Megama Yeruka* (The Green Trend) and *Tnu La'Chayot Lichyot* (Let the Animals Live), have clashed with such organizations as *Hevra Le'Haganat Ha'Teva* (Society for Protection of Nature in Israel), which was founded in 1952 and has extensive relationships with government authorities. In some instances, however, the older institutions have adopted some of the strategies and agendas of the newer organizations. *WIZO* and *Na'amat*, for example, added programs in the 1990s to protect battered women, and the Society for the Protection of Nature in Israel has been working more assertively to preserve environmental quality.

The growth of the third sector in the pluralist period has also been spurred by the advent of new funding sources. In 1980, the New Israel Fund (NIF) was established in response to rifts in Israeli society and their consequent effects on funding from American Jews. The foundation offered an alternative fundraising system to the institutionalized approach of the Jewish Agency, which had been the dominant fundraiser among Diaspora Jews for years.[44] The establishment of the NIF reflected a different set of funding priorities among a new generation of U.S. donors with different values and agendas than those of their parents. Thus, the NIF has provided financial and technical support (e.g., organizational consulting) to social-change organizations with a leftist-center orientation that are not part of the establishment, including some Arab organizations that never received funding from the Jewish Agency. The NIF's activities raised criticism among donors to the Jewish Agency, who either stopped contributing funds to the agency or called for greater involvement in deciding how their donations would be spent. As a result, the Jewish Agency has created programs that promote closer ties between donors and recipients and give donors greater control over the manner in which their donations are used. These include Project for Neighborhood Renewal, established in 1978, and Partnership, founded in 2000. In addition, the number of Israeli donors has begun to increase significantly. With the debut of the *Teletrom* program in 1981, the radio was used for the first time to raise contributions for third sector organizations. Donations from the Israeli business sector have also increased, and citizens have become more interested in fostering the work of Israeli foundations. For instance, the Van Leer Institute established the Israeli Foundations Forum in 1994 to create liaisons and coordinate activities among Israeli foundations.

Another fundamental change within the third sector has been a trend towards organizational stabilization. Since the early 1980s, there have been attempts at coordinating organizations and voluntary associations within the Israeli third sector. Some examples of organizations that have coalesced around a specific issue include the Women's Network, which was created in 1984; the Council for Religious and Cultural Freedom (*Hemdat*), a coalition of organizations that oppose religious coercion; *Bat Adam*, a group of organizations combating violence against women that was founded in 1988; and the Forum of Voluntary Associations for Immigrant Absorption, which was established in 1989. Likewise, an umbrella organization was instituted in 1986 that addresses the entire third sector: the Joint Distribution Committee's Nonprofits and Voluntary Sector has been developing and fostering voluntary activities and initiatives, lobbying the government and the Knesset to promote collaboration and coordination among its member associations, fostering public awareness of the importance of voluntary endeavors, and developing professional leadership and training courses. In addition, the New Israel Fund established *Shatil*, which has been involved in organizational consulting to advocacy and social change organizations. All of these developments have signified a process of increased professionalization within the third sector.

Despite all of these changes and the significant growth within the third sector, the relationship between third sector organizations and the Israeli government has remained unchanged in many respects. The government has continued to regard the third sector as inferior to the public sector and has maintained its view that third sector organizations are primarily service providers. Indeed, much of the considerable economic growth within the third sector can be attributed to an expansion in the types of state-funded services these organizations have provided. Thus, the pattern has continued in which the government uses voluntary endeavors and donations for its own purposes. For example, the state founded the National Organization for Promoting Voluntary Activities on Issues of Society and Welfare in 1981 to promote and coordinate voluntary activities aligned with government policies and priorities. By establishing this organization, the government was in essence attempting to retain the policy it had developed during the statehood period when the prime minister's office created the Center for Voluntary Services in 1972. Likewise, the Libi Foundation for Israel's Security was established in 1982 to compensate for cuts in the defense budget (particularly in areas pertaining to soldiers' wellbeing); public donations to the foundation, however, may be channeled to the current budgets of the Israeli Defense Forces (IDF) and the Ministry of Defense (Ben-Meir, 1988, p. 110). In addition, in order to influence the activities of third sector organizations, the government enacted the Law for Volunteers' Insurance in 1976 and the Law of Associations in 1980,[45] which provides the government with greater supervision over the internal activities and management of associations (Bar-Mor, 1997).

Ultra-Orthodox and Arab Third Sector Organizations in the Pluralist Period

During the pluralist era, the ultra-Orthodox population has significantly increased its power and consequently its ability to obtain larger amounts of public funding. This situation has resulted from the meteoric ascent of the Haredi Mizrahi party, *Shas*, as well as the inclusion throughout the 1980s and 1990s of Haredi parties in various political coalitions that have enabled them to tip the political scales. Since the Haredi population has lacked a business/economic infrastructure, all of the funding that it has received has been channeled directly to third sector organizations, particularly those involved in ultra-Orthodox education. Moreover, because Shas has refused to sign any contractual agreements with the state that would create open and transparent budgets within their organizations, public funds have been transferred in a variety of ways that have allowed the recipient organizations to evade submitting full and complete reports of their operations.

The Haredi population has used these public funds to simultaneously strengthen the ultra-Orthodox community and Shas' power. Yishai (1998) distinguishes between a regular party, which appeals to a wide electoral body, and a "movement party," such as Shas, which represents a specific social group that is trying to make inroads with the dominant political stratum in order to increase its policy-making power. While a regular party has a broad platform that includes various social, economic, and security-related issues, a movement party inevitably has narrow goals, focusing upon a pivotal issue or trajectory around which it structures its political platform. Rahat (1998) notes that the strategies and tactics of the Shas party (including its use of third sector organizations to buttress its political power) are similar to those of the Labor party and the Histadrut during the statehood and Yishuv periods, respectively. The Shas party has recruited voters by offering to help anyone in need and using the "member brings a buddy" method. Those who have used the Shas' services join a constantly widening circle of potential voters who have spread the word about the movement among their friends.

Shas has offered a wide variety of services to potential voters. One of the most extensive has been the Haredi educational system, *Ma'ayan ha'hinuch ha'Torani*, whose benefits include a long school-day, extra Bible classes, short vacations (the summer vacation is only three weeks instead of 2 months in the public school system), breakfast and lunch, transportation to and from school, and often textbooks and notebooks. Members pay either nothing or a symbolic fee to use these services. In 1998, there were 40,000 students enrolled in Shas Haredi educational system. This system of free (or almost free) schooling has created a strong line of communication not only among children but also their parents and has built a future generation of children and adult supporters of Shas.

In addition, Shas has provided ancillary educational services for children and adults, including evening Torah lessons, after-school activities, booster classes, training, and books. These services have been extremely popular: *El Ha'ma'ayan* (the Shas organization that provides educational services) has had close to 300,000 Torah students throughout Israel and has maintained a presence in almost every Israeli city. *Shas* also has run a network of organizations intended to gain potential voters: *Ma'ayanei Hityashvut*, which has targeted residents of *moshavim* (agricultural settlements); *Bnei Chayil*, a youth movement; *Margalit—Em b'Yisrael*, a women's organization; *Netzach Margalit*, which has provided medical equipment to the needy; and *Shitat Beit Yosef, Yehuda Ya'aleh*, a nationwide advice bureau with local councils to handle complaints from the public. Additionally, Shas has allocated substantial budgets for such services as taking thousands of women to summer-camps and hosting families during the Sabbath. Shas has assumed that the recipients of these activities will return the favor by voting for them on election day (Rahat, 1998, pp. 367–368).

Despite the preponderance of organizations that have been established to promote the Shas party, there have been a number of Haredi third sector organizations that have broadened their frameworks in order to serve the entire Israeli population. The most noteworthy example is *Yad Sarah*, an organization that lends medical equipment to people in need. This organization has achieved impressive success in developing a new area of activity within the third sector. Likewise, the Haredi organization, *Ezer mi'Zion*, has expanded its medical consultation services to the broader population.

Like the Haredi community, the Arab population in Israel has also experienced significant social, economic, and political changes since the late 1970s. These developments have resulted in the formation of a middle-class, an autonomous economic foundation, and increased political power. Consequently, there has been an intensification of attitudes challenging the Israeli establishment, which in turn has led to the development of an infrastructure for an autonomous third sector. Since the Law of Associations was enacted in 1980, the number of Arab organizations has increased "by thousands of percentages, relative to the period that preceded it" (Zeidan and Ghanem, 2000, p. 10). Many organizations have been established to nurture the social and cultural advancement of Arab communities, including service-provision organizations that exist primarily at the local level and in fields where state services were either non-existent or inappropriate. However, a number of organizations have been formed with distinct political goals that criticize the state's discrimination against Arabs, including the Association for the Preserving and Protecting of the Rights of the Bedouin in Israel, the Committee for Defending Arab Land, and the Arab Organization for Human Rights. *Itijiya*, an umbrella organization for all of these organizations was founded in 1995. Some Arab organizations have countered the ideological underpinnings of the Jewish state.

The Islamic movement has been an important factor in propelling voluntary activity among the Arab population. The movement has successfully developed an organizational framework that provides welfare, education, and health services chiefly to the poor and handles social problems, such as juvenile delinquency, drug abuse, alcoholism, and prostitution. Generally operating at the local level, the movement has filled a vacuum left by the limited number of state welfare institutions within the Arab population. Since the Islamic movement has a political party and formal political powers, its service provision work has been perceived in the same way as the Shas party's work: the Islamic movement has developed totalitarian frameworks and a clientelistic approach with the expectation that recipients will respond with a political payback on election day in return for the services provided. The most striking difference between the Islamic movement and *Shas*, however, is that the Arab organizations intentionally have maintained their autonomy from the Israeli state. Their endeavors are funded exclusively by donations obtained chiefly from the Palestinian Diaspora but also from Islamic Arab groups in the United States. Their autonomy has allowed the Arab third sector organizations to present themselves as an alternative to the state and to combine the provision of social services with a radically critical approach to the Israeli government.

CONCLUSION

Both Kramer (1976), writing in the 1970s, and Silber and Rosenhek (1999), writing two decades later, have used the term "paradox" to explain, on the one hand, the existence of a large, vibrant, and variegated third sector throughout the course of Jewish/Israeli history, and, on the other hand, the lack of a democratic western tradition that has emphasized individualism, localism, and distrust of the government in determining society's direction. The authors also marvel at the remarkable way in which communal/voluntary systems have been run in the Jewish tradition so that there has been no distinction between activities that have been undertaken voluntarily or under coercion. The answers to these apparent inconsistencies may lie in the history of the Israeli third sector. When Israel was first formed it was necessary to create a variety of third sector organizations to meet a wide range of needs; therefore, there was no need or room for an anti-etatist philosophy. This type of ideology became more appropriate during the pluralist period when it was necessary to consolidate an array of third sector organizations as individuals and their problems (rather than the collective) became more prominent. Thus, over long periods of time, Jewish history provided the conditions for third sector organizations to fulfill these contradictory roles.

Likewise, the seemingly paradoxical combination of voluntary activities and coercive methods of participation have stemmed from developments dating as far back as the Middle Ages when ideological disputes led to a multiplicity of organizations with various orientations that were either supportive, contradictory, or neutral towards the status quo. The lack of a sovereign system for enforcing the decisions of the dominant leadership resulted in the development of coercive frameworks without a clear distinction between these frameworks and the voluntary sector. Furthermore, inter-organizational relations were at times cooperative and at other times antagonistic and competitive, depending upon the circumstances.

Thus, the traditions of running third sector organizations in the Diaspora were re-created and even significantly improved upon in Israel during the Yishuv period. Sovereign independence in 1948 and the accompanying statist ideology failed to alter these patterns. This is evidenced by the developments within the Israeli third sector over the past two decades of the pluralist period. With the waning of the statist ideology, the number and variety of third sector organizations has increased with the attendant division of these organizations into societal sectors. The blurring of the public and voluntary sectors and the counter-reaction to statist attempts to demarcate these boundaries has led to a reinforcement of a sectoral structure, which third sector organizations have further strengthened (minus the politic and consociational culture that was a feature of the Yishuv period). Therefore, an examination of the third sector in Jewish history since the Middle Ages reveals a consistent organizational pattern of multiplicity and variety that represents a continuous Jewish tradition. Over the past twenty years, this tradition has adopted a fresh perspective through the influence of current global social and economic trends, as is the case with many third sectors in other countries.

This analysis of the Israeli third sector also reveals three historical legacies. First, it appears that in the Jewish/Israeli tradition, the ability to create associations has played a central role in providing a perception of freedom within adverse political or administrative situations. Both Israeli and Diaspora Jews have expressed their liberation from governmental/administrative constraints through the formation of a range of third sector organizations, such as charity organizations, trade unions, political organizations, and membership associations, that for the most part were formed at the same time in history but with little coordination between them. For example, this process occurred when the Jews left the ghettoes in Europe during the Enlightenment period (Eisenstadt, 1989, pp. 80–85), again when the Turks left Palestine after WWI (Segev, 1999),[46] and later when the Law of Associations was enacted in 1980, marking an end to the moral and administrative constraints on the freedom of association that characterized the statist period and leading to the establishment of numerous nonprofit organizations. This pattern suggests that at certain junctures in Jewish history a "social pressure-valve" has been released resulting in a flood of organizations where they had previously been restricted.

Second, throughout its history Israel's third sector has been marked by pluralism. The periodization approach of our historical analysis shows that most third sector organizations have been able to adapt to the principal forces directing societal development. This has been primarily due to the allocation of resources to the sector for the promotion of specific goals. At no period, however, has this led to an exclusive trajectory: in conjunction with those organizations within the central system and its institutions, other organizations have always sprung up that have either challenged the central system or chosen to remain outside of it in order to deal with private or professional issues without losing their focus and autonomy. Hence, over the years, third sector organizations have simultaneously preserved the societal and political infrastructure and brought about ferment, change, and innovation. These trends have resulted in a legacy of pluralism in the functions, organizational forms, and spheres of activity of third sector organizations that has been evident throughout each period of Israeli history. Thus, the pluralism that has flourished since the late1970s in Israel is also part of a continuing legacy in which the third sector has played diverse roles throughout its history.

Third, there is a certain ambiguity in Israel regarding the definition of "voluntarism," which is a key concept and an essential ideological infrastructure for the development of a third sector. This lack of clarity can be linked to the absence (until 1948) of a "public sector," the existence of which enables an autonomous voluntary sector to thrive. In addition, after statehood, the need to develop a "public sector" based upon the existing infrastructure of voluntary organizations from the Yishuv period further clouded the distinction between the two sectors. Additionally, there has been the influence of the Jewish tradition, which stresses communal/collective frameworks rather than the individual. Thus, defining voluntarism as part of an array of *mitzvot* (precepts) and a behavior that is expected of individuals within a communal system has blurred the distinction between individual free will and enforced activity, as well as between donated funds and funds paid through taxes. In contrast to the Anglo-Saxon tradition, there has been no dichotomous separation in the Jewish political tradition between "voluntary" organizations (based on philanthropic inputs) and governmental (or communal) organizations and leadership based on taxes and the enforcement of coercive laws.

Kramer (1976) argues that this lack of separation between the state and the third sector has been clearly manifest in modern Israel where the prevailing ideology does not place any particular value on the kind of voluntarism that is based on an anti-etatist philosophy and therefore opposes the broadening role of the central government. On the contrary, government intervention has been considered desirable in Israel. Evoking a paternalistic approach, the accepted attitude and expectation has been that "the government will take care of things." There has been a clear preference for handling social problems with combined forces, making no distinction between the public and voluntary frameworks. Thus, the state's encouragement of voluntary activity has not been considered paradoxical. Unlike the U.S. or the UK, the government has been neither for nor against a voluntary effort—on the contrary, the two sectors have been considered a single entity. Furthermore, at the individual level, Kramer notes that voluntarism in Israel has been based on collective responsibility, in which members of a voluntary framework have had reciprocal-collective responsibilities towards the frameworks and each other, as opposed to the personal-individual responsibility of autonomous individuals who are unmediated by any framework. All of these attitudes have led to the development of overly close relations and a lack of distinction between the public and the third sectors, which in turn has resulted in the formation of frameworks for "collective voluntarism" and unfortunately at times has given rise to negative consequences (e.g., abusing the NPO status).

Thus, despite the great diversity of the Israeli third sector today, the prevailing attitude remains that the state should be the primary funder of the third sector rather than private donations, that the government is responsible for setting policy for the sector, and that the overlap between the public and third sectors is appropriate. The voluntary system is still considered a tool for solving the problems of the state and the collective. In many cases, voluntary efforts are defined as collective efforts "for the good of the state" or "for society's sake." While this situation is not unique to Israel, what is unusual is that in other countries this type of government control and intervention is usually considered unconscionable; in Israel, however, the blurred boundaries and reciprocal relationship between the state and civil society are viewed as desirable.

NOTES

29   This form of "internal" government also led to the development of unique Jewish traditions and culture (Katz, 1958). The combination of these factors has resulted in the creation of a "Jewish political culture" (Elazar, 1997), with specific patterns of governance that continue to impact the political environment in Israel (Eisenstadt, 1989).

30   See, for example, Silber and Rosenhek (1999).

31   These organizations guaranteed burial and prayer services to the dead, including the poor. They subsequently spread to other Jewish communities throughout the world.

32   Loewenberg (1997) uses the term, "non-voluntary voluntarism" to describe the Jewish percep-
     tion that as the world's resources (e.g., capital, time, and control of human actions) are in God's
     possession, man cannot invest these resources voluntarily since he does not possess them. In
     other words, a human being's investment in any goal merely expresses his commitment to a set
     of precepts established by God, which is intended for the realization of these goals.

33   There are some researchers who disagree. For instance, Silber and Rosenhek (1999) argue that
     the dominant Zionist organizations gradually adopted features of a public system, including
     centralization, supervision of the population, and control of financial and political resources,
     which led to a general framework resembling a "proto-state." Likewise, Kimmerling (1995)
     posits that the development of sectoral services with a political and ideological basis helped to
     mobilize, centralize, and develop a "consensual attitude" among the people that resulted in a
     "proto-state" system that was necessary in order to gain control under the British Mandate. We
     recognize the existence of some "state organizations" (e.g., the Zionist Organization, the Jewish
     Agency) but argue that other organizations, such as the Histadrut (a system of organizations
     that offered services to members of the Labor party) fit the definition of the third sector used
     in this book.

34   It is important to note that the institutional framework of a "sector" during the Yishuv period
     included a variety of institutions, not only those that we would classify today as being part of
     the "third sector."

35   The term "civil" in the Yishuv period referred to those circles that were not part of the Labor
     movement. The connotation of the word "civil" at that time was being of the "bourgeois"
     (Horowitz and Lissak, 1977, p. 102).

36   This type of system is evident today in such countries as Switzerland and Belgium, in which
     the populations are fairly heterogeneous.

37   This situation is expressed in a booklet published in 1946 summarizing the first decade of activity
     of the organization, *Mishan*, in Haifa: "There is a danger that the help extended to a member
     which is basically socialistic help based on the principle of mutual aid will turn into philanthropy
     that debases and leads to a moral decline" (*Bemaagal Ha'ezra Hahadadit*, 1946, p. 12).

38   According to Divshoni (1928), money was collected by a variety of means:

> Letters are sent in large numbers to various donors overseas. Each and every institution
> has a book of addresses . . . [which is] prepared mainly on the basis of American
> telephone directories or [is] bought from "holders of fund-raising drives" . . . [In
> addition] one institution may sell [address books to] another institution . . . Most
> of the kolelim and institutions [also] use the services of emissaries . . . [some of
> whom] . . . receive fixed salaries [and others who] . . . are paid a percentage of their
> revenues . . . Well-known institutions . . . pay 30 percent [of the emissaries' revenues];
> new and less well-known institutions . . . sometimes [pay] up to 80 percent of the
> money collected by the emissaries . . . boxes . . . are [also] placed in synagogues . . . [and]
> in private homes, etc . . . [and] in Eretz Yisrael, there people [who] approach the tourists
> [for money]. Twenty Jerusalem institutions even have special offices in America for the
> collection of funds (p. 4).

39   Another famous argument erupted over abolishing the sectoral military/defense organizations
     and establishing the IDF.

40   The total budgets for the 162 voluntary organizations do not include all such organizations that
     existed at that time. A large portion of the total budgets for these organizations is derived from
     a small number of organizations, including the Youth Immigration and Immigrant Absorption
     Divisions of the Jewish Agency, Malben, and WIZO International, all of whom obtained the
     majority of their funds from overseas donations.

41 The Companies Ordinance also provided a legal framework for third sector organizations that could register as "limited liability associations" but be subject to wider public supervision.

42 Ralph Kramer is an expert in the field of voluntary organizations in the U.S. and has analyzed third sector organizations in Israel according to this perspective. In addition to a "technical" analysis of the management and funding patterns of third sector organizations, Kramer emphasizes the principles and ideas upon which the voluntary sector is based. His research represents the first systematic attempt to distinguish the Israeli third sector (from the public sector) in a consistent and comprehensive manner and to investigate its components in the context of the sector itself, the broader society, and the sector's relationships with the government. His study covers the time frame between the "statist" and the "pluralist" periods and is based on data collected from 1971–1972.

43 For example, during his research, Kramer requested data from a senior official at the Ministry of Welfare on the ministry's budget allocated to voluntary organizations for handicapped people. The official claimed that they did not draw such distinctions stating that, "It makes no difference, in both cases it's money from the Jewish people." This type of holistic system contrasts with the dualist system characteristic of Holland, for example.

44 It should be noted that the New Israel Fund was never actually described as an "alternative" to the Jewish Agency.

45 The Law of Associations replaced the Ottoman Law of Associations of 1906.

46 As Segev (1999) states: "As soon as the Turks left the country, from out of the small and sparse Jewish community sprang up dozens of associations and councils and unions and alliances, clubs for sports, and consumers, trade unions and ethnic committees and parties: all of them conducted general meetings, all organized elections. All competed with each other in displays of patriotic Zionism" (p. 85).

Chapter 5

The Welfare State and the Third Sector in Israel

INTRODUCTION

The contributions of nonprofit organizations prior to, and since, the establishment of the welfare state in Israel have been largely ignored by researchers. Moreover, it was only in the 1990s when changes started to take place within the welfare system that researchers began to focus on the role of the third sector within the Israeli welfare state system. The processes of privatization, decentralization, and globalization that have occurred within Israeli society over the last two decades have led to changes in the division of labor between the public, voluntary, and business sectors. As a result of these changing relationships, the power and influence of the voluntary and business sectors has increased significantly. In this chapter, we describe and analyze the relationship between the Israeli welfare state and the third sector. We first examine the role of third sector organizations in the development of the welfare state. We then present data pertaining to the third sector's involvement in three primary service provision areas: education, healthcare, and social services.[47] In particular, we analyze the relationship between third sector organizations and the Ministry of Labor and Social Welfare. We conclude by examining the role of the third sector in the development of the Israeli welfare state, particularly within the context of the changes that occurred during the 1990s.

THE ROLE OF THE THIRD SECTOR IN THE DEVELOPMENT OF THE ISRAELI WELFARE STATE

Third sector organizations have played an important role in the formation and structure of the Israeli welfare state (Neipris, 1984). Even before the state was established, third sector organizations offered a variety of welfare services to the Jewish population in Palestine (Gidron, 1997). Despite the pervasive collectivistic ideology that existed after the state was formed and the push to establish statutory welfare services for the entire population, the government allowed third sector organizations to continue to provide a wide range of services. The most prominent of these organizations were those involved in health services (e.g., the Kupot Holim), as well as voluntary groups involved in education, welfare, and pension funds. Thus, although the government pushed for the provision of welfare services through statutory systems, the mere existence of third sector organizations meant that many services were provided outside of the public sector. To a large extent, this situation was due to the social and political powers of the organizations themselves, particularly the Histadrut, the largest trade union in the country that strenuously opposed the nationalization of healthcare services for years. Nevertheless, the government maintained close supervision over these organizations and was the primary funder of their activities.

The very existence of these voluntary organizations during the pre-state era promoted the creation of a welfare state with a "mixed market." The Israeli welfare state differed from the "mixed welfare market" characteristic of the U.S., in which third sector and for-profit organizations both play a key role in the provision of welfare services, and the corporatist welfare market distinctive of Germany and France, where third sector organizations provide many welfare services and, in turn, play a key role in the policy-making processes with little government intervention (Esping-Andersen, 1990; Salamon, 1995). In the Israeli mixed welfare market, the state determined policy without any involvement from the third sector, which provided services that the government financed and closely monitored. As a result, third sector organizations became the executive arm of the state welfare system, while the distinction between the two sectors—in terms of the funding, organization, structure, and delivery of services—remained blurred.

This situation continued throughout the 1960s and 1970s when, in addition to the existing organizations, other service-providing associations were established that offered daycare centers for working women, the elderly, and the disabled (Kramer, 1981). The majority of these organizations continued to rely upon the government for financial support but remained "outsiders" in terms of their ability to make decisions regarding the provision of social services (Yishai, 1990). Thus, by the end of the 1970s, there was an extensive system in Israel in which third sector organizations provided most of the services while the government maintained control through funding and supervision.

The situation began to change in the 1980s when new arrangements between the third sector and the welfare state began to evolve (Katan, 1996). While the government was essentially forced to rely upon third sector organizations in the early years of statehood, the situation became intentional during the 1980s. Like other countries at this time, Israel was influenced by neo-conservative policies that promoted the privatization of social services and limitations on the role of the state in their provision (Doron, 1989; 1999). This trend was the result of several factors: the desire to lower costs by providing services through non-governmental organizations; the availability of domestic and foreign resources that were inaccessible to the government; dissatisfaction with the management and bureaucracy of public welfare services; the need for services that the government did not supply or only partially provided; and a political atmosphere that supported decreased government involvement in favor of privatization (Ajzenstadt, 1996; Gal, 1994; Katan, 1996).

Thus, during the 1980s and continuing into the 1990s, government agencies, municipalities and local councils, established, funded, and supervised associations that worked closely with the public systems (e.g., Eshel, the Association for the Planning and Development of Services for the Elderly, and Ashalim, the Association for the Planning and Development of Services for Children). Nevertheless, as Ajzenstadt (1996) notes, privatization in the Israeli welfare state remained limited since the government continued to fund and supervise these organizations. Therefore, the primary development during these years was the increased involvement of third sector organizations in the provision of services within the Israeli welfare state.

The relationship that formed between the Israeli welfare state and the third sector during the 1990s appears on the surface to be cooperative, with a clear division of labor between the two sectors: the government funded, initiated, and supervised third sector organizations, which in turn provided services to the public. Although such arrangements are usually considered cooperative in other countries (Salamon, 1995), it is difficult to characterize the relationship between the Israeli welfare state and third sector as one of cooperation. Since the state was not only the primary funder of third sector organizations but also the sole determinant of policy and legislation, it appears that a situation of state control over the third sector developed. Over the years, the state was able to "recruit" the third sector to fulfill its service-providing functions. Health, education, and welfare services were mostly managed under the state umbrella and, in many areas, the organizations that provided these services had become the government's executive arm, acting under its overwhelming control (Yishai, 1990; Gidron, 1997). This arrangement was possible primarily because of the welfare state's financial power: as long as the state had sufficient resources, it could continue to dominate over the associations, using their activities to promote its own agenda. The situation started to change when cutbacks in the welfare development budgets coupled with the need to satisfy new and diversified needs led to the deeper involvement of the third sector in the welfare state.

One might have expected the government's attitude towards the third sector to change during this time since it was becoming increasingly dependent upon the sector to fulfill its service provision mission, but this was not the case. Instead, the welfare state remained centralistic, with marked signs of dominance towards the third sector. The government developed new control mechanisms, including the increased cooptation of associations, the creation of "monopolies" of service-providing associations in various areas, and a preference for working with bigger and older associations with conformist attitudes towards the state rather than newer, more entrepreneurial organizations whose activities could be viewed as challenging existing services. In the case of the Home Care Law, the state preserved its control over third sector organizations through legislation. As Ajzendstadt and Rosenhek (2000) have noted, by transferring its service-provision function to extra-governmental bodies, the state actually detached and protected itself from consumer pressures and demands while at the same time it preserved its control through funding and legislation. Thus, privatization did not necessarily weaken the state; instead, the government found new ways to exert its control and involvement.

One noteworthy exception to this arrangement occurred within the Haredi independent educational system. The Haredi independent educational system was developed through political compromises that originated in the pre-state era. As the Haredi political parties strengthened their power during the 1980s and 1990s (particularly the Shas party) and became an instrumental factor in political decisions, the two largest political parties became increasingly dependent upon the Haredi for their votes in the Knesset. This situation led to a strengthening of the relations between the Israeli government and the leaders of the Haredi educational system.

Thus, unlike the public educational system, the Haredi system remained essentially independent, even though its primary source of financing continued to be government funding. This freedom was most conspicuous in the Haredis' ability to decide their own curriculum, procedures, teaching methods, management processes, and student characteristics. Although a supervisory mechanism existed within the Ministry of Education that would have allowed the government to oversee the Haredi educational system, all of the supervisors were members of the Haredi community (Shiffer, 1998). Moreover, although the Haredi received substantial funding from diverse government resources, with allowances that significantly exceeded those provided to public education students, it is difficult to estimate the volume of this support due to a lack of data that may have been intentionally obscured (Shiffer, 1998). Thus, within the Haredi educational system, it appears that third sector organizations became more powerful than the state. Not only did these organizations play a significant role in deciding relevant policy, but to a large extent they were the sole determiners and directors of the Haredi educational system. This situation is reminiscent of the relationship between the Israeli welfare state and the Histadrut during the 1950s.

The fact that this type of close relationship between the government and the third sector survived over the past 50 years emphasizes the importance of the sector's political qualities. The third sector remained dominant in a vast variety of areas by providing services to the entire Israeli population. Throughout the years, the sector was able to maintain its power as long as it did not clash with the political interests of the state. In the case of the Haredi educational system, the state would have preferred to play a greater role in its management; however, the influence of the Haredi political parties was an important factor in the state's decision not to intervene. Thus, even though the state exercised significant control over the third sector as a whole, the Haredi educational system was an exception. In this situation, the opposite was true: third sector organizations within the Haredi educational system exerted significant control and dominated all decision-making processes.

THE THIRD SECTOR'S INVOLVEMENT IN EDUCATION, HEALTHCARE, AND SOCIAL SERVICES

The data presented in this section demonstrate the considerable involvement of third sector organizations in the Israeli welfare state, particularly over the past two decades. Like other welfare states, Israel has developed a "mixed welfare market" over the years. Although we only focus the provision of educational, health, and social services in this chapter, it is important to note that third sector organizations are prominent in other areas of the Israeli welfare system, including housing, culture, the absorption of immigrants, and religion (Gidron and Katz, 1999). In addition, we do not address a number of government agencies that provide funding to third sector organizations involved in the provision of welfare services, such as various government ministries (i.e., Religion, Immigrant Absorption, Housing), the NII, and local municipalities. Therefore, it is safe to assume that the third sector's involvement in the Israeli welfare state is even broader than what we describe here.

Education

Background

The educational system that was developed in Israel after statehood built upon the existing educational institutions from the pre-state (Yishuv) era. This earlier system consisted of three systems corresponding to the main ideological branches: the religious, the Labor, and the general (Gaziel, 1996). Although this pre-existing system was well functioning, highly developed, and able to absorb the tens of thousands of new immigrants that poured into the country, its components were organizationally and ideologically diverse and often competed to promote their own interests (Alboim-Dror, 1998). When the Compulsory Education Law was enacted in 1949, education became mandatory in Israel and the state assumed responsibility for providing educational services. The government maintained the three existing ideological divisions and added a fourth: *Agudat Israel*, the collection of independent, ultra-Orthodox educational organizations that had operated as private institutions in the Yishuv period. Thus, shortly after the establishment of the state, the educational system in Israel was divided into four main groups that operated distinct schools with separate curriculums (Dror, 1998).

Not surprisingly, the divided political and organizational structure of the educational system led to conflicts between the state and the authorities of the distinct educational centers, who had enjoyed considerable autonomy prior to the establishment of the state. In addition, the challenges that the new state faced, particularly the absorption of a large number of immigrant students with differing scholarly levels and cultures, both reinforced the need for a central managerial system and placed the needs of the state above those of the various sectors, further restricting their independence (Gaziel, 1998). With the enactment of the National Education Law in 1953, a national educational system was established. Although this law negated the previous divisions within the educational system and appeared to create one that was more centralistic (Gaziel, 1996), in fact the newly established system remained divided and the subsystems within it—the national, the national-religious, the independent ultra-Orthodox, and the settlement (i.e., Kibbutzim) educational institutions—enjoyed a considerable measure of autonomy (Dror, 1998).

In particular, the 1949 Compulsory Education Law and the 1953 National Education Law had the most profound effect upon the ultra-Orthodox educational institutions. While the national, national-religious, and settlement educational organizations had operated within the pre-state system for years, the private Haredi institutions had not. With the Compulsory Education Law, the Haredi schools received government funding for the first time and were able to expand their programs considerably. In fact, after the law was enacted, 70% of Agudat Israel's budget stemmed from government support (eventually, Agudat Israel would be financed almost entirely through government funds) (Friedman, 1991). Once the National Education Law was passed, Agudat Israel established itself as an independent educational network with its own separate curricula. Thus, although Agudat Israel operated closely with the national system, it slowly developed an independent educational system comprised solely of nonprofit associations.

The educational system in Israel remained relatively stable until the 1980s and 1990s when major changes began to occur, including increased privatization and reduced centralization of the system, greater parental involvement, and the implementation of an expanded and more diverse curriculum (Inbar, 1989; Harrison, 1993; Yogev, 1999). "Specialized schools" were developed around a unique core educational or conceptual philosophy, and enrolled students outside of their catchment areas (Shapiro, 1989). For the most part, these schools were absorbed into the national educational system, although parents played a significant role in their operations. Some of these schools were incorporated as amutot (nonprofit organizations) in order to raise funds to support enrichment activities related to their special programs (Shapiro, 1989).

Likewise, complementary educational programs, also known as "gray education," were initiated during the 1980s. Although the Ministry of Education considered these programs to be supplementary educational hours and did not provide them with any government funding, they were required to obtain the Ministry's approval prior to implementation. In 1988, 27% of these programs were incorporated as amutot. During the 1990s, the Ministry of Education also contracted with both nonprofit and business organizations to implement new large-scale projects for which the Ministry had no available infrastructure (Segan et al., 1996). The Haredi educational system also grew significantly during these years (Shiffer, 1998). The Shas party (a Haredi political party that gained considerable power throughout the 1980s and 1990s) managed to enroll many non-Haredi students into its educational programs (Sheleg, 2000).

Third Sector Involvement in Education. In 1998, 5,284 third sector organizations or approximately 18% of all third sector organizations were engaged in educational activities in Israel. Most of these associations operated as Torah learning centers (2,664 organizations) or preschool, elementary, and high school educational institutions (494 organizations). Overall, third sector organizations involved in education employed approximately 95,000 people or 37% of the entire Israeli labor force working in education. Many of these organizations received substantial government support: throughout the 1990s, approximately 70% of their total annual income stemmed from government funds. This trend is also evident when we examine income according to the type of educational institution. As Table 7 shows, most third sector organizations involved in education received more than half of their funding from the government in 1996. Since these figures do not include income that these organizations derived from the "sale" of their services, it is likely that the amount of government support was even higher since the state increasingly became the largest consumer of third sector educational services throughout the 1990s.

The government provided most of its financial support to third sector organizations operating in the independent ultra-Orthodox, higher, and settlement (kibbutzim) educational systems.[48] In this section, we present data on government funding to the first two categories. In 1997, there were 140 schools and 50,198 students in the independent Haredi educational system, which is wholly comprised

Table 7. Sources of Income of Nonprofit Educational Organizations, by Type of Educational Institution, in Million Shekels, 1996[1]

Institutions	Government*	Local Municipalities*	Sales of Services	Donations**	Interest	Portion of Total Income from Government & Municipalities**	Total
Pre-Schools	169	27	161	41	0	49%	398
Elementary Schools	745	52	12	20	1	96%	830
High Schools	1,108	48	180	90	10	80%	1,436
Vocational, Marine, & Agricultural Schools	1,630	51	75	31	5	94%	1,792
Teachers' Training Seminars	115	0	57	9	2	63%	183
Post-High Schools	254	16	283	52	15	43%	620
Higher Education	3,315	0	1,371	592	109	61%	5,387
Yeshivas & Kolels	231	0	60	177	6	49%	474
Other Educational Facilities	39	2	1	9	1	79%	52

[1] It should be noted that in this table, we placed schools from the independent educational network in the "elementary" and "high school" categories (as opposed to the "yeshivas and kolels" category). This accounts for the relatively high rates of government support among elementary and high schools.
*Including capital transfers.
**Income from service provision also includes services that the government purchased; thus, it is safe to assume that the total volume of government transfers to these organizations was even larger.

Table 8. Government Funding of Higher Education Institutions, Thousands Shekels[1]

Year	Total Budget of Higher Education Institutions	Amount of Total Budget from Government Sources	Portion of Total Budget from Government Funding
1980	1,136	800	70%
1985	568,572	315,360	55%
1990	1,462,609	936,263	64%
1992	2,079,694	1,525,349	73%
1993	2,483,175	1,693,672	68%
1994	3,146,593	2,637,335	84%
1996	4,130,600	3,561,585	86%

[1] Amounts are based on current values.
Source: Higher Education Budget Proposal, 1998.

of nonprofit associations. The substantial government support that these organizations receive often exceeds the amounts provided to institutions within the statutory educational system. Despite the large amounts of government support, financial data on the Haredi educational system are scarce. For both historical and political reasons (see Chapter 4), the Haredi are exempt from the laws governing the statutory educational system and therefore may appoint their own inspectors. According to Shiffer, "the budgets of the Haredi educational system are an especially unique example of a hidden process...so as not to allow the accurate figuring of its volume...it seems that this vagueness is not necessarily accidental but sometimes rather intentional" (1998, p. 29).

Like the Haredi educational system, all of the institutions within the system of higher education that receive government funding are third sector organizations, including seven universities, the Open University, and 11 non-university institutions (primarily colleges).[49] All of these organizations are subject to the Higher Education Law of 1957, which requires every degree-awarding institution to be authorized by the Council for Higher Education and regulates government support to these institutions. In 1998, the higher educational system received 4.5 billion shekels in government funding. As Table 8 shows, the amount of government support to these institutes of higher learning has increased substantially over the last 20 years, rising from 70% of their total budgets in 1980 to 86% in 1996.

Thus, although the Israeli educational system has traditionally been viewed as being government-operated, in reality the number of third sector organizations involved in the provision of educational services in Israel has been increasing since the 1980s. This trend is most obvious within the independent and higher educational systems.

Healthcare

Background

Like the Israeli educational system, the healthcare system in Israel is rooted in frameworks dating back to the pre-state era. By the time the state was established in 1948, these organizations had coalesced into a well-developed, nationwide, independent healthcare system. When the state assumed control of the healthcare system, a compromise was necessary between the government, which aimed to develop an egalitarian system that would provide services to all Israelis, and the existing institutions, which desired to preserve their autonomy. The resulting healthcare system included a variety of organizations operated by different groups that came together under one umbrella. The primary organization within this system was the Histadrut's Kupat Holim (a health insurance fund) that was established as a nonprofit organization in 1911.[50] As the system evolved, other Kupot Holim were established, as well as a number of public hospitals. Most of these organizations were financed through a combination of membership dues and government support.

When the National Health Insurance Bill was passed in 1994, the Israeli healthcare system changed substantially to one of controlled competition: citizens now belong to a kupa (company) of their own choice that in turn provides a unified "basket of healthcare services."[51] The system is financed through a progressive health tax collected by the National Insurance Institute and through state support (Gross, Rosen and Shirom, 1999). There are four active Kupot Holim in Israel: the General Health Services fund, the Maccabi Health Services fund, the United Kupat Holim, and the National Kupat Holim. All of these organizations are subject to government supervision. Despite the fact that the Kupot Holim are registered as nonprofit associations, these institutions do not fit the definition of third sector organizations used in this book (see Appendix 2) since their activities are essentially non-voluntary: by law, every Israeli citizen is required to join a kupa that offers a standardized "basket of healthcare services" (Gidron and Katz, 1998).

The Israeli healthcare system also includes a large number of hospitals and other service provision organizations that are incorporated as nonprofit organizations. The best known of these are Hadassah, Bikur Holim, Sharei Tzedek, and Red Magen David. Thus, the Israeli healthcare system is characterized by pluralism, which Schwartz (2000) views as both a strength and weakness. For many years the large number of diverse organizations within the healthcare system prevented the legislation of a national health insurance bill; nevertheless, the system created free competition that enabled the development of independent health institutions and offered consumers a wide range of organizations from which they could obtain healthcare.

Table 9. National Expenditures on Healthcare by Sector

Year	Government and Local Municipalities	Health Funds (Nonprofits)	Other Nonprofits	Business	Total
1990	21.5%	41.4%	12.7%	24.3%	100%
1991	21.5%	41.6%	12.7%	24.3%	100%
1992	22.5%	39.9%	12.7%	24.8%	100%
1993	20.4%	43.7%	12.1%	23.8%	100%
1994	21.6%	43.4%	12.2%	22.8%	100%
1995	21.9%	41.6%	12.3%	24.1%	100%
1996	21.8%	41.7%	12.1%	24.3%	100%
1997	21.15 (6,445 m. shekels)	42.7% (13,056 m. shekels)	11.8% (3,610 m. shekels)	24.4% (7,445 m. shekels)	100% (30,566 m. shekels)
1998	21.2%	41.7%	12%	25.1%	100%

Source: The Annual Statistical Report, 2000, The Central Bureau of Statistics

Third Sector Involvement in Healthcare

The third sector plays a prominent role in the Israeli healthcare system. Third sector organizations account for most of the national healthcare expenditures in Israel. Of the 30.5 billion shekels spent on healthcare in 1997, third sector organizations spent approximately 16.5 billion shekels (of this amount, the Kupot Holim spent 13 billion), while the business and public sectors spent only 7.5 and 6.5 billion shekels, respectively. As Table 9 shows, the implementation of the National Health Insurance Bill in 1994 had little effect upon third sector expenditures on healthcare throughout the 1990s.

The third sector also owns most of the hospitals and hospital beds in Israel. As Table 10 indicates, the number of third sector hospitals has increased substantially since the state was established. In 1948, only 28 hospitals were registered as third sector organizations; by 1999, 177 hospitals were incorporated as third sector organizations, an increase of more than 1,000%. Most of this growth occurred during the 1980s and 1990s when the number of third sector hospitals increased by 124% while the number of private hospitals increased by only 23% and the number of government-owned hospitals decreased by 25%. Likewise, third sector organizations own most of the hospital beds (41%) in Israel compared to the government (33%) and private companies (26%). While third sector organizations possess considerably more beds in rehabilitation hospitals and facilities for the chronically ill, third sector organizations own a relatively small number of beds in mental health hospitals.

Third sector organizations also receive most of the government funding for healthcare in Israel. This is primarily due to the fact that the four main Kupot Holim

Table 10. Number of Hospitals by Ownership[1]

Ownership	1948	1950	1960	1970	1980	1990	1996	1997	1999
Third Sector Organizations									
Klait Health Fund	10	12	16	16	14	14	14	14	13
Maccabi Health Fund	–	–	–	–	–	–	9	7	9
United Health Fund	–	–	–	–	–	–	4	4	4
Christian Church related	5	6	8	9	7	7	7	7	7
Other Third Sector	13	15	15	26	29	65	132	126	144
Government									
Central Government	7	20	37	38	35	29	28	28	26
Municipal Government	–	–	–	2	2	2	2	2	2
Commercial	31	30	57	69	57	70	122	116	122
Total	66	83	133	160	144	187	318	304	327

[1]The National Kupat Holim is not listed in this table because it does not own any hospitals.
Source: The Annual Statistical Report, 2000, The Central Bureau of Statistics.

in Israel (the General Health Services fund, the Maccabi Health Services fund, the United Kupat Holim, and the National Kupat Holim) are nonprofit associations, which the government is mandated to support according to the Health Insurance Bill. In 1998, the government spent 16.786 billion shekels, which amounts to most of the Ministry of Health's annual budget, to support the kupot holim. The government also provided 886 million shekels to third sector public hospitals, 30.5 million shekels to third sector organizations that provide mental health services, and 11.4 million shekels to third sector organizations involved in public health services. Thus, overall the government spent an estimated 18 billion shekels, or approximately 60% of its health services budget, on nonprofit health organizations in 1998.

The government provides less support to the 357 third sector organizations engaged in the treatment and prevention of mental and physical health problems in Israel (Gidron, Katz and Bar, 2000). These organizations receive most of their funding from local and foreign donations. Most notable among these organizations are those that tailor their services towards individuals suffering from specific diseases, such as the Cancer Society, the Diabetes Association, the AIDS Task Force, and the Israeli Union for Rare Diseases. The majority of these groups are also engaged in advocacy work on behalf of their members. For example, the Israeli Health Consumers' Organization fought for the Patients' Rights Bill that passed in 1996. Some of these organizations also supplement the services that the government provides. For instance, Yad Sara lends medical equipment and engages in rehabilitation of the elderly and infirmed, Ezer MiZion is a support center for the sick and needy, and Ezra leMarpe and Kav LeHaim offer home medical equipment and domestic support that the government does not provide.

Thus, the third sector organizations involved in healthcare can be divided into two categories: (1) larger and more institutionalized organizations (e.g., the Kupot Holim, hospitals) that are engaged in the provision of extensive primary healthcare services, and (2) smaller groups that offer services that support, complement, or expand upon those services that the government provides. While the larger organizations are more dependent upon the government for funding, the smaller associations rely upon other sources of support and are more likely to be engaged in advocacy work and to involve "health consumers" and patients in their activities.

Social Services

Background

One of the most important trends that developed during the 1980s and 1990s in Israel was the privatization of welfare services, with the government transferring most of its service provision duties to nongovernmental organizations. During this time, organizations that provide public welfare services also began to employ various business practices characteristic of the private sector (Gal, 1994; Doron, 1999; Katan, 1996). As a result, the third sector's involvement in the provision of social services within the welfare state grew significantly. This is evident in the substantial payments that the Ministry of Labor and Social Welfare made to third sector organizations in 1998. For instance, payments to the third sector equaled 71% of the budget for the Department of Rehabilitation, 56% of the budget for the Department for the Mentally Disabled, and 53% of the budget for the Department of Corrections and Runaway Youth.[52] Overall, the Ministry of Labor and Social Welfare supported more than 1,000 third sector organizations in 1998. These data indicate that third sector organizations have become a major part of the welfare system by fulfilling many of the services that the Ministry is obligated to provide.

Third Sector Involvement in Social Services

Currently, third sector organizations supply the majority of personal welfare services in Israel. Overall, there were 3,807 third sector organizations in the "welfare" category of the Israeli Third Sector Database in 1998; this equals approximately 13% of all registered third sector organizations. According to the definitions used in this book, 90% or 3,403 of these organizations were civil society organizations rather than organizations integrated within the welfare state system (see Chapter 3 and Appendix 3), as indicated in Table 11. Thus, only 10% of third sector organizations involved in the provision of welfare services had binding contracts with the government either through legislation, or other forms of funding (usually long-term contracts). Moreover, since the government only provided funding to 33% of all third sector organizations involved in the provision of welfare services in 1998, it is clear that most of the third sector organizations involved in welfare activity in Israel do not receive state funding or support.

These data contradict the long-standing notion that voluntary welfare organizations in Israel are tightly linked to and funded by the welfare state. Instead, it appears that two separate but concurrent trends are occurring within Israeli society: (1) there is a small group of well established third sector organizations that have a close relationship with the state and are supplying a considerable portion of the welfare services that the government is required to provide; these organizations receive generous support from the government, and, to a large extent, are linked to the state, which supervises and regulates their daily activities; and (2) there is also a diverse group of civil-society organizations that are undertaking extensive welfare activity in a variety of areas and are neither connected to nor funded by the state but receive most of their funding through donations or fees; while these organizations lack the universalism characteristic of those third sector organizations that receive substantial government support, they provide a variety

Table 11. Third Sector Organizations Involved in the Provision of Welfare Services,
by Specific Area of Activity, 1998

Area of Activity	Organizations Integrated within the Welfare State System		Civil Society Organizations		Total	
Children & Youth	27	12%	197	88%	224	100%
Families	6	3%	175	97%	181	100%
Handicapped	92	29%	223	71%	315	100%
Elderly	86	23%	283	77%	369	100%
Women	21	15%	116	85%	137	100%
New Immigrants	12	4%	276	96%	288	100%
Police, Soldiers, & Wardens	30	43%	39	57%	69	100%
Addicts	8	10%	71	90%	79	100%
Convicts & Felons	15	27%	41	73%	56	100%
Other Welfare Services	19	6%	301	94%	320	100%
Financial Support	36	3%	1,211	97%	1,247	100%
In-Kind Support	4	2%	178	98%	182	100%
Other Support	13	4%	290	95%	304	100%
Total	369	10%	3,403	90%	3,772	100%

Source: ICTR database

of alternative solutions to Israelis who are dissatisfied with the government's system.

The organizations that receive substantial funding from the state operate in a variety of fields. In 1998, the Department of Rehabilitation spent 71% of its budget on third sector organizations that provide (1) employment and placement services, rehabilitation services (e.g., vocational training courses in rehabilitation centers), and boarding schools for the handicapped; (2) services to the blind, including employment programs, clubs, and rehabilitation activities; (3) services to the hearing-impaired, including the purchasing of equipment; (4) out-of-home and community rehabilitation services for handicapped children and adults; (5) employment to the mentally disabled; (6) aid to handicapped immigrants; and (7) specialized services (e.g., A Step Ahead, which trains brain-damaged children in the Peto Method).

In 1998, the Department for the Mentally Disabled spent 56% of its budget to support third sector organizations involved in community and domestic treatment, including daycare centers, schools, services, employment rehabilitation projects, summer camps, clubs, and trips. While third sector organizations provide most of the community and domestic treatment programs for the mentally disabled in Israel, for-profit companies operate the majority of institutions: of the 54 active institutions in 2000, 33 were privately owned, 12 were registered as third sector organizations, and 9 were government-owned. Thus, although the state funds, legislates, and supervises most of the services for the mentally disabled in Israel, third sector and private (for-profit) organizations actually initiate, develop, and implement the majority of these activities.

The Department for the Elderly gave substantial support to third sector organizations involved in community assistance to the elderly in 1998. In particular, third sector organizations operated 92% of all day care centers for the elderly in 1997. Associations also provided clubs, home care, personal care, domestic help, medical assistance, transportation to medical appointments, household items, and hot meals. Six thousand older adults utilized these services per month in 1998. In addition, the Department for the Elderly provided funds for protected housing, an arrangement that offers independent older adults special apartments within close proximity to the services they utilize. In 1998, third sector organizations managed 19% of these housing arrangements, while the government operated 64% and private companies managed 16% of these facilities.[53] Third sector organizations were especially active in the field of long-term care services; over the last two decades, third sector organizations have owned close to 50% of the beds in long-term care facilities for the elderly. Likewise, since the 1980 Home Care Law mandated that nongovernmental entities are responsible for providing home care services, third sector organizations have become more active in this field (Katan and Loewenstein, 1999). Nevertheless, of the 150 private and third sector organizations involved in home care in 2000, for-profit companies provided 67% of all home care service hours.

The Department of Personal and Social Services dedicated over half of its budget to nonprofit associations that operate boarding schools, provide "communal activities for children," offer services to at-risk children, provide community support services for families in distress (e.g., recovery programs for alcoholics, programs for the homeless), operate summer camps, and provide domestic help to veterans and new immigrants with family problems. Likewise, the Youth Protection Authority spent a significant portion of its 1998 budget on third sector organizations that operate accommodations for at-risk and homeless children and youngsters, such as shelters (e.g., the Shanti House, Elem), boarding houses, and hostels. In recent years, the government has also significantly increased its support for third sector organizations that provide help for abused women and girls; in 1998, 75% of the budget for the Department for Distressed Women and Girls went to associations running shelters and transitional apartments for battered women, treatment centers, girls' shelters, and other community support services. Additionally, since the 1998 amendment to the Child Adoption Law stipulated that only third sector organizations can handle international adoptions, third sector organizations have become active in this field. In 2000, the Ministry of Labor and Social Welfare and the Ministry of Justice approved 21 third sector organizations to conduct international adoptions in Israel and abroad; as of June 2000, Israeli families had adopted 367 foreign children.

Third Sector Organizations and the Ministry of Labor and Social Welfare

As is the situation between the government and most third sector organizations in Israel, the Ministry of Labor and Social Welfare maintains an ambiguous policy towards nonprofit associations. In a 2001 budget proposal, the Ministry stated that "[in order to promote] efficiency in the headquarters' activities, administration, and services, including improving client service, [there is a need to transfer] government institutions for the mentally disabled and institutions for vocational training to outside bodies" (Budget Proposal 2001, p. 43). Other than these types of ambiguous goals delineated in the Ministry's financial reports, there is very little evidence of a clear, formal policy towards the third sector.

Nevertheless, when we examine elements of the Ministry's approach to the third sector over the years, it is possible to discern some indications of a latent policy towards the sector. For instance, the Home Care Insurance Law of 1986 and the 1998 amendment to the Adoption Law legally defined the relationship between third sector organizations and the state. In both instances, privatization was clearly the intended outcome: from the outset, legislators decided that the state would fund and supervise home care and adoption services but nongovernmental organizations would be responsible for supplying them. Although the Home Care Law permits both nonprofit and for-profit organizations to provide these types of services, the amendment to the Adoption Law explicitly stipulates that only third sector organizations may handle international adoptions.

Another indication of the Ministry's approach towards the third sector is evident in the establishment of the Department for Resource Development in 1994. The goal of the Department is to encourage donors and foundations to support various projects that the Ministry is interested in promoting, most of which are initiated and implemented by third sector organizations.[54] The Department was established after budget cuts began to impact the development of new services and the Ministry became increasingly aware that funding nonprofit organizations was an effective way to fulfill its service-provision function (Cnaan and Dror, 1997). Although the Department's budget equaled only 39 million shekels in 2000, it received over 200 million shekels from external resources (e.g., donors, government and public foundations, associations) that were used to fund over 600 projects. Thus, despite its limited means, the Department of Resource Development is seriously trying to create intermediary frameworks between the government and the third sector. In the process, the Department has become a model for cooperation between the government, foundations, and third sector organizations. Moreover, by creating the Department of Resource Development, the Ministry has given its tacit consent to developing innovative projects that could not have been previously realized due to a lack of resources.

Further evidence of the Ministry's stance towards the third sector is evident in the establishment of a subcommittee within the *Kadima* project to determine whether local third sector organizations could be developed to protect at-risk children in the community ("Developing Local Associations for Children at Risk," The Ministry of Labor and Social Welfare, 2001). The Kadima project is a major component of the Ministry of Labor and Social Welfare's overall plan to track and prevent problems with at-risk children and domestic violence, and to encourage community development to address these concerns.

Thus, although there are signs that the Ministry of Labor and Social Welfare has increasingly recognized the necessity of promoting third sector organizations in order to fulfill its service obligations, the government's policy towards third sector organizations remains vague. Overall, this ambiguity impedes nonprofit associations as they attempt to operate within the broader ministerial and national policy environment (Telias, Katan, and Gidron, 2000). For instance, certain aspects of the relationship between third sector organizations and the government are regulated while other parts are not. Although the Home Care Law legally defined interactions between nonprofit associations and the state, these same third sector organizations often provide other services that fall under the jurisdiction of the Department of Rehabilitation (e.g., supervising homes for the elderly or mentally disabled). In these instances, the relationship between third sector organizations and the state is legally controlled in one sphere of operation but remains amorphous in another area. As a result of this ambiguity, the state often prefers to support well-known, veteran associations with which it has been collaborating for years rather than establish new relationships with smaller, younger, and innovative groups.

One of the primary problems in the relationship between the government and third sector organizations is the lack of regulated supervision. Although limited data are available, State Comptroller reports from the 1990s clearly show a lack of supervision among the departments that comprise the Ministry. For instance, a 1996 report found that all of the housing facilities for the handicapped and mentally disabled were operating without a license and lacked proper safety and security operations (State Comptroller, 1997). Likewise, a 1998 report showed that half of all religious and Haredi boarding schools for 12- to 18-year-olds lacked required permits and had recurring problems with malfunctioning equipment (State Comptroller, 1999). Similar lapses were found among emergency centers providing physical protection and first-aid treatment to at-risk children and among organizations serving the blind: 1998 and 1999 reports showed that none of these organizations was tendered, as is required by law, and that inspections of these organizations were never undertaken (State Comptroller, 1999). Furthermore, organizations serving the blind and those serving troubled adolescents inaccurately reported the number of clients that they had served, resulting in inappropriate reimbursements from the government (State Comptroller, 2000; State Comptroller, 2001). Finally, a 2000 State Comptroller's inspection report revealed that most adoption organizations failed to make appropriate payments to their clients and to submit required data on adopted children, including the medical tests that they had undergone (State Comptroller Report, 2001).

The scenarios outlined here constitute only a few of the State Comptroller's findings on the nature of the relationship between third sector organizations and the Ministry of Labor and Social Welfare.[55] The many breaches and irregularities described in the State Comptroller's reports are evidence of the numerous hurdles that currently exist when third sector organizations provide welfare services. Despite the deep involvement of associations in the provision of welfare services and the Ministry's growing dependency upon these organizations to fulfill its service obligations, the state has failed to develop an appropriate policy towards the third sector at either the macro-governmental or ministerial levels. Moreover, the semi-familial nature of the relationships that currently exist also explains why the Ministry often prefers to support veteran associations while the various departments are often inaccessible to smaller organizations. Unfortunately, this vague situation is likely to result in continued abuses on both sides.

THE CURRENT ROLE OF THIRD SECTOR ORGANIZATIONS IN THE ISRAELI WELFARE STATE

Today, the Israeli welfare state faces a paradoxical situation: although budgetary pressures have forced the government to turn to outside organizations to fulfill its service provision duties, it still aims to remain centralized and dominant. The state's attempts to maintain control crumble in the face of reality, however, since the very existence of a large number of associations in a variety of areas results in a de facto policy. As Katan and Loewenstein (1999) have noted, although the Home Care Law was intended to preserve the state's dominance while legislating relations between the state and extra-governmental service-providing organizations, in fact it led to the creation of a multitude of third sector and for-profit organizations whose sheer numbers have hindered efficient state supervision. Thus, although the state remained dominant towards the third sector until the 1990s, the relationship between the two sectors has been evolving since that time. This adjustment has not necessarily stemmed from a change in attitude on the part of the welfare state but rather from various external constraints, including the large number of associations that are now engaged in the provision of welfare services and their increasing desire to influence policy. In other words, the growing impact of third sector organizations in the welfare state is not necessarily a result of the government's desire to cooperate, but is a reflection of the increased power of these organizations.

Although the government has increasingly recognized the value of collaborating with third sector organizations in recent years, it is difficult to characterize this relationship as cooperative (Cnaan and Dror, 1997). This situation highlights the need to re-evaluate the definition of cooperative relationships with regards to the Israeli welfare state. In general, a dominant welfare state does not necessarily have to be destructive to the third sector. There is nothing wrong with and there might even be an advantage to establishing a strong welfare state that is capable of organizing all of the various components of the system. Unfortunately, this is not the situation with the Israeli welfare state where the urge to control and dominate has led to a scenario in which the unique characteristics of the third sector are overlooked and even harmed. The government has viewed the third sector as a cheaper and more efficient means of providing services but not necessarily as: 1) an entrepreneur that is capable of better expressing the needs of a variety of population groups, some of whom are excluded from mainstream society, 2) an intermediary between the state and consumers, and 3) a means for social change in accordance with the welfare state's goals.

This approach has ultimately harmed both the welfare state and the third sector. By disregarding the unique characteristics of the third sector, the government has been unable to utilize associations to solve difficult problems, such as budgetary cutbacks or rising ideological opposition to government activity. The damage to the third sector has been even greater: over the years, associations have learned that there is no need to develop the distinctive features typical of third sector organizations, such as targeting special population groups, engaging in social entrepreneurship and change, developing special services, and expanding volunteerism; instead, these organizations have realized that the government supports associations that conform with the state. Thus, the Israeli welfare state's approach has significantly contributed to the development of a third sector that is primarily characterized by state-funded service provision activity (Gidron, Katz, and Bar, 2000; Gidron and Katz, 1999).

The government's policy has also created a significant division within the third sector: on the one hand, the sector is comprised of larger, well established organizations that provide services on behalf of the state; on the other hand, the sector also consists of smaller, newer organizations that are not part of the welfare state system but have preserved those special qualities characteristic of the third sector. Although the larger organizations, such as the health funds, public hospitals, independent and boarding schools, and day care centers for the handicapped and mentally disabled, are legally part of the third sector, they greatly resemble government agencies. These associations have been interconnected with the welfare state system for many years, and in numerous instances have become an integral part of the welfare state. In contrast, the smaller, less established organizations are characterized by special traits that are almost never found in government agencies.

In general, the third sector can: (1) serve as a substitute to the welfare state, (2) cooperate with it, or (3) complement the services that it provides (Salamon, 1995; Young, 2000; Katan, 1988). In Israel, it is difficult to consider the third sector as complementing the services that the welfare state provides since many third sector organizations are almost an integral part of the state. Likewise, the third sector does not act as a replacement for the welfare state because Israel has developed a comprehensive and centralistic welfare system that is primarily state supported. Furthermore, the sector's cooperation with the welfare state appears to be limited. Therefore, the unique situation in Israel warrants the development of a fourth type of relationship model in which the third sector is a part of and controlled by the state in the same way as public agencies. This status, in which many third sector organizations have become an "internal" part of the welfare state, has provided a stable and continuous source of funding to these organizations but has distanced them from the unique characteristics of the third sector: volunteerism, innovativeness, the representation of and provision of unique solutions for special population groups, and the promotion of civil engagement (Katan, 1988; Kramer, 1988).

In light of the privatization ideology of the 1980s and the 1990s, the Israeli welfare state consciously chose to focus on the third sector as a means for providing efficient, low-cost services rather than its other special abilities (Doron, 1999); as a result, the government lost a potential partner in promoting the Israeli welfare state. The state's continual attempts at centralization have hurt both the state and the third sector, particularly as the balance of power has shifted and the state now desperately needs the third sector to provide a variety of services. Moreover, the process of privatization in Israel remains limited since the state continues to act as the primary funder, policymaker, and supervisor of all welfare-related activities (Katan, 1996; Ajzenstadt, 1996).

The main problem, however, is not whether the state has "left the picture," but rather the fact that it has never succeeded in forming a clear-cut policy towards the third sector. On the one hand, the state wants to continue exercising control over the third sector; on the other hand, it is beginning to recognize the sector's increasing influence on welfare policy. Clearly, the state is beginning to acknowledge the special characteristics of third sector organizations, but there has been no preference for utilizing third sector organizations over for-profit organizations when the two operate in the same service-provision areas. Moreover, while the state is interested in expanding the activity of the third sector, it is having difficulties maintaining its supervisory capacity. Thus, the evolving policy is full of contradictions, with a screeching dissonance between goals and modes of action (Telias, Katan, and Gidron, 2000). A coherent policy is absolutely necessary to improve both the functioning and relationship between the welfare state and the third sector; this policy must be operative and go beyond general declarations.

CONCLUSION

In conclusion, it appears that the third sector has had a significant impact on the development of the Israeli welfare state. Many of the voluntary arrangements that were established before statehood continued to operate after the state was formed; in addition, third sector organizations initiated other services that the state later adopted. But the state also had considerable influence on the development of the third sector. The state has formed close relationships with specific third sector organizations and this situation has led to a distinction between two types of organizations within the sector: (1) older organizations that are fewer in number but larger in size, receive extensive government funding, resemble public agencies, have close government connections, and operate as the welfare state's executive arm; and (2) smaller, less established service-providing organizations that do not receive extensive public support and are not tightly linked to the welfare state. Paradoxically, the goals and activities of these latter organizations more closely resemble the goals of the welfare state than the larger organizations: they promote social change and equality, provide solutions to a variety of special needs, and aspire to empower the community and to expand social integration. These organizations receive almost no preferential treatment from the welfare state, which at best considers them worthy of periodic support and at worst as a threat to its status.

Although the Israeli welfare market has changed throughout the years, the role of the third sector has remained central. Recent changes in the welfare state support the contention that the third sector's role in providing welfare services will continue to grow. This situation calls for the establishment of an appropriate policy towards the third sector. An amorphous and inconsistent strategy is problematic and hurts the goals of the welfare state: to provide efficient services, narrow social gaps and inequality, and prevent distress. Current circumstances require the Israeli welfare state to reach a quick decision on its approach towards the third sector and to act accordingly. Indecisiveness will continue to be destructive to the sector, as well as to the welfare state.

NOTES

47   All of the data on third sector organizations and government budgets presented in this chapter are based on 1998 figures, unless otherwise noted.

48   The government also provided substantial amounts of support to informal educational programs run by the Community Centers Association and youth movements.

49   The government does not support private institutes of higher learning or branches of foreign universities, which have become more common in Israel in recent years.

50   The Histadrut was an umbrella framework of organizations that provided services to members of the Labor party.

51   Health insurance tax is universal and progressive (by income). It is deducted from the employee and paid to the NII by the employer.

52   These amounts include both payments for contract services and support for third sector organizations operating in these areas.

53   The Department for the Elderly also supported protected housing arrangements that were jointly run by third sector and private (for-profit) organizations.

54   The information presented here on the activities of the Department of Resource Management within the Ministry of Labor and Social Welfare is mostly based upon personal communication with Ms. Nili Dror, the head of the department. It is important to note that the Ministry of Labor and Social Welfare is the only government agency that is promoting this type of resource development activity.

55   It is important to note that the findings from the State Comptroller's reports are not unique to the Ministry of Labor and Social Welfare and are not necessarily reflective of the Ministry's overall supervisory system but pertain exclusively to interactions with third sector organizations. As a result of the numerous criticisms mentioned in the reports, the Ministry has improved its inspection methods in recent years.

Chapter 6

The Third Sector and Civil Society in Israel

INTRODUCTION

This chapter focuses on the associational aspects of the third sector in Israel, with particular emphasis on the subcategory of "civil society organizations" that comprise the sector. The third sector in Israel consists of a large group of organizations that share a similar legal status but differ greatly in terms of their areas of activity and the manner in which they operate. In general, third sector organizations can be classified into two major categories according to the types of activities in which they are engaged: (1) service-providing organizations, and (2) organizations that focus on developing civil society (Anheier, 1995; Boris, 1999; James, 1997). These organizations can also be categorized by their attitude towards the state: (1) organizations that oppose the government; these are generally advocacy and social change organizations; (2) organizations with a neutral stance towards the government or its policies; these associations usually focus their activities on the interests of their own members rather than those of the general public (e.g., bird-watching, diving, singing, and self-help groups); and (3) organizations that identify and cooperate with the government; these organizations usually provide public or quasi-public services with funding from the government.

The Israeli third sector consists of a combination of these classifications. On the one hand, it includes organizations that are integrated into the welfare state system and receive government funding in order to provide services that either supplement or replace those of the state; we have termed this group as "organizations integrated within the welfare state system" (IWSSs). On the other hand, the Israeli third sector also includes autonomous organizations that do not receive government funding, are independent from the state, and adopt either a challenging or neutral stance towards government policy.[56] Since the organizations in this latter category operate outside of the state system and are, by and large, voluntary, their overall role is to foster civil society. Therefore, we have termed this group as "civil society organizations" (CSOs).[57] Given the Israeli history of significant government involvement in third sector activity, it is particularly important to distinguish between IWSS organizations, which are actively linked to the welfare state, and CSOs, which are independent.

Kimmerling (1995) defines civil society as "all [of] the social activities that are performed outside of the state's direct instructions, and beyond family or primordial frameworks" (p. 69). This definition encompasses the principal political-social role of the third sector (Smith and Lipsky, 1993). Thus, civil society organizations are a necessary component of civil society in Israel: they are actively involved in the preservation of specific values, the promotion of citizen involvement and participation, the representation of the interests of special population groups, and the monitoring of government activities and policies. (Berry, 1977; Boris, 1999; Eran, 1992).

It is important to note that CSOs in Israel are formal associations; that is, they have been registered in one of the third sector registries in Israel. One of the most significant features of these associations is that they lack any ongoing, binding legal or economic relationships with the state.[58] Thus, CSOs are engaged in activities that are independent from the state institutions; have been established voluntarily by people who are interested in advancing similar values, perspectives, ideas, and identities; and supply resources and services to their members or to other population groups (Herman, 1995; Lyons, 1996). These organizations also deal with a wide range of topics related to public, private, individual, or group issues that often resonate with people at a personal level; as such, they are able to attract human and monetary resources, generally from individuals.

In our discussion of civil society organizations, it is also important to distinguish between "civil society" as an analytical term that describes a situation or specific social sphere, and "civil society organizations." Civil society organizations are a concrete, organizational manifestation of "civil society"; that is, these associations reflect those areas of activity that participants choose to place within a framework that will ostensibly allow for their continual operation. Clearly, civil society organizations constitute only one aspect of the many diverse factors that comprise civil society. In this chapter, we outline the development of civil society in Israel, present data on the characteristics of Israeli civil society organizations, examine the patterns of giving and volunteering in Israel as a manifestation of civil society, and analyze the impact that civil society organizations have had on Israeli society, in general, and Israeli civil society, in particular.

THE DEVELOPMENT OF CIVIL SOCIETY IN ISRAEL

In describing the development of civil society in Israel, we must first note that there is a disparity in the existing literature: most studies deal with advocacy and social change organizations, which tend to attract a great deal of public attention,[59] while very little has been written about the endeavors and traits of other types of associations. Thus, a literature review on this topic is significantly biased in one direction. Moreover, the definition of the concept of "civil society" that most authors use is skewed towards organizational activities that challenge state or government policy; generally the definition employed does not include endeavors that are separate from the state but are not necessarily antagonistic towards it.

Yishai (1998) has identified three major developmental stages of civil society in Israel. The first phase, termed "active inclusion," began with statehood in 1948 and continued until the late 1960s. During this time, the state was a major factor in mobilizing Israeli society. Through its official institutions and in conjunction with the political parties, the state served as the prime agent for socialization. Citizens became subjects who depended upon state authorities to fulfill many of their needs (e.g., healthcare, education, pensions). Most of the organizations that operated as part of civil society were professional groups that worked closely with the state and adhered to its goals. The majority of these organizations were linked to various political parties (e.g., the Histadrut Labor Federation, the Farmers' Association) while the number of autonomous groups were few. In addition, most of the protest activity that occurred during this time was related to specific cases rather than general issues (Herman, 1995). Yishai maintains that the process of state building required strong proximity between the state and civil society in order to advance nation-building and cope with various internal and external challenges. As a result, the boundaries between civil society and the state became blurred, and there was considerable state intervention in civil society.

The second phase, termed "active exclusion," began after the Six Day War in 1967 and continued until the early 1980s. This stage was characterized by a transition within Israeli society towards greater materialism; thus, the ideological principles of the previous period gradually lost their appeal and large segments of the population became increasingly interested in achieving economic growth, as evidenced in a growing rate of consumption. At the same time, the power of the political parties started to wane (Gal-Noor, 1996) while the influence of the state bureaucracy and the army began to increase. The growing materialism, on the one hand, and the decline of the political parties, on the other, impacted the civil arena and led to the rise of various public interest groups, many of which were established in response to the Six Day War. Of these, the two most prominent were the Greater Israel Movement (later known as *Gush Emunim*) and Peace and Security (later termed *Peace Now*).

The burgeoning protest movements that were becoming a global trend also had an impact on Israeli society during this time. Of particular significance were the environmental protest organizations. Although the size and number of such organizations increased, they continued to work closely and comply with the state. Two notable exceptions were the feminist and social protest organizations. Until the 1970s, most of the women's organizations had been linked to the political parties and complied with national goals. In the early 1970s, however, several feminist organizations were established that challenged the patriarchal structure of Israeli society by furthering the interests and equality of women. Likewise, the Black Panthers group, which was founded by second-generation *Mizrahim* (immigrants from Middle Eastern countries) who grew up in Jerusalem's distressed neighborhoods, accused the Israeli establishment of intentional discrimination against their community (Bernstein, 1979). While the Panthers successfully spurred many young people into action, their protest activities led to violent demonstrations and vigils, as well as clashes with the police.

In response to these protest activities, the state adopted an approach of active exclusion. The authorities rejected the claims of both groups and excoriated them. The Israeli public, as a whole, vilified feminism, which was viewed as a foreign import that threatened both society and the goals of the Jewish state. Likewise, Golda Meir, who was the prime minister of Israel at the time, reacted to the Black Panthers with the phrase, "They are not nice guys," which succinctly summarized the establishment's attitude towards the group's activities. Soon after, the state attempted to de-legitimize the movement and its leaders, who were characterized as criminals that threatened the Jewish state. Despite the public vilification of these two groups, they had an impact on Israeli society. The Black Panthers highlighted the social divide that existed in Israeli society, with broad sections of the population living in poverty and distress. In fact, the movement was one of the factors that led to the establishment of a special government commission in 1972 to deal with the problems of distressed children and youth.

The third phase in the development of civil society began in the early 1980s and is continuing today. This period has been characterized by a shaky coexistence between civil society and the state. During this time, there has been accelerated economic growth in Israel, a rise in the standard of living, a less centralized economic structure, and the unceasing privatization of public services. There have also been significant changes in the electoral system, with the implementation of direct personal elections for the prime minister and primaries for the parties' candidates. As a result, sectoral parties have gained control while the large political parties have begun to lose power. Yishai argues that these changes have led to a blurring of the boundaries between the political parties and CSOs as the parties have started to represent specific rather than diverse interests. As such, the parties' activities have shifted from the political arena to that of civil society.

During this time, there has been a corresponding rise in the number of associations and the scope of their activities. This increase is due in part to Israel's transition from a collectivist society to one that is pluralistic, allowing for more open expression from various groups such as women's and environmental organizations (Fogel-Bijaoui, 1992; Gidron, 1997). Likewise, among the Israeli public, national goals have been superseded by social and personal interests that do not necessarily correspond to the "national interest." These changes have been reflected in the often defiant and oppositional strategies that CSOs have employed: there has been an increasing number of demonstrations and public protests, some of which have turned violent (Lehman-Wilzig, 1992). Thus, today a variety of associations representing different population groups and goals are working within the framework of civil society in Israel, which Yishai describes as vibrant. As a result, CSOs have gained greater access to powerful decision-makers, have been able to implement a variety of challenging strategies, and have managed to impact public policy in Israel (e.g., changing the electoral system, annulling legislation for capital gains tax).

Despite these changes, Yishai argues that civil society in Israel is still vastly different from civil society found in most Western nations. The strong bond between the state and the Israeli public remains and a truly pluralistic civil society has been difficult to establish due to the fundamental values underlying Israeli society, particularly paternalism and collectivism (Yishai, 1999). Although Israeli civil society has appeared to be transitioning "towards a society that is citizen-oriented and not state-oriented" in recent years (Yishai, 1998, p. 48) and more active expression has been permitted among individuals and groups, Israeli citizens continue to rely upon a strong state.

Other researchers view civil society in Israel in a different light (Ben-Eliezer, 1999; Fogel-Bijaoui, 1998). They agree that changes in Israeli society have led to increased numbers of associations; however, they maintain that these organizations have had limited success challenging the establishment. For instance, Ben-Eliezer argues that:

> Even if the politics of associations yields, here and there, genuine achievements at the level of rights and legislation, it has nothing to do with the establishment of civil society—a society that by its very definition widens the public domain by attempting to bring significant and major issues to a more *public* and less *state* decision, by enhancing the involvement and influence of the public. The growth in the number of associations does not in itself attest to Israel's having been transformed into a multicultural society or even the widening of the foundations of Israeli democracy, for the associations themselves are not involved in the goal of changing reality, they have no vision of the common "good"—even arguments about it are non-existent, and they remain, for the most part, in their fragmented and pluralistic position. Thus, hand in hand, the associations

march alongside the state mechanisms and together with the market forces, towards an Israel that is more liberal, but not necessarily freer (1999, p. 87).

Sasson-Levi, who studied the activities of the Twenty-First Year protest movement, which was founded 21 years after the Six Day War to oppose the Israeli occupation, agrees with this point of view: "Sometimes groups that challenge the hegemony of the state in fact also serve that same hegemony, the same subjugated power relations isolating and distancing specific populations in order to perpetuate the power of the center and its ideology" (1995, p. 134). Likewise, Fogel-Bijaoui, who studied women's organizations in Israel, contends that "most [of the] women's organizations, especially the central ones, are uninterested in, or are incapable of, confronting the gendered order in Israel. This is because in fact they operate inside its framework, and also contribute to its reinforcement" (1998, p. 66). According to Fogel-Bijaoui, women's organizations are situated at the center of the national consensus and only raise issues in public debates that do not threaten the establishment. Thus, this group of researchers argues that the associations operating in Israel have been unable to generate awareness of the "social order" in Israel rather than the "state system" and have been drawn into the consensus without succeeding at genuinely challenging it; as such, they have failed to establish civil society in Israel (Ben-Eliezer, 1999).

The few studies dealing with the nature of civil society in Israel in recent years have only focused on certain aspects of associations in order to test the hypothesis regarding the existence of civil society. Yishai (1998) has examined the activities of and the relationship between interest groups, social movements, and identity groups and the state to determine whether changes in civil society have occurred. Likewise, Ben-Eliezer (1999) has studied the level of instrumental success of the activities of associations as a measure for the existence of civil society.

THE CHARACTERISTICS OF CIVIL SOCIETY ORGANIZATIONS IN ISRAEL

Distribution, Employees, and Areas of Activity

Most of the registered third sector organizations in Israel are civil society organizations by our definition. Of the 29,000 third sector organizations that were registered at the end of 1998, 83% or 25,730 were CSOs; the remaining 5,436 associations were IWSS organizations. Despite these figures, the proportion of active CSOs is actually quite small relative to the proportion of active IWSS organizations.[60] As Table 12 indicates, 60% of IWSS organizations (3,271 organizations) were active in 1998 compared to only 26% of CSOs (6,030 organizations). Nevertheless, CSOs constituted almost two-thirds (65%) of all active third sector

Table 12. Registered Civil Society and IWSS Organizations that Are Active, 1998

	Civil Society Organizations	IWSS Organizations	All Third Sector Organizations
Registered Organizations	23,547 (81%)	5,500 (19%)	29,047 (100%)
Active Organizations	6,030 (65%)	3,271 (25%)	9,301 (100%)
Proportion of Registered Organizations that are Active	26%	60%	32%

organizations in Israel in 1998. In particular, the number of CSOs within the Arab community is considerable: 85% of all registered Arab third sector organizations in Israel were CSOs in 1998. Despite high employment rates within these organizations, only 21% of these organizations were active.

In 1998, over 30,000 salaried employees worked in civil society organizations compared to over 115,000 in IWSS organizations.[61] Thus, civil society organizations employed only 21% of all third sector employees, while the remaining 79% worked in IWSS organizations. In addition, civil society organizations benefited from the efforts of an unknown number of volunteers. As Figure 8 shows, over 40% of all civil society organizations did not employ any salaried workers in 1998 versus 24% of IWSS organizations, and the majority of CSOs employed less than 10 workers. Only 8% of all civil society organizations employed more than 10 employees compared to 35% of IWSS organizations in 1998.

As Figure 9 shows, 25% of all CSOs were active in the field of religion in 1998 compared to 21% of IWSS organizations. These CSOs were predominantly places of worship (e.g., synagogues, churches, mosques) but also included multi-purpose religious institutions, such as the *Ateret Yehuda* association, which establishes Torah institutions that provide charity, good deeds, and aid to the poor and needy; and the Association for Fostering Torah Institutions of the Religious Kibbutzim, which engages in religious, educational, cultural, scientific, nursing, and sports activities. Sixteen percent of CSOs concentrated their activities in the field of education and research versus 36% of IWSS organizations. These CSOs included parents' associations; the "TALIM" Association for Educating Children with Special Needs, which encourages specialization in and public awareness of special education methods; and the Israeli Association for Studying Labor Relations, which initiates and advances theoretical and empirical research in the fields of labor and industrial relations.

Seventeen percent of CSOs were engaged in welfare activities (versus 8% of IWSS organizations), including the Handicapped Association, which promotes employment, housing, and welfare for handicapped people; the Women of Valor Organization, which helps needy families and women after childbirth; the Israeli Association for Family, Marriage, and Domestic Matters; and the Tova Arman

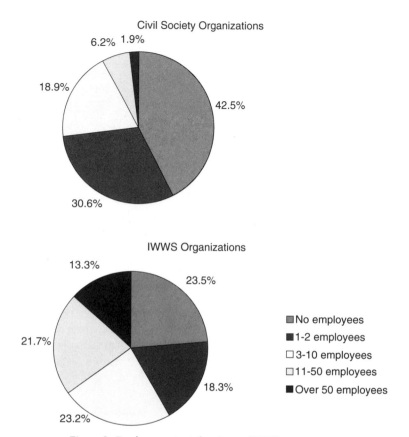

Figure 8. Employment in civil society and IWSS organizations

Association for Free Loan Funds of Agudat Israel Women—Jerusalem, which provides interest-free loans to the needy. Of the 16% of CSOs that were involved in culture and leisure in 1998 (compared to 20% of IWSS organizations), some examples include Next Generation—the Lovers of Yiddish Association, which encourages, promotes, teaches, and disseminates the Yiddish language and culture; the Association of Stamp Collectors from Holon and Bat-Yam, which encourages stamp-collecting through meetings and lectures; and the Artists Association of Mitzpeh Ramon, which aims to establish a local museum, gallery, and studio in order to create a dynamic dialogue between artists and the community.

Only 6% of CSOs and 7% of IWSS organizations were involved in philanthropy in 1998. Most of these CSOs were foundations, such as the Dov Bernard Rakovsky Foundation, which awards grants to Torah institutions, LIBI (a fund that supports the Israeli defense forces), and the Holocaust memorial, Yad Vashem; the

Civil Society Organizations

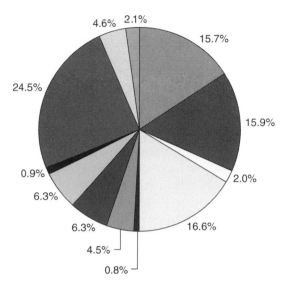

IWSS Organizations

■ Culture & leisure

■ Education & research

□ Health

□ Welfare

■ Environment

■ Housing & development

■ Advocacy, social & political change

□ Philantropy

■ International activity

■ Religion

□ Professional & commercial associations

■ Commemoration & other

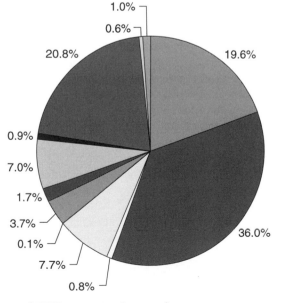

Figure 9. Civil society and IWSS organizations by areas of activity

Association of Friends of the Gesher Theater, which supports the Gesher Theater Company; and the Ruth Lev Scholarship Foundation, which grants scholarships to needy students at the ORT School for Girls and the WZO Ramat-Gan Vocational School for Girls. Examples of the 6% of CSOs that were engaged in advocacy and social and political change (compared to only 2% of IWSS organizations) include the Lilach Association, which generates public debate on the moral, social, and legal aspects of medical treatment for patients with terminal and irreversible conditions and short life-expectancies; the Association for the Advancement of Women in Science, Engineering, and Technology, which promotes, encourages, and motivates young women to enter into the fields of science, engineering, and technology; and the Association for Encouraging Leadership, which encourages political involvement and fosters leadership among young people of Mizrahi origin.

Approximately 5% of CSOs and 4% of IWSS organizations were involved in housing and development. Examples of such CSOs include Young People for Jaffa C South, which aims to increase housing construction for citizens of the Jaffa C neighborhood; Avoka (Torch)—Association for Development Endeavors in Arab Towns and Villages, which promotes the economic, social, and cultural development of Arab towns and villages and a peaceful coexistence between Arabs and Jews; and the Tent Movement, which aims to advance social and community development in disadvantaged neighborhoods and development towns. Nearly 5% of CSOs were active as commercial and professional associations compared to less than 1% of IWSS organizations. Such CSOs include the Football Players Organization of Israel, a professional association of football players; the Organization of Former Employees of Israel Discount Bank, which promotes the economic and social well-being of its members and offers professional study courses; and the Ice-Cream Manufacturers Club in Israel, which promotes the economic and professional interests of the Israeli ice-cream industries.

Two percent of CSOs and less than 1% of IWSS organizations were involved in the field of health in 1998. Some examples of these CSOs include the Association for the Advancement and Institutionalization of Chinese Medicine in Israel, which aims to legitimize traditional Chinese medicine; the Arab Association for Combating AIDS, which works within the Arab community to educate about, dispel prejudice against, and assist patients with AIDS or HIV; and IGA—the Israeli Association for Growth and Development, which fosters research, information, and education in the field of normal and abnormal growth and development. Examples of the 2% of CSOs that were involved in memorial activities in 1998 (compared to 1% of IWSS organizations) include the Association for the Commemoration of The Nahal Brigade; and the Committee of Bereaved Families Resulting from Acts of Terror, which aims to construct a monument to commemorate the victims of terrorist attacks and to establish memorial foundations. Approximately 1% of CSOs and IWSS organizations were engaged in international activities. Some examples of CSOs include the Association for Encouraging Israeli-Turkish Relations; and the Association for Dissemination of Radiophonic Information from Jerusalem, which was established to disseminate reliable and corroborated radiophonic information in order to provide a true picture of events in Israel and the Middle East. Finally, less than 1% of CSOs and IWSS organizations promoted the environment in 1998. Examples of such CSOs are the Four-Legged Friends Shelter for Abandoned Animals, which chiefly tends to abandoned cats and dogs; and Blue and Green—the Association for the Environmental Quality of the Carmel Coast.

Major Organizational Functions

We divided the organizational functions of civil society organizations into three primary categories: (1) service provision (e.g., in welfare, education, health); these organizations are characterized by an organizational infrastructure that is based on professionals or volunteers, and have mechanisms that enable the organizations to work and interact with service recipients; (2) advocacy; these organizations have an organizational infrastructure that is based on their efforts to generate social change and are engaged in activities that will influence public opinion and policymakers, such as organizing demonstrations and lobbying;[62] and (3) funding; these organizations (usually foundations) have an organizational infrastructure that enables them to channel funds to support individuals or other organizations. It is important to note that organizations often fulfill more than one function; for example, some organizations may be involved in both advocacy and service provision. We categorized organizations based upon their primary central function.[63]

As Figure 10 shows, 78% of all CSOs functioned as service provision organizations in 1998. Examples of such organizations include *Menucha Nechona—Tel-Aviv*, which establishes, maintains, and manages secular cemeteries; the Institute for the Teachings of the Sages, which researches community life in the Diaspora and the history of the Jewish Sages; the Hannah Shohat Home—A Shelter for Children, which runs shelters for children with special needs; and Open Door, which provides help to the aged, especially those living in the Rehavia neighborhood of Jerusalem.

Only 6% of CSOs fulfilled an advocacy function in 1998. Such organizations include The Association for Teaching of Jewish Values, which works to incorporate Jewish values in all areas pertaining to the Torah, the Land of Israel, and the Jewish people; and The Tent Movement for Social Renewal in Israel, which aims to advance social and community development in disadvantaged neighborhoods and development towns. Some advocacy organizations focused their activities upon a specific population group, such as The Feminist Movement in Israel, which promotes equality and equal opportunities for women in Israel. Other organizations concentrated their efforts on a specific issue, such as The Drivers' Association for

Civil Society Organizations

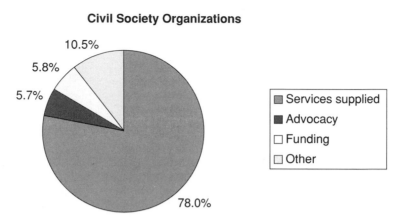

Figure 10. Civil society organizations by major organizational function

Combating Road Accidents, which aims to establish a state commission to investigate those responsible for road accidents. There were also advocacy associations with a regional nature, such as the Association for the Welfare and Prosperity of Kamanah Village, which works towards improving the living conditions of the village's residents. Only 6% of CSOs were involved in funding activities in 1998. As we noted in the previous section, examples of such organizations include the Dov Bernard Rakovsky Foundation; the Association of Friends of the Gesher Theater; and the Ruth Lev Scholarship Foundation.

GIVING AND VOLUNTEERING IN ISRAEL

Giving and volunteering are two key characteristics of civil society. In 1997, 75% of all adult Israeli citizens (over the age of 21) made some kind of monetary contribution to third sector organizations (Shye, Lazar, Duchin, and Gidron, 1999). Total donations to the third sector from individuals and households equaled NIS 465 million. The vast majority of people donated small sums of money: over 60% donated less than half a percent of their income and the median annual household contribution totaled NIS 50.[64] Almost all of these donations were channeled to organizations in four areas of activity: welfare, religion, health, and education. Large, well-known service-providing organizations received the majority of these contributions, including the Israel Cancer Association (whose budget is based solely on donations), the large organizations for the handicapped, the Association for the Welfare of Soldiers and LIBI (both of which are linked to the army), and other large-scale associations.

The donation rate—that is, those who made any contribution at all—was significantly higher among the religious population than the secular and traditional communities.[65] Within the religious population, the rate of individuals who made large donations—exceeding NIS 750 each year—was also significantly higher. It is important to note that religious donors gave almost exclusively to religious institutions.

There were also differences between the rates of giving among the Jewish and Arab populations, with the Arab community making significantly fewer donations to third sector organizations.[66] As with the religious populations, Arabs tended to donate money to organizations that were close to them—that is, they preferred to support Arab organizations. These trends reflect both the minority status and the collective identities of the religious and Arab communities, respectively. Patterns of giving also were related to donors' educational and income levels. Individuals with higher educational levels were more likely to make a donation and to give relatively larger sums of money to third sector organizations than individuals with less education. Likewise, the rate of giving among individuals with higher income levels was close to 90% compared to 60% for those with lower levels of income; 40% of individuals with higher incomes also made larger donations compared to 16% of individuals with lower incomes.

The rate of volunteerism in Israel is impressive: one-third of all adults were involved in some form of volunteer activity in 1997. Overall, volunteers devoted 72 million hours to these pursuits. Of these hours, 56 million were spent working for third sector organizations; this is roughly valued at NIS 840 million (in 1997 values). However, the vast majority of volunteers contributed only a few hours per week, and in fact less than one-fifth of volunteers fulfilled two-thirds of all volunteer activity in Israel. The average volunteer in Israel worked 160 hours per year (roughly 3 hours per week) in 1997. However, a high rate of this volunteer activity occurred within the field of security (e.g., firefighters, civil defense), which is comprised of very few third sector organizations. Excluding the security services field, 55% of the volunteer activity took place in welfare organizations in 1997 and 27% in health organizations. Thus, rates of giving and volunteerism in Israel clearly demonstrate that there is extensive civil involvement in third sector organizations.

THE CONTRIBUTION OF CIVIL SOCIETY ORGANIZATIONS IN ISRAEL

The data that we have presented in this chapter clearly demonstrate that formal organized civil society activity exists in Israel. Clearly, an analysis of these data does not constitute a comprehensive representation of the entire Israeli civil society; however, given that the limited number of studies on civil society in Israel are based on examinations of specific organizations, phenomena (e.g., protest activity), or history, the data we present provide a new and unique understanding of the structure and activity of Israeli civil society.

Our analysis reveals a complex picture, however. Ostensibly, it appears that there is substantial independent civil activity in Israel. An analysis of the associational aspects of the third sector shows that it is primarily comprised of independent organizations that do not rely extensively upon direct government funding. In addition, the fact that 32% of the adult population in Israel is involved in volunteer activities and 75% contribute monetarily to third sector organizations clearly demonstrates that the Israeli public is heavily involved in civil endeavors (Shye et al., 1999). Likewise, it appears that CSOs are engaged in a broad range of activities within a variety of areas. All of these facts indicate that as opposed to the typically centralistic and state-controlled civil society that existed in Israel up until the 1980s, Israeli civil society currently appears to be very vibrant, independent, and diverse.

A closer examination of civil society organizations, however, reveals a different picture. Unfortunately, many CSOs are unable to sustain themselves adequately after they have been established, resulting in lower levels of activity and government support. These low activity rates could be the effect of limited funding. Unlike the organizations that have close relationships with the state and receive significant government support, most CSOs in Israel receive very little government funding and this could hinder their ability to remain active. In addition, the organizational characteristics of some of these associations may limit the amount of activity they are able to undertake. This is particularly true among Arab CSOs in which the rates of activity are especially low due to limitations in the process for registering these organizations, as well as other economical and organizational factors. In many cases, CSOs in Israel are relatively small and their endeavors do not generate income. For example, neighborhood and communal associations, parent-teacher associations, and self-help groups are considered economically "inactive" because they have no economic activities to report to the tax authorities. The relatively low ratio of economically "active" organizations suggests that although more and more CSOs are being established and registered, many cease their operations after a short time. Thus, although these groups are registered as CSOs, their genuine contribution to civil society in Israel is limited.

The picture becomes even more complicated when we look at advocacy organizations. Although 6% of CSOs are engaged in advocacy work, there has been a significant increase in their numbers and areas of activity since 1990. For example, prior to 1990, there were only a few organizations that advocated to protect the environment; starting in 1989, however, their numbers increased considerably: 2 organizations were registered in 1989, 9 were registered in 1994, and 18 were registered in 1998. This growth in the number of advocacy organizations and the broadening of their fields of interest is highly significant for Israeli society, which previously was characterized by an ideology of consensus and collectivity. As such, the increase in organizations with a confrontational stance towards issues of politics, policy, security, and society constitutes a major change.

The data on volunteering add to the complexity of the situation. Though rates of giving and volunteering in Israel are very striking, donations are usually small and are mostly made to large, well-established organizations, many of which are state-supported. Most volunteers dedicate a small amount of time to voluntary endeavors and are most active in the field of security, which does not include many third sector organizations. In addition, most voluntary activity occurs within organizations that receive generous government funding (e.g., welfare and health organizations) and within only a few areas in which CSOs predominately operate.

These findings raise questions regarding the significance, influence, and scope of civil society organizations, their basic role within the third sector, and the contributions of the growing numbers of advocacy organizations that were established during the 1990s on civil society in Israel. Israeli society has undergone significant changes over the past two decades. Essentially, until the mid-1970s, the social, cultural, and political patterns in Israel were characterized by centralism, political directives, the channeling of resources to national and security-related needs, and an ideology focused on others and the collective solidarity (Horowitz and Lissak, 1989; Knei-Paz, 1996; Lissak, 1998); since the 1970s, however, Israel has transitioned to a divided, sectoral society that encompasses diverse identities and resembles societies of the West, with a high degree of democracy, an emphasis on citizens' rights, a free economy, increased protest activity, pluralism, individualism, and the organizing of parties along ethnic, religious, and class orientations (Knei-Paz, 1996; Aharoni, 1998; Lehman-Wilzig, 1992; 1999; Herman, 1996; Avineri, 1996; Yishai, 1998). Many of these changes stem from the aftermath of the Yom Kippur War when large numbers of Israeli citizens became disillusioned with the political system; these feelings intensified over time until the 1990s when many Israelis felt a sense of powerlessness in terms of their ability to influence government policy (Gal-Noor, 1996; Arian, 1997). This distrust may explain the significant levels of citizen involvement in non-governmental organizations and movements as an means to influence policy.

These developments have coincided with a decline in the power of some important institutions that have previously been considered central to, representative of, and influential in Israeli society: the army, the kibbutzim, the Histadrut, the Knesset, and the political parties (Knei-Paz, 1996). Public confidence in these institutions has waned considerably (Ya'ar-Yuchtman, 1998). Whereas public criticism of some of these institutions, such as the army, had previously been taboo, expressions of disapproval are now considered legitimate and even desirable (Yishai, 1998). As Knei-Paz notes, the changes that have swept through the Israeli political system in recent years and particularly "the weakening of the parties, the political institutions, the Histadrut, and the other economic organizations, impl[ies] the creation of a more independent civil society [that is] less dependent on the political and economic center" (1996, p. 426).

Within this new social and political landscape, particularly the vacuum left by the parties, third sector organizations have assumed the role of mediator between society and state. This is partly the result of changes that have occurred within the third sector during the last twenty years, including: (1) growth in the number and variety of third sector organizations; (2) the increased numbers of social movement and advocacy organizations within the third sector that deal with such issues as peace, security, women's issues, social protest, the structure of the government, and environmental quality; and (3) the impact of CSOs on politics and society in Israel, particularly in terms of introducing into the agenda and dealing with a broad variety of new issues, such as environmental quality in Israel, violence against women, children's rights, and discrimination against the handicapped. For instance, Deri (1992), who studied the homeless in the early 1990s, notes: "'The tent' protests without doubt brought the problem of the homeless onto the public agenda" (1992, p. 1).

In some instance, the effects of these activities have extended beyond simply introducing a new issue into the national agenda. Over the last two decades, the decision-making institutions in Israel have become more amenable to different perspectives. Political power and influence in Israel have become more egalitarian due to professionalization in the civil service, the communications revolution, sharp public criticism of various governmental institutions, the Supreme Court's juridical activism, the strengthening of citizens rights, and the growing regard for public opinion in policymaking (Smooha, 1999). Thus, new opportunities have become available for CSOs and, in some cases, the endeavors of these organizations have had an impact on policymaking, particularly as the power of the political parties and the Histadrut has weakened (Zalmanovich, 1998). One manifestation of these changes is the advent of "alternative politics" in Israel (Lehman-Wilzig, 1999): citizens who want to change existing policies are organizing activities and proposing alternative options to government services and processes (e.g., alternative religious institutions, alternative educational and cultural institutions, new welfare services, and attempts to establish a constitution for Israel). These endeavors have resulted in far-reaching reforms in many public spheres, including legislation of the National Health Insurance Law, initiation of a longer school day, and amendments to Basic Laws.

Another example of the changing decision-making environment is evident in the fact that members of Knesset committees and other bureaucratic mechanisms now tend to consult with consumer groups and other organizations when discussing relevant policy issues. In contrast to previous practices, the government now considers the opinions of these types of organizations an important aspect of policymaking (Nachmias and Sand, 1999). In particular, Ben-Aryeh (1999) found that Knesset members frequently consulted with and incorporated the opinions of welfare organizations when determining welfare policy. Likewise, Bar (1999) found that welfare organizations have become more involved in and have had greater influence on policymaking regarding handicapped children since the mid-1980s through personal contacts; meetings; correspondence with Knesset members, senior political officials and executives; and use of the media. The joint endeavors that these welfare organizations have undertaken with Knesset members have turned out to be an extremely effective and mutually beneficial strategy for changing policy: the organizations are represented in the Knesset and are able to advance relevant legislation, while Knesset members gain the vital public recognition and support from different population groups that are necessary to win elections. Bar found that these welfare organizations were able to influence the actual process of policymaking towards handicapped children and their families not only by introducing an issue into the agenda but also by being actively involved in the formulation, approval, and implementation of new policy. Kadman (1992) noted a similar process among organizations advocating for children's rights that were instrumental in shaping the 1989 Law for Prevention of Abuse of Minors and Dependents. These changes partly resulted from the more confrontational approach that these organizations adopted towards the policymaking institutions during the 1980s and 1990s, as well as the activities of other advocacy organizations.

The influence of CSOs on the policymaking process in Israel reflects the increasing openness of government institutions towards these organizations, which they consult on a regular basis regarding a variety of issues. Clearly, such openness is the result of several factors, including changes in the structure and status of the public sector. However, the activities of CSOs were also influential in bringing about these changes. Since policymakers often lack the resources to collect comprehensive information on specific topics, CSOs have become an important source of information. For instance, think tanks are becoming increasingly numerous in Israel, offering policymakers empirical expertise on a variety of issues. In addition, increasing numbers of CSOs are offering insight into and alternative solutions to various policy issues.

Civil society organizations also have had a wide-ranging social impact on Israeli society. Organizing and forming associations has become a common pattern for dealing with the problems of specific population groups. This has been particularly evident in the growing numbers of self-help organizations operating in Israel (Ramon, 1997). A wide variety of associations has been established to offer support for various health or social problems, including multiple sclerosis, epilepsy, divorce, and alcoholism. Likewise, new associations that offer cultural, educational, and self-help activities were established during the 1990s to aid immigrants from the former Soviet Union who found the government services lacking (Horowitz and Leshem, 1998). During the 1990s, the number of Arab associations increased significantly, as well, providing alternative educational, health, cultural, and welfare services to those provided by the state (Zeidan and Ghanem, 2000); some of these organizations were established to deal with social needs and problems that the state had largely ignored. These associations have become an important source of employment for educated Arabs, who lack adequate employment resources in the Israeli economy. While most of the Arab organizations that have been established are engaged in service-provision activities, an increasing number of advocacy organizations have been formed to defend the rights of Arab citizens in Israel. Finally, CSOs have also served as a source of identity for various population groups within Israeli society. For instance, as Helman and Rappaport (1997) have noted, the protest activities of Women in Black laid the foundation for a collective identity among Israeli women who united to in order to put an end to the marginalization of women within Israeli society.

The specific contributions of civil society organizations to "civil society" in Israel are somewhat dependent upon the definition of civil society that is employed. According to Foley and Edwards (1996), civil society can be divided into two categories: (1) civil society I, which is an independent domain that is separate from the state, pluralistic in nature, involves voluntary action, and encourages independent and participatory citizen activity, and (2) civil society II, which includes a domain in which the principal goal is to change the political and social order primarily through confrontation. If we examine Israeli civil society according to the definition of civil society II, the contributions of CSOs appear to be bleak (Ben-Eliezer, 1999). The major function of most CSOs in Israel is service provision; only a minority of organizations is engaged in advocacy with the goal of creating social change. Most of the organized activity within Israeli civil society is not confrontational in nature. Moreover, the majority of organizations that have adopted a confrontational approach target specific issues rather than the broad social and political order. The few organizations that deal with general, comprehensive issues represent populations with unique problems and attempt to amend policies that affect those particular populations (e.g., promoting the rights of the disabled, women, Arabs, the unemployed). Although some of these organizations have made major strides, this was not their primary objective. Thus, a civil society that is largely confrontational and challenges the existing social and political order is largely absent in Israel.

On the other hand, if we examine Israeli civil society according to the definition of civil society I, it appears that the contributions of CSOs to the promotion of civil society in Israel are significant and have been growing. For example, the considerable increase in the number of self-help groups in Israel indicates that forming organizations has become a common strategy among Israelis for dealing with various problems (Ramon, 1997). Whereas Israelis used to turn to the government, today citizens are creating organizations in order to solve their own problems or those of specific population groups (Kramer, 1981). Thus, within Israeli society, there is a domain of independent collective action that is positioned between the state and the individual. This is evidenced by the large number of CSOs within the third sector. One of the most significant attributes of these organizations is their independence from the government: there are no laws governing their activities or their relationship with the government; most of their resources stem from donations or self-generated income (e.g., sale of services, membership fees) rather than government funding; and close to a half have no salaried employees and rely exclusively upon volunteers. Thus, although the Law of Associations outlines considerable state intervention into citizens' organizations, in actuality the level of government interference is minimal (Yishai, 1998). Clearly, the tremendous growth in the number and scope of CSOs during the 1990s contributed significantly to the development of civil society in Israel that is characterized by independence, and the expression of diverse interests, opinions, and needs.

It is important to note, however, that the pluralism that exists within Israeli civil society is not necessarily correlated with another characteristic of civil societies: tolerance for other opinions, groups, and organizations. The most striking example is the fact that Prime Minister Yitzhak Rabin was assassinated during a protest demonstration in the heart of civil society. Although generally there is little major friction between CSOs in Israel, there have been incidents of violence and sabotage between rival organizations during election periods.

In addition, Israeli civil society is lacking another quality common to civil society: self-regulation. The organizations that operate within civil society have been unable to establish a clear-cut set of rules to govern their activities due to in large part to the patronizing culture of the government, the close ties between many third sector organizations and the state institutions, and the statist atmosphere within which most organizations have been developed. As a result, the government has determined most of the rules by which CSOs must operate. Moreover, most organizations do not identify themselves as being part of a distinct sector (i.e., the third sector) and consider the state to be the primary regulator of their activities.

Additionally, civil society in Israel has not developed into an arena for wide-ranging public debate and negotiations over values and norms. Although the public debates in Israel have moved beyond the limitations imposed by the state, the mass media has largely been responsible for this change rather than the CSOs (Yadger, 1998). Moreover, competing interpretations of crucial public issues are not being presented, nor are significant alternatives being explored. While CSOs have succeeded in becoming more actively involved in policymaking, their impact usually has been limited to the public institutions where policies are determined rather than the broader realm of public debate.

Israeli civil society is also limited in that it is not entirely inclusive, with equal access for all citizens and widespread civic participation. Unfortunately, individual citizens and marginalized population groups often are excluded from civil society. In a study of the Twenty-First Year protest movement, Sasson-Levy discovered that "the social structure of the movement reflected the elite of Israeli society: the movement was comprised of Ashkenazi Jews, with higher education levels, who belonged to the new middle-class. There were no Palestinian activists in the movement and a negligible percentage of Mizrahim. Although women constituted the majority within the movement, they mostly filled administrative roles, while men assumed the representative, ideological roles" (1995, p. 5). Likewise, in their study of the Women in Black protest movement, Helman and Rappaport concluded that "examining the regular profile of a 'Woman in Black' reveals that these women are well-endowed with personal resources and have a similar ethnic and class background attributing them to Israel's socio-cultural elite: the 'Woman in Black' is secular, of Ashkenazi origin, holds Israeli citizenship, is educated, relatively mature, and works for her living... indeed members of Women in Black perceived themselves as elite and defined their advantage over their spectators and over other women in terms of perseverance, determination, internal morality, and particularly in terms of a developed conscience and a high moral standard" (1997, p. 177). Fogel-Bijaoui (1998) also points out that most leaders and activists in Israel's leading women's organizations share a similar ethnic and class background: most are middle- and upper-class Ashkenazi Jews. Mizrahi and Arab women have not obtained leadership positions within these organizations. Moreover, the agendas of most of the women's organizations in Israel often reflect class interests that are not relevant to the majority of women in Israel. Similar demographic characteristics are also apparent among the activists within other CSOs engaged in welfare, environmental protection, health, and educational activities. These findings are not surprising given that Israelis of Ashkenazi origin with higher levels of education are most likely to volunteer their time and skills to third sector organizations (Shye et al., 1999).

Another important factor that must be considered is the distribution of third sector organizations in Israel. Clearly, most of the organized civil activity occurs in the geographical center of Israel (Gidron, Katz, and Bar, 2000). As a result, people from weaker minority groups who live in the outskirts are unable to advance their integration into society. Recent developments seem to imply that this trend is changing: various organizations that represent vulnerable or excluded population groups have succeeded in bringing specific issues into the public agenda. Some examples include organizations that assist foreign workers, organizations for the disabled, and community organizations working in various distressed neighborhoods in Israel. Nevertheless, for the most part, marginalized groups have less opportunity to participate in the public debate occurring in Israeli civil society. Thus, CSOs in Israel have not necessarily been successful at promoting equality and the participation of excluded population groups.

Finally, although civil society activity generally includes a range of interpersonal interactions that encourage the development of social capital such as trust, cooperation, and tolerance (Putnam, 1993), this has not been the case in Israel. While Israelis have high levels of trust in their political and public institutions, trust in other people is low: in a recent study, over 60% of respondents said that people should not be trusted (Yishai, 2001). In particular, the social divides between secular and religious Jews, Arabs and Jews, and Mizrahi and Ashkenazi Jews have hampered the development of acceptance and trust. The lack of familiarity between these various social groups has resulted in low levels of tolerance and in certain instances has even bred hatred. Moreover, although the act of associating in an organization may appear to be an expression of collaboration and cooperation between people, the fact is that formally associating does not necessarily imply that collaboration exists between the different members participating in the organization. Nevertheless, it appears that the activities of CSOs in Israel have encouraged citizens to act not only for their own good, but also for the good of others. Furthermore, the impressive rates of organizing and volunteerism that have recently been recorded demonstrate a desire among the Israeli public to make a contribution and help others. Clearly, this issue warrants further investigation to determine whether CSOs in Israel are actually adhering to democratic principles and to examine the levels of cooperation among members in executing the organizations' activities. In the absence of studies on social capital in Israel, it is difficult to determine the extent to which these activities have promoted collaboration among Israelis and, if so, how and within which social circles this phenomenon has evolved.

CONCLUSION

It is clear that civil society organizations have significantly impacted the development of Israeli civil society over the last decade. The substantial number of CSOs that have been established during this time, the broad scope of the areas and activities in which they are engaged, the diverse strategies that they employ including protesting against and challenging the government, their impact on policymaking, and the high rates of volunteerism among the Israeli public undoubtedly indicate the central role that these organizations have played in creating and empowering an independent civil society in Israel. Moreover, for the most part, these organizations appear to represent the true values of civil society: they enable citizens to express opinions, promote interests and values, form identities and a sense of belonging, help and be helped by others, and create alternative solutions and services to those of the state. Furthermore, contrary to the prevailing public opinion, these organizations also comprise most of the third sector in Israel.

NOTES

56   In this definition, we exclude occasional funding that does not require extensive conformity with welfare state policy.

57   For a description of the methods used to make the distinction between IWSS and civil society organizations, see Appendix 3. It should be noted that civil society organizations could be further divided into two sub-groups based upon their stance towards the government: (1) organizations that challenge the government and/or its policies, and (2) organizations that are neutral towards the government and/or its policies. At this stage of our research, we cannot distinguish between these two sub-categories when presenting data.

58   These associations may obtain public grants from time to time; the distinction is that they do not receive public funding on a regular basis.

59   In fact, attracting public attention is often an overt objective and strategy of these types of organizations.

60   Active organizations file annual reports to the income tax authorities.

61   This is the equivalent of 2,600 full-time positions, according to the weighted ratio of workers-to-jobs in the various areas of activity within the third sector, as calculated during the Hopkins Project in Israel.

62   The term "advocacy" is defined here as "any attempt to influence governmental or institutional decisions in order to promote an objective or a collective interest" (Jenkins, 1987; Boris and Mosher-Williams, 1999; Reid, 1999). The term pertains to the broader political activity of the organization, and not necessarily to its "advocacy" efforts, which focus on defending and advancing the rights of deprived populations (Kramer, 1998).

63   We determined an organization's central function not by studying the organization's actual activities but by analyzing the organization's goals, as written by the organization's founders.

64   Although the average donation was NIS 530, this number was skewed upwards by a small number of relatively large donations.

65   In studies on Israeli population it is usually divided into four categories: secular, traditional, religious, and ultra-Orthodox.

66   It is important to note, however, that the rate of informal donations—that is, donations that are not made to organizations—is almost identical between the Jewish and Arab populations.

Chapter 7

Summary and Conclusion

The Israeli public's renewed interest in the third sector is reflected in a headline article about two accomplished generals who retired from the Israeli Defense Forces and decided to forego politics in favor of public activity:

> They are both charismatic people who are convinced their public duty is not done yet. Both resolved not to join the political system as civilians after leaving the army. These are two people who could have filled a frontline position in the political arena: one was offered the position of Secretary of Defense and the other a senior position in one of the political parties. Their reasons for not joining the political system were identical: in the present situation they feel they can contribute much more to society outside the political arena. They want to meet people, to join non-political movements, to speak and listen, learn and contribute. They believe this is not done in the Knesset nor in the party headquarters ... nowadays non-governmental organizations address nearly every public issue from Jewish-Arab relations to a new secular-religious "treaty." All the issues that have never been mentioned in the election campaigns, all the gaps and rifts that are really important to our life here and no prime minister has addressed in the past twenty years, all these are discussed by and within the civil society arena (Shelach, 2001).

Although it may appear that this interest in third sector organizations is a new phenomenon, the data presented in this book demonstrate that for the past 50 years, third sector organizations have been active in the fields of health, education, welfare, culture, the environment, recreation, housing, law, and politics. These organizations have been an integral part of the lives of all Israeli citizens: often this involvement starts with birth in a hospital that is owned by Kupat Holim or another nonprofit organization, and continues with recreation activities in local community centers or clubs, membership in a trade union or workers' committee, PTA membership in children's school, involvement in a social change movement, nursing services in old age, and finally ends with burial by the Chevra Kadisha

Burial Society. Israelis both partake in the services that third sector organizations offer and personally participate as volunteers, members, or protestors.

Given the prevalence of these organizations in the lives of Israeli citizens, it is surprising that there has been limited research and public interest in the third sector. Only in the last two decades have researchers, politicians, journalists, and the general public begun to focus their attention on this sector as a result of the social, political, economic, and demographic changes in Israel that we have described in this book. Today, it is nearly impossible to fully comprehend Israeli society without an understanding of the third sector. That is the primary objective of this book: to bring this important phenomenon to the attention of the public and the research community. Our central argument is that formal nonprofit organizations in Israel have unique legal and organizational characteristics that place them in a distinct category that is separate from the state—namely, the third sector. While the Israeli third sector was viewed as peripheral in the past, today it is a major social and economic force that cannot be overlooked.

While we have presented significant data on the Israeli third sector throughout this book, it is important to note that our analysis serves as a first step towards a discourse on the issue and does not represent a comprehensive view. In this concluding chapter, we summarize the data that we have presented throughout this book, discuss the implications of our findings on public policy towards the third sector in Israel, and consider how the Israeli third sector corresponds with various theories on the third sector and Israeli society, in general.

PRIMARY FINDINGS ON THE ISRAELI THIRD SECTOR AND THEIR IMPLICATIONS

The Two Faces of the Israeli Third Sector

The Israeli third sector is comprised of a large group of organizations that are active in a wide variety of areas, contribute significantly to the Israeli economy, and in specific areas, such as education and health, utilize extensive volumes of resources and labor. A closer examination reveals that the sector actually consists of two sub-sectors: (1) a relatively small group of organizations (20% of all registered organizations) that are "integrated within the welfare state system" (IWSS); that is, they receive substantial funding from and work closely with the public sector in terms of providing services that complement or are a substitute for those offered by the state; and (2) a relatively large groups of "civil society organizations" (CSOs) that are independent from the state; that is, they generally are established and operated by citizens, receive little government funding, and are not solely service-providing organizations but deal with a wide variety of issues.

The classification of the Israeli third sector into organizations that are IWSS and CSOs corresponds with the two dominant approaches to third sector research today. During the 1980s, researchers in the U.S. realized that a "third sector" approach that primarily focuses on the economic aspects of the third sector did not sufficiently explain the activities of third sector organizations. Thus, researchers developed the "civil society" approach in order to examine patterns of activity within third sector organizations. In Israel, researchers adhered to the third sector approach until the second half of the 1990s when it became apparent that it was not possible to study the Israeli third sector without considering the civil society approach.

In particular, researchers began to realize in the mid-1990s that the composition of the Israeli third sector had changed and was now comprised of two very different types of organizations. This was not the case in the early history of the Israeli third sector. Many IWSS organizations were established prior to statehood in order to meet the welfare needs of the Jewish population in Israel; these organizations fulfilled statutory functions in the absence of a central government and built the foundation for welfare services in education, health, and culture. Once the state was established, these existing organizations continued to act as the primary service providers. Despite the push for nationalization of welfare services, many of these service-providing organizations remained within the third sector, primarily for political reasons. Thus, shortly after statehood, the third sector in Israel was primarily composed of IWSS organizations that provided pseudo-public welfare services. These organizations and consequently any newly established associations fell into a pattern in which they acted as the government's executive arm.

Over the years, third sector organizations expanded their fields of activity to include education (e.g., higher, Haredi, agricultural, and boarding school education), health (e.g., primary healthcare, public health, hospitals, and nursing organizations), personal welfare services (e.g., homes for the elderly, rehabilitation services), and services for new immigrants. Over time, the central role of IWSS organizations in providing welfare services expanded so that eventually these organizations were recognized as an integral part of the Israeli welfare state. The goals of the IWSS organizations also coincided with the pervasive national-collective ideology in Israel during the first two decades of its existence; by collaborating with rather than challenging the state, these organizations gained extensive support. Thus, until the mid-1970s, organizations that were IWSS dominated the Israeli third sector and provided services to the population in conjunction with or in lieu of the state.

Although civil activity existed in Israel during this time, it was relatively scarce, disorganized, and sporadic. During the mid-1970s, however, the number of civil society organizations began to increase in Israel. Most of these organizations did not necessarily engage in service provision activities; those that did so directed their services to specific population groups whose needs the state had not addressed. Instead, some of these associations undertook activities that challenged the state in order to change government policies. The increased numbers of such organizations resulted from changes in Israeli society, including a decline in the national-collective ideology, a rise in the standard of living, the revolution in the media, and a trend towards increased privatization. Thus, during the 1980s and 1990s, the composition of the Israeli third sector changed: most of the active organizations in Israel were independent associations rather than organization that were IWSS.

Today, two sub-sectors operate within the Israeli third sector: one consists of large organizations that often employ hundreds or thousands of employees, receive funding from the state, and act as the government's executive arm; the other is comprised of smaller organizations that are based primarily on volunteerism rather than paid labor and receive funding from sources other than the state. The existence of two sub-sectors within the third sector is also reflected in the government's de-facto policy towards the sector: IWSS organizations receive extensive direct and indirect funding from the government while CSOs receive almost no public support whatsoever. Likewise, most of the third sector organizations that the state consults or collaborates with are almost exclusively IWSS organizations. The current policy almost completely ignores the existence of CSOs and the state's approach towards these organizations is vague and unclear. Thus, although third sector organizations in Israel share the same legal status, there are considerable differences between IWSS and civil society organizations.

Within the category of civil society organizations, two additional sub-groups can be identified: (1) a small number of advocacy or social change organizations whose primary goals are challenging the state or a specific policy; and (2) a large group of citizen-initiated associations that focus their activities on the interests of their members rather than social or political change (e.g., self-help groups, trade/professional associations, recreation groups). As in other countries, research on the Israeli third sector generally has focused on organizations that are IWSS and on CSOs with an advocacy or social change orientation, rather than the numerous associations founded by citizens to promote their specific interests (Smith, 2000). Most of these studies have concluded that there is no independent civil society in Israel and that advocacy organizations have had very little impact on policy and the decision-making processes (Yishai, 1987; 1999; Ben Eliezer, 1999).

However, a closer examination reveals the existence of extensive civil activity in Israel in a wide variety of areas. Israel is, in fact, characterized by a vivacious civil society, with an associational rather than a confrontational focus. Although these associations have little immediate impact on government policies and tend to be ignored in the research on third sector organizations because they do not have large budgets and are not engaged in political activities (Smith, 2000), they have significantly affected Israeli society, including the political culture, democracy, and relations between citizens and government institutions. As Putnam (1993; 2000) has demonstrated the important role that these organizations play in preserving and nurturing democracy and democratic values, such as pluralism and tolerance. Thus, it is important that future research focus on the contributions of these organizations in order to provide a comprehensive conceptualization of the Israeli third sector.

The Impact of the Israeli Third Sector

In general, most of the research literature on the third sector has focused on how various factors affect the sector rather than the impact that the third sector has had on society.[67] In this approach, the third sector has been characterized as passive, with very little influence. In contrast to this depiction, our analysis reveals the Israeli third sector to be very active and influential. The third sector organizations that existed in Palestine prior to the establishment of the state significantly affected the subsequent development of the welfare system after statehood. Nongovernmental organizations initiated hospitals; higher, Orthodox, boarding school, and settlement educational systems; daycare centers; rehabilitation services; nursing homes; and burial services. After Israel was established, the state did not assume control of these organizations but legally classified them as third sector associations. This arrangement created strong links between the Israeli welfare state and third sector organizations, which received substantial government funding in exchange for providing services on behalf of the state.

Later, third sector organizations involved in advocacy, social change, and protest activities succeeded in changing government policy on a large variety of issues, including the Israeli-Palestinian conflict; the rights of women, children, and the mentally disabled; and the environment. In many instances, third sector organizations were instrumental in bringing these issues to the public agenda for the first time and influenced the relevant decision-making processes. Moreover, in many instances, third sector organizations have not only started to influence government policy regarding service provision, but they have significantly affected the manner in which these services are delivered since they are responsible for their actual implementation. Thus, it appears that the third sector in Israel is an active rather than a passive force. Research in this area has only just begun and it is important to continue to examine the impact of the third sector on Israeli society.

THE APPLICATION OF CURRENT THEORIES TO THE ISRAELI THIRD SECTOR

Nonprofit Theories

In general, the Israeli third sector does not appear to correspond with any of the predominant economic theories on the third sector organizations. Most of these theories illuminate only one particular aspect of a much larger picture.

Those theories that focus on demand side consider the growth of the third sector to be the result of failures in the public and business sectors (Weisbrod, 1977; Hansmann, 1987). In these models, consumers influence the development of the third sector by preferring one type of organization over another. These theories only partially explain the development of the Israeli third sector. For instance, the choice to maintain the existing system of third sector organizations after statehood had nothing to do with satisfying the "average voter," who was not ready to fund "specialized" services using tax-payers' money (Weisbrod, 1977).[68]; rather, the decision was based primarily upon political considerations. Likewise, Hansmann's theory regarding consumer preferences for third sector organizations because they are perceived as being more trustworthy than for-profit organizations is not completely applicable to the situation in Israel.[69] Given that a number of third sector organizations have been linked to cases of corruption, it is difficult to assume that Israeli consumers trust these organizations simply because they do not distribute profits. In fact, the opposite situation is more likely to be true: Israeli consumers generally trust businesses over third sector organizations.

On the other hand, "government failure" theory does help to explain the increased number of third sector organizations that were established during the 1980s and 1990s in response to the privatization of public services, decreased government involvement in welfare activities, and the increased legitimization of citizen-based organizations (e.g., complementary educational programs, services for AIDS patients, cultural services for new immigrants). Israeli society became more pluralistic during this time as an increasing number of service-providing CSOs were established without any government initiatives or public funding. Similarly, theories that emphasize the supply side of economics by claiming that third sector organizations are established in order to attract potential adherents to a particular political or religious ideology (James, 1987) help to describe the establishment of many service-providing organizations during the pre-state period. During that time, the various ideological movements in Israel established service-providing third sector organizations in order to obtain political support. Later, during the 1980s and the 1990s, the Shas party and the Islamic movement employed similar tactics. Thus, in accordance with these theories, at various times in Israel's history, sectoral organizations have been developed to provide welfare, educational, cultural, and health services in exchange for support.

Social Origins Theory

Social origins theory offers a much more comprehensive approach for understanding the Israeli third sector since it focuses on a variety of influences rather than a single perspective (e.g., economics) in explaining the sector's development (Salamon and Anheier; Esping-Andersen). As we have shown throughout this book, a range of social, political, religious, economic, and cultural forces have

Table 13. The Influence of Various Forces on the Israeli Third Sector during
Four Historical Periods

	State	Religious Institutions	Philanthropy from the Diaspora	Trade Unions
Diaspora Period	Indirect	Extensive	Extensive	N/A
Pre-State Period	Indirect	Small	Extensive	Extensive
Statist Period	Extensive	Small	Small	Extensive
Pluralistic Period	Extensive	Extensive	Extensive	Small

shaped the third sector in Israel. Despite its broad applicability, however, social
origins theory is most effective at explaining: (1) the economic rather than the
associational aspects of the third sector; and (2) the situation in countries with
clear democratic processes, where the influence of traditional (e.g., the church)
and contemporary (e.g., trade unions) forces have been integrated into the system
of government.

In this context, Israel presents a unique model for several reasons: (1) the
country's history began outside of its current territorial boundaries; (2) a large
Diaspora has supported the Jewish community in Israel as far back as the period
after the destruction of the First Temple; (3) there is no separation between religion
and state in Israel; and (4) since some basic issues remain unresolved (e.g., relations
between Israel and its neighbors, the Israeli-Palestinian conflict, relations with
the Jewish Diaspora), Israeli society is somewhat fluid and is therefore subject
to new influences that find expression in the third sector. Because all of these
factors have significantly impacted the Israeli third sector, it is necessary to adopt a
dynamic approach to social origins theory when examining Israeli society. Utilizing
Salamon and Anheier's model (1998), we have identified four factors that have
continuously affected the Israeli third sector throughout its history: the state, the
religious institutions, Jewish philanthropy from the Diaspora, and the trade unions.
As Table 13 demonstrates, these four factors have had varying degrees of influence
on the third sector during different periods of Israel's history.

During the Diaspora period, the Jewish population living in what is now Israel
developed mostly service-providing third sector organizations that were primarily
linked to traditional religious frameworks, received most of their funding from the
Jewish Diaspora, and helped the Jewish community maintain a sense of identity.
Although these organizations were subject to the rules of the Ottoman Empire,
the state's influence was fairly indirect. Likewise, during the pre-state period, the
influence of the British Mandate on third sector organizations remained indirect.
During this time, the primary goal of the Zionist community in Israel was to establish third sector organizations that would mobilize human and financial resources
in order to establish the State of Israel. The major forces in these new organizations
were the trade unions (particularly the Histadrut) and the Diaspora Jewish

funders who provided philanthropic support. The ultra-Orthodox Jews were not actively involved in these new organizations and maintained their traditional institutions within their separate communities. During the statist period, government involvement in the third sector increased significantly as the third sector organizations that were active in the pre-state period became the primary service-providing organizations in the new state. During this time, the trade unions remained active in the third sector and received substantial financial support from the state. Although massive amounts of money continued to flow in to Israel from the Diaspora, these philanthropic funders had little influence on how the money was spent. As in the pre-state period, the ultra-Orthodox Jews maintained influence over the third sector organizations within their own separate communities. Finally, during the pluralistic period, the power of the Histadrut began to decline. In contrast, the ultra-Orthodox communities gained power and were able to direct more state funds towards their respective organizations. Likewise, the Jewish Diaspora was able to channel its philanthropy to specific organizations and directed more support to CSOs. Clearly, different factors have had varying degrees of influence on the third sector at different times during Israeli history. As such, the Israeli third sector only partially fits into the social origins model presented by Salamon and Anheier.

Civil Society

From a social scientific research perspective, the literature on civil society does not at this point lend itself to specific theoretical formulations; that is, the literature does not offer specific theories regarding the factors that contribute to the development of civil society. Thus, it is not possible to apply specific theories on civil society to the Israeli third sector. Moreover, the data presented in this book only pertain to the formally organized aspects of civil society in Israel; clearly, we cannot undertake a comprehensive analysis of Israeli civil society without complete data.

Nevertheless, we found the conceptual framework put forth by Edwards and Foley (1996) to be very helpful in terms of analyzing CSOs in Israel. Edwards and Foley divide civil society into two domains: civil society I, an independent domain that is separate from the state, pluralistic in nature, involves voluntary action, and encourages independent and participatory citizen activity; and civil society II, a domain in which the principal goal is to change the political and social order primarily through confrontation. Since the 1970s, there has been significant growth in the number of civil society organizations in Israel that are independent from the state. Still, to date, it has not been possible to distinguish between those independent associations in Israel that are engaged in advocacy and social change versus those that espouse a neutral stance towards the state since many organizations alter their strategies over time and must be examined on a long-term basis. Likewise, a lack of sufficient data on the Israeli third sector prevents us from applying Putnam's concept of social capital, in which interpersonal interactions in the third sector encourage the development of trust, cooperation, and tolerance.

Based on the existing data, we can at best make the following hypothesis regarding Israeli civil society: according to patterns of giving and volunteerism among the Israeli public, it appears that associations are formed on the basis of identity (e.g., religion, ethnicity, or class) rather than more comprehensive, generic attributes that encompass a broader portion of society (e.g., by profession or residential neighborhood). This trend is particularly evident among the Orthodox/Haredi and Arab communities where the geographic distribution of the population overlaps with the sense of communal identity. Similar trends also appear to be occurring among the new immigrant populations from the former Soviet Union. By forming associations, these minority population groups are able to (1) obtain specialized services that are otherwise not available or inappropriately provided for by the state; and (2) preserve their collective identities.

Theories on Israeli Society

As we noted in the first chapter of this book, there are three major sociological schools of thought on the evolution of Israeli society: (1) the Jerusalem school, which was propounded during the 1950s; (2) functionalism revisited, which was dominant in the 1970s; and (3) critical sociology, which developed during the 1990s. To a large extent, these theories correspond to the evolution in contemporary thinking about Israeli society. The Jerusalem school, which considers the government to be the primary determinant of all major economic and social systems in Israel, corresponds to the economic structure of the third sector. For instance, the state grants the third sector very little independence: the government's system of financial support and supervisory mechanisms has virtually transformed many third sector organizations into public services. Likewise, the centrality of the state was evident when the National Institutions controlled donations from the Diaspora and channeled the funds to third sector organizations that the government favored. Furthermore, the fact that up until now the government has been the primary source of funding for nonprofit organizations perpetuates the idea that associations should be established to serve public rather than private issues and that their existence and survival depend upon the government.

The changes that have occurred in Israeli society over the last twenty years correspond with functionalism revisited, which recognizes and accentuates the growing diversity in Israel society. The multi-faceted nature of Israeli society was legally acknowledged when the government enacted the Law of Associations (Amutot) in 1980. As hundreds of new CSOs have been established among many different population groups (particularly among the ultra-Orthodox community), the third sector has become an arena in which societal differences and alternative voices can be expressed. Still, the law stipulates that associations cannot be incorporated if their goals and/or activities contradict the Jewish nature of the state or its democratic regime. Thus, even though the third sector is multi-faceted and represents diverse interests and orientations, it still must operate within the accepted framework of the state. Furthermore, the fact that the third sector continues to be dependent upon and to identify with the government (as reflected in the large numbers of organizations applying for government support) indicates that the state remains at the political center of Israeli society.

Finally, in contrast to functionalism revisited, adherents of the critical sociology school of thought maintain that the development of society is driven by the elite, class relations, group interests, and power struggles. Such processes were evident in Israeli society during the first thirty years of statehood when the closed nature of Israeli society enabled its leaders to shape institutions to maintain their advantage. The elite used nonprofit organizations to control the population and to maintain political support, as evidenced by the large numbers of service-providing associations during this time and the paucity of organizations that challenged the state. Although Israeli society has changed over the last twenty years, the proponents of critical sociology do not consider the large numbers of new associations to be indicative of a genuinely critical civil society (Ben Eliezer, 1999). These researchers argue that the new associations have failed to develop an awareness of the social order among the Israeli public rather than the state system, and that they have been pulled into the consensus without succeeding at genuinely challenging it.

In addition to these predominant sociological schools of thought, researchers have put forth a number of models explaining the changes that Israeli society has undergone over the past twenty years from a political science perspective. While a number of leading veteran political scientists (e.g., Akzin, 1955; Elazar, 1986; Arian, 1972) have focused on the structural properties of the democratic regime in Israel (e.g., the major branches of the government, the free and open elections every four years, the multiple party system, the independence of the judicial branch), Galnoor (1982) argues that up until the mid-1960s a participatory democracy in Israel was lacking. In fact, the Israeli bureaucracy actually opposed and prevented citizen participation in policymaking and implementation. In doing so, the government assumed a role of supremacy, in which it presumed to know what was best for the Israeli public (Doron and Kramer, 1991). This was also the reality in the third sector until the 1970s, as Kramer (1976) has noted in his pioneering study of voluntary organizations dealing with different types of disabilities. Likewise, Yishai (1990; 1998) found that no direct lines of communication existed between Israeli interest groups and decision-makers in the Israeli government; interest groups were only able to present their legitimate demands through the political parties, thereby perpetuating a paternalistic/clientelistic culture.

These trends have also been evident in the political culture, as reflected in the Israeli population's attitudes towards the government, during various times in Israeli history. It is well accepted among political scientists that after fulfilling the Zionist dream of statehood the level of trust in the political leadership and its institutions (e.g., the Knesset, the political parties, the public administration, and to a lesser extent the army and the court system) during the statist period was high, even though public opinion surveys and other such studies were rare during this time. This high level of regard declined sharply during the 1970s, however, especially after the Yom Kippur War, and has never been restored. While attitudes towards the government have varied over time, in general, the level of confidence in the political system today is relatively low compared to the previous era. As a result, various population groups have resorted to forming CSOs in order to solve their collective problems on their own. For example, when the Ministry of Education cut its budget in the 1980s and closed many enrichment programs in schools, parents organized to fill that void. Since the early 1980s, thousands of new citizen-initiated nonprofit organizations have been established, some of which have even challenged the government and its policies.

Likewise, the political parties that were formed around a particular ideology during the pre-state era have been in decline since the 1970s. In the past, each party promoted a broad political platform that was inclusive (e.g., socialism, liberalism) and with which a large number of voters could identify. Over the past 20 to 30 years, however, sectoral parties have emerged that have built their political platforms around one particular issue or that represent specific groups. Thus, although religious parties have been in existence since the inception of the state, in the past several elections new parties representing ethnic groups (e.g., Russian immigrants, North African immigrants, Arabs), the elderly, proponents of the legalization of soft drugs, or supporters of the environment have run for the Knesset and increased their electoral power. These trends clearly have impacted the third sector. In the past, the political parties served as intermediaries between the government and the population; today, nonprofit organizations have assumed this role. Associations now represent and increasingly advocate for specific interests.

CONCLUSION

In conclusion, it is obvious from a review of the literature that, to date, no theory has been developed that clearly explains the distinct development and nature of the Israeli third sector. If such a theory were to be conceived, it would have to be extremely complex and would likely encompass numerous disciplines, including political science, sociology, and economics, in order to describe the unique features of the Israeli third sector. Whether or not such a theory is ever developed, we believe that our analysis contributes to the theoretical discussion on the third sector by elucidating the two distinct types of organizations that comprise the third sector in Israel—namely, IWSS organizations and CSOs—and by presenting a methodological system that enables researchers to quantify and measure these two components. This work could be the first step in the long road that researchers of the Israeli third sector will face in the coming decade.

NOTES

67   An exception is the social science research examining the influence of interest groups on government policy and the characteristics of different regimes. In addition, Putnam (1993; 2000) has examined the impact of civil activity on government systems and political culture.

68   Weisbrod maintains that when services are public in nature, but specialized, the public sector generally cannot provide the services due to a lack of support from the legislature, which will only approve funding for services that cater to the "average (or mean) voter"; in such instances, the nonprofit organizational form is used to provide the specialized services.

69   Hansmann maintains that the nonprofit organizational form is generally used in instances where there is an asymmetry of information between the service provider and recipient, wherein the recipient is unable to judge the quality of the service provided (e.g., old-age homes, nursery schools). In such cases, forming a nonprofit association is preferable since the "owners" of the organization have no incentives to "cut corners" in order to maximize their profits at the expense of consumers.

Appendices

APPENDIX 1. INFORMATION ABOUT THIRD SECTOR ORGANIZATIONS IN ISRAEL

Although various public agencies collect information on third sector organizations in Israel, these data have several limitations:

1. Every public agency collects different types of data, using incompatible computing systems;
2. Different public agencies assign different identification numbers to the same organizations;
3. The information collected is seldom current;
4. Part of the data are not available to the public;
5. Public information systems are sometimes extremely outdated; and
6. Only seldom is there a clear distinction between different types of organizations, making identification of third sector organizations nearly impossible.

In order to overcome these obstacles and obtain integrative and longitudinal information about Israeli third sector organizations on a long-term basis, we developed The Israeli Third Sector Database, a new information system housed at The Israeli Center for Third Sector Research. The database integrates for the first time existing data collected from various public agencies' databases. For example, the database gathers information from the registries of Amutot (nonprofit associations) within the Ministry of Interior Affairs, the registries of public endowments and public utility companies within the Ministry of Justice, the Income Tax Commission, the Accountant General in the Ministry of Finance, the Bequests Fund, etc. From these various sources, the database collects the registration details of all the organizations listed in the various third sector organizations' registries, as well as information on the organizations' public funding, staff, employee compensation, mission, activities, social affiliations, and geographical locations. In addition to the data gathered from these sources, we added to the database information on the organizations' fields of practice, organizational functions, religious or ethnic affiliations, geo-coding, etc. The system allows the user to examine each organization in the database from various aspects, combining different data from various sources. We did not include in the database information on local governments, national lotteries, the national institutions, or any private organizations, such as umbrella organizations or foundations.

APPENDIX 2. AN OPERATIONAL DEFINITION OF THE ISRAELI THIRD SECTOR

In this book, we use the structural/operational definition of third sector organizations that was formulated by the Johns Hopkins Comparative Nonprofit Sector Project. The Hopkins definition is comprised of various terms that were used to define and characterize third sector organizations among the 36 different countries that participated in the project. The Hopkins Project identified five major features of third sector organizations that were evident across all of the participating countries. Hence, the third sector includes organizations that must be:

1) **Formal**—The organizations must be institutionalized to some extent. This does not necessarily imply that the organizations must be formally registered; however, they must have a minimal level of stability and formality. Thus, informal gatherings, or temporary or ad hoc endeavors do not qualify as third sector organizations.
2) **Nonprofit Distributing**—The organizations cannot distribute profits to their founders or directors. If any operational surpluses exist, they must be reinvested back into the organizations.
3) **Private**—The organizations must be institutionally separate from the government and not subject to the control of any public agency (although they can enjoy public finding).
4) **Independent**—The organizations must have mechanisms for self-rule and cannot be controlled by external entities.
5) **Voluntary**—The organizations must have at least minimal philanthropic inputs (e.g., donations, volunteers, and/or voluntary membership).

According to the Hopkins definition, the decision of whether to include religious sacramental organizations (e.g., synagogues, churches, mosques, etc.) or political parties in the third sector should be determined by the local circumstances of each country.

This definition corresponds with the characteristics, accepted perceptions, and frameworks of what normally is considered the third sector in Israel. The inductive approach of this definition is particularly useful given that neither the nonprofit organizations, government officials, nor the general public consider the third sector to be a distinct entity in Israel. However, there are some unique issues in Israel that make it difficult to clearly delineate the third sector and these need to be addressed.

First, we do not consider those organizations that are known collectively as the "National Institutions" to be part of the third sector, particularly those that served as the executive branch of the Jewish community in the pre-state era, such as The Jewish Agency, the Jewish National Fund (*Keren Kayemet l'Israel*), and the Jewish Foundation Fund (*Keren Hayesod*). Although these organizations meet some of the criteria listed above, they are not private, nor are they institutionally distinct from the government. They originally were founded in the pre-state era as public agencies operating as the *de facto* government of the Jewish community and helped to create the infrastructure for the state. When Israel was established they were not dissolved, and the government delegated to them certain public functions (e.g., the absorption of immigrants, settlement in the periphery areas, forestation, etc.). Their governing mechanisms are based on the Israeli party system and the government in power has major influence in deciding the leadership of these entities. Thus, although the "National Institutions" may be formally separate from the government, they cannot be considered private. For these reasons, we did not include them in our analysis. In fact, the Central Bureau of Statistics treats these organizations as non-profit-making institutions in their national accounts, but places them in a separate category between government and other nonprofit organizations.

Until 1994, the health funds (i.e., health insurance and service organizations) met all five of the criteria in the Hopkins definition. The enactment of the "National Health Insurance Law" in 1995, however, created a system of health care in which the existing sick funds began to deliver state health services. While citizens are entitled to choose the specific fund they wish to join, they cannot opt out of the system—membership in a health fund is obligatory and if a person does not choose a fund, the authorities will do so for him/her. Furthermore, the law enacted a system of payments based on a "Health Insurance Tax," which replaced the health fund membership fees. Thus, the mandatory nature of membership in these organizations deviates from the "voluntary" condition in the definition and they cannot be considered part of the third sector.

Since the Hopkins definition requires that local circumstances determine whether political parties and sacramental organizations should be included in the sector, we decided to omit the former and include the latter, provided that they met the five criteria in the definition. The legal status of political parties in Israel is altogether different from that of nonprofit organizations. They are registered separately, have a distinct law regulating them, and have a different tax status. For the most part, the government finances them, according to procedures and criteria specified by law. The law also strictly regulates their receipt of contributions. This alone sufficiently indicates that they are not institutionally separate from the public sector. Therefore, they are not compatible with the structural/operational definition of nonprofit organizations and we did not include them in our analysis. Since there is no separation between religion and the state in Israel, religious organizations are an important venue for civic participation and community action, flourishing despite the government's extensive involvement in the religious life of the people.

Also, while many religious organizations are informal and unincorporated, they comprise a large share of the Israeli third sector and provide various social services that are intertwined with their religious activities. Therefore, in order to present a realistic picture of the Israeli third sector, we included these organizations in our analysis.

APPENDIX 3. OPERATIONAL DEFINITIONS OF ORGANIZATIONS THAT ARE INTEGRATED WITHIN THE WELFARE STATE SYSTEM AND CIVIL SOCIETY ORGANIZATIONS

The Israeli Third Sector Database includes data on all nonprofit organizations in Israel that are legally registered as either associations, foundations, or public benefit companies—none of which are part of the business or public sectors. The information collected in the database allowed us to divide these organizations into two categories: (1) those organizations that are Integrated within the Welfare State System (IWSSs), and (2) civil society organizations (CSOs).

We used three guidelines to distinguish between IWSS organizations and CSOs. The first guideline takes into consideration the form of government funding an organization receives: if an organization obtains public funding through a long-term contract for services that are considered part of the welfare state's responsibilities, this organization is considered an IWSS organization.[70] There are instances where the services that an organization provides are considered part of the welfare state's responsibilities, but primarily for political reasons the public funding these organizations receive is given in the form of grants. We also categorized these organizations as being IWSS. The second guideline considers whether the services that the organization provides are determined by law. Under these circumstances, the organizations have no discretion over the type, amount, or price of the services that they are mandated to provide.[71] In such cases it is clear that the organization is not independent of the welfare state and is therefore classified as an IWSS organization. The third guideline focuses on the founders of the organization. In the many cases where public agencies have established third sector organizations to perform some of their functions,[72] the public agencies have most of the control over decision-making and policies; therefore, despite being nonprofit, these organizations are actually part of the welfare state apparatus, and as such are classified as IWSS organizations. Similarly, when an IWSS organization establishes a secondary organization over which it has control,[73] the latter is not considered a civil society organization.

Thus, the application of this operational definition enabled us to divide the organizations comprising the Israeli third sector into the two categories defined below:

1. **Organizations Integrated within the Welfare State System (IWSS)—**
   These organizations either supplement or replace public services and actually are integrated into the welfare state system in different areas such as health, education, welfare, culture, burial, etc. They are bound by contract with the state to deliver these services and are sometimes

perceived as the state's or the municipality's "executive arm." This group can be further divided into four sub-groups:

a. Organizations involved in long-term contracts with the government.

b. Organizations providing services that are considered to be part of the welfare state but for political reasons receive compensation for these services through grants.

c. Organizations established by public agencies.

d. Organizations that conduct some civil society activities but are otherwise substantially engaged with the welfare state apparatus.

2. **Civil Society Organizations (CSO)**—These organizations are not connected to state institutions in any long-term or substantial way.[74]

It should be noted that the distinction between IWSS organizations and CSOs is not dichotomous. Rather than perceiving them as two discrete categories, it is helpful to view them as being located at different places on a continuum. Although IWSS organizations are primarily government-funded and perform government functions, they sometimes conduct activities that are normally attributed to civil society organizations and occasionally act in direct opposition to government policy. For example, while the Israeli Association for Disabled Persons (ILAN) provides public services that are stipulated by law, it also advocates and organizes its constituents to protest against certain government policies.

Within the Israeli Third Sector Database, we identified IWSS organizations using data collected on organizations that receive any form of government funding. To identify the CSOs, we had to combine social-change organizations and associations since the database could not distinguish between these two categories. Thus, this combined category represents the civil society component of the Israeli third sector that is both legally and financially independent from the state.[75] Improvements in the data on third sector organizations in Israel in the future may allow researchers to distinguish between social change organizations and associations within this group.

NOTES

70   Examples of such organizations include The Association for the Elderly, national and local sports associations, community centers, the major women's organizations that provide day care services, the Associations of the Handicapped, etc.

71   For example, these would include services mandated by the nursing services law, the national health insurance law, and some residential services for mentally or physically disabled children.

72   For example, municipalities establish nonprofits to provide welfare and education services, national lotteries establish foundations to distribute their monies, and the police establish organizations to provide social benefits to policemen.

73   Examples of such organizations would include friends associations of IWSS organizations, scholarship foundations established by public schools, etc.

74   In order to verify our results, we put civil society organizations to two additional tests: 1) the funding test—if an organization is extensively funded by the state from any source whatsoever, it cannot be defined as a civil society organization; and 2) the size test—since civil society organizations that are very large and employ hundred of workers are rare, if an organization is big and receives sizeable amounts in public grants, it is thoroughly examined and when appropriate classified as an IWSS organization.

75   European scholars also distinguish between organizations that are integrated within the state welfare system and civil society organization since this distinction applies to the third sector in their countries, as well (see Zimmer and Priller, 2001:232).

APPENDIX 4. CLASSIFICATION OF THIRD SECTOR ORGANIZATIONS IN ISRAEL BY FIELD OF PRACTICE

The classification of third sector organizations that we use in this book is based on another element in the shared research tools of The Johns Hopkins Comparative Nonprofit Sector Project—that is, The International Classification of Nonprofit Organizations (ICNPO). This scheme, in turn, is based on the UN International System of Classification (ISIC), which is used to classify activity throughout the economy. The ICNPO divides the third sector into twelve fields of practice according to their major goals. Each of the main groupings is further broken down into sub-groups.[76] The twelve main groups of the ICNPO are:

1. Culture and Recreation
2. Education and Research
3. Health
4. Welfare and Social Services
5. Environmental and Animal Protection
6. Housing and Development
7. Law, Advocacy and Politics
8. Philanthropy and the Promotion of Volunteering
9. International Activity
10. Religion
11. Commercial Organizations, Trade Unions, and Professional Associations Other Organizations

In general, the ICNPO is compatible with the types of organizations that exist in Israel. However, we adjusted the framework to incorporate fields of nonprofit activity that are unique to Israel. Thus, we added Ultra Orthodox religious educational organizations and memorial organizations to the ICNPO. The following is the Israeli version of the ICNPO that we used in our study:

1. Culture and Recreation
    1.1 Culture and Arts
        1101 Communications and Publishing
        1102 Plastic and Visual Arts
        1103 Theatrical Arts
        1104 Historical, Literary, and Humanistic Societies
        1105 Museums
        1106 Parks, Zoos, and Aquariums
        1107 Libraries
        1108 Other Art and Culture

1.2 *Recreation and Clubs*
    1201 Sport Clubs and Organizations
    1202 Cultural, Youth, Sport, and Community Centers
    1203 Social Clubs
    1204 Youth Movements

2. Education and Research
   2.1 *Schools and Kindergartens*
    2101 Nursery, Elementary, and Secondary Education
   2.2 *Higher Education*
    2201 Universities and Colleges
   2.3 *Ultra-Orthodox Education*
    2301 Yeshivot and Kolelim (Post-Primary)
    2302 Talmud Torah (Primary)
    2303 Other Ultra-Orthodox Education
   2.4 *Other Education*
    2401 Vocational Education
    2402 Adult Education
    2403 Local Authorities' Educational Organizations
    2404 Parents' Organizations and Committees
    2405 Other Educational Institutions
   2.5 *Research*
    2501 Research: Medical
    2502 Research: Science and Technology
    2503 Research: Social and Political Science
    2504 Research: Judaism
    2505 Research: Other

3. Health
   3.1 *Health Services*
    3101 Health Funds and Primary Health Services
    3102 General Hospitals
    3103 Rehabilitation Hospitals
    3104 Psychiatric Hospitals
    3105 Geriatric Hospitals
   3.2 *Health Organizations*
    3201 Health Organizations (Preventative Treatment, Mental and
        Physical Health)
    3202 Other Health Organizations

4. Welfare and Social Services
   4.1 *Social Services*
    4101 Children and Youth
    4102 Family
    4103 Disabled Persons

4103.1 Disabled Persons—Sheltered Facilities

4103.2 Disabled Persons—Open Facilities

4104 Senior Citizens

4104.1 Senior Citizens—Sheltered Facilities

4104.2 Senior Citizens—Open Facilities

4105 Women

4106 Immigrants

4107 Police, Soldiers, and Prison Workers

4108 Substance Abuse

4109 Prisoners and Criminals

4110 Other Welfare Services

4.2 Financial and In-Kind Aid (Faith-Based)

4201 "Gemilut Hesed": Financial Aid

4202 "Gemilut Hesed": In-Kind Aid

4203 "Gemilut Hesed": Mixed and Other

5. Environmental and Animal Protection

5101 Environment Protection

5102 Animal Protection

5103 Other Environmental Organizations

6. Housing and Development

6101 Housing and Construction

6102 Economic and Local Development

6103 Vocational Retraining and Rehabilitation

6104 Other Housing and Development

7. Law, Advocacy and Politics

7101 Civil Organizations and Special Groups

7101.1 Ethnic and Immigrants Associations

7101.2 Special Groups

7102 Law, Consumer Protection

7103 Social Change

7104 Support of Political Parties and Politicians

7105 Other Civil Organizations

8. Philanthropy and the Promotion of Volunteering

8.1 Foundations

8101 Foundations that Support Many Organizations

8102 Foundations that Support Specific Organizations

8103 Foundations Supporting Individuals

8104 Other Foundations

8.2 Philanthropic Intermediaries

8201 Philanthropic Intermediaries and Umbrella Organizations of Philanthropic Organizations

8202 Other Philanthropic Organizations

9. **International Activity**
   9101 Exchange Programs, International Friendship Societies, and Chambers of Commerce
   9102 International Jewish Organizations
   9103 International Development and Aid Organizations
   9104 Other International Organizations

10. **Religion**
    10.1 Jewish
    10101 Jewish Institutes of Worship (Synagogues)
    10102 Jewish Religious Organizations
       10102.1 Jewish Religious Organizations: Religious Services
       10102.2 Jewish Religious Organizations: Religious Activities
       10102.3 Jewish Religious Organizations: Multi-Purpose
    10.2 Non-Jewish Religions
    10201 Non-Jewish Institutes of Worship (Mosques, Churches, etc.)
    10202 Non-Jewish Religious Organizations

11. **Commercial Organizations, Trade Unions, and Professional Associations**
    11101 Commercial and Business Associations
    11102 Unions
    11103 Professional Associations
    11104 Retired People's Associations
    11105 Other Commercial Organizations, Trades Unions, and Professional Associations

12. **Other Organizations**
    12.1 Memorial Organizations
    12101 Memorial Organizations for Victims of the Holocaust
    12102 Memorial Organizations for War and Terrorism Casualties
    12103 Other Memorial Organizations
    12.2 Others and Unclassified
    12201 Road Safety
    12202 Not Classified Elsewhere
    12203 Quasi-NGOs

NOTE

76   For a more elaborate description of the ICNPO, see Salamon and Anheier (1996) *Defining the Nonprofit Sector*, Manchester University Press.

References

CHAPTER 1

Anheier, H. K. (2000). *The CIVICUS Civil Society Diamond*. London: London School of Economics, Center for Civil Society.

Anheier, H. K. and W. Seibel (2001). *The Nonprofit Sector in Germany*. Manchester, Manchester University Press.

Archambault, E. (1997). *The Nonprofit Sector in France*. Manchester and New York: Manchester University Press.

Cohen, J. L. (1995). "Interpreting the Notion of Civil Society," in M. Walzer. (ed.) *Toward a Global Civil Society*. Oxford: Berghahn, pp. 35–40.

Coleman, J. (1990). *Foundations of Social Theory*. Cambridge: Belknap.

Dahrendorf, R. (1997). *After 1989: Morals, Revolution and Civil Society*. London: Macmillan.

De Tocqueville, A. (1959). *Democracy in America*, New York, Doubleday, Anchor Books.

Eisenstadt, S. N. (1954). *The Absorption of Immigrants*, London: Routledge.

Etzioni-Halevy, E. (1977). *Political Culture in Israel*, New York, Praeger.

Foley, M. W. and B. Edwards (1996). "The Paradox of Civil Society," *Journal of Democracy* 7(3), 38–52.

Foley, M. W. and B. Edwards. (1998). "Beyond Tocqueville: Civil Society and Social Capital in Comparative Perspective," *American Behavioral Scientist* 42(1), 5–20.

Gidron, B. (1992). "A Resurgent Third Sector and its Relationship to Government in Israel," in B. Gidron, R. Kramer and L. Salamon (eds.). *Government and the Third Sector – Emerging Relationships in Welfare States*. San Francisco: Jossey-Bass Publishers, pp. 176–195.

Hansmann, H. (1980). "The Role of Nonprofit Enterprise," *Yale Law Journal*, 89, 835–901.

Hansmann, H. (1987). "Economic Theories of Nonprofit Organizations," in W. W. Powell (Ed.) *The Nonprofit Sector: A Research Handbook*. New Haven: Yale University Press, pp. 27–42.

James, E. (1987). "The Nonprofit Sector in Comparative Perspective," in W. W. Powell (Ed.). *The Nonprofit Sector: A Research Handbook*. New Haven: Yale University Press, pp. 397–415.

James, E. (1989). "Economic Theories and the Nonprofit Sector," in H.K. Anheier and W. Seibel (eds.)*The Nonprofit Sector: International and Comparative Perspectives*, Walter de Gruyter and Co.

Kimmerling, B. (1983). *Zionism and Territory: The Socio-Territorial Dimension of Zionist Politics*. Berkeley: University of California Press.

Kimmerling, B. (1995). *Between State and Society: The Sociology of Politics*. Tel-Aviv: The Open University (Hebrew).

Lissak M. and D. Horowitz (1989). *Trouble in Utopia: The Overburdened Polity of Israel*, Albany, NY, SUNY Press.

Minkoff, D. C. (1997). "Producing Social Capital: National Social Movements and Civil Society," *American Behavioral Scientist* 40: 606–619.

Putnam, R. D. (1993). *Making Democracy Work.* Princeton: Princeton University Press.

Putnam, R. D. (2000). *Bowling Alone: The Collapse and Revival of American Community.* New York: Simon and Schuster.

Ram, U. (Ed.) (1994). *The Israeli Society: Critical Aspects.* Tel-Aviv: Breirot (Hebrew).

Salamon, L. M. (1994). "The rise of the nonprofit sector," *Foreign Affairs*, July/August, 109–122.

Salamon, L. and H. K. Anheier (1998). "Social Origins of Civil Society: Explaining the Nonprofit Sector Cross-Nationally," *Voluntas*, 9(3), 213–248.

Shapira, Y. (1991). *Elite Without Followers.* Tel-Aviv: Am Oved (Hebrew).

Smooha, S. (1978). *Israel: Pluralism and Conflict.* Berkeley: University of California Press.

Swirski, S. (1989). *Israel: the Oriental Majority.* London: Zed.

Walzer, M. (1995). "The Concept of Civil Society," in M. Walzer (Ed.) *Toward a Global Civil Society* Oxford: Berghahn, pp. 7–28.

Weisbrod, B. A. (1977). *The Voluntary Nonprofit Sector.* Lexington: Lexington Books.

Weisbrod, B. A. (1988). *The Nonprofit Economy.* Cambridge: Harvard University Press.

Yamamoto, T. (1998). *The Nonprofit Sector in Japan.* Manchester and New York: Manchester University Press.

CHAPTER 2

Anheier, H. K. (2001). "Measuring Global Civil Society," in Anehier, H.K., Glasius, M. and Kaldor, M. (Eds), *Global civil society 2001.* Oxford: Oxford University Press: pp. 221–230.

Anehier, H.K., Glasius, M. and Kaldor, M. (Eds), (2002). *Global civil society 2001.* Oxford: Oxford University Press.

Brenner, Nava (2002). *Satellite Account For The Non-Profit Sector In Israel—Main Findings.* Jerusalem: the Central Bureau of Statistics (unpublished).

Burger, A. and Dekker, P. (2001). *The Nonprofit Sector in the Netherlands.* The Hague: SCP: pp. 57–61.

Central Bureau of Statistics (1996). *Nonprofit Institutions in Israel, 1991.* Jerusalem: the Central Bureau of Statistics.

Donoghue, F., Anheier, H. K. and Salamon, L. M. (1999). *Uncovering the Nonprofit Sector in Ireland.* Dublin: National College of Ireland.

Gabay, Y. and Brik, E. (2002) "Salary Structure in the Third Sector in Israel," Beersheba: Ben Gurion University, Israeli Center for Third-sector Research (Hebrew).

Ghanem, A. (2001). "Civil society in the Arab-Palestinian Population in Israel," in *ICTR Annual Conference Proceedings*, Beersheba: Ben Gurion University, Israeli Center for Third-sector Research.

Gidron, B. and Katz, H., (1998). *Defining the Nonprofit Sector: Israel.* Baltimore: The Johns Hopkins University, Institute for Policy Studies.

Gidron, B. and Katz, H. (1999). "Israel," in Salamon, L. M., Anheier, H. K., List, R., Toepler, S., Sokolowsky S.W. and Associates, *Global civil Society: Dimensions of the Nonprofit Sector,* Baltimore: The Johns Hopkins University, Institute for Policy Studies.

Gidron, B. and Katz, H. (2001). "Patterns of Government Funding to Third Sector Organizations as Reflecting a De-Facto Policy and their Implications on the Structure of the Sector in Israel," *International Journal of Public Administration*, 24 (11) 2001: 1133–1160.

Gidron, B., Katz, H. and Bar, M. (2000). *The Israeli Third Sector 2000: Roles of the Sector.* Beersheba: Ben Gurion University, Israeli Center for Third-sector Research.

Gidron, B., Katz, H. and Bar, M. (2001). "Characterizing Israeli Civil Society," in *ICTR Annual Conference Proceedings*, Beersheba: Ben Gurion University, Israeli Center for Third-sector Research.

Gidron, B., Katz, H., Anheier, H. K. and Salamon, L. M. (1999). *The Israeli Nonprofit Sector: an Overview of Major Economic Parameters.* Beersheba: Ben Gurion University, the Israeli Center for Third-sector Research.

Hall, M., McKeown, L. and Roberts, K. (2001). *Caring Canadians, Involved Canadians: Highlights from the 2000 National Survey of Giving, Volunteering and Participating.* Ottawa: Statistics Canada.

Ibrahim, S. E., Adly, H. Shehata, D. (2002). *Civil Society and Governance in Egypt.* Brighton: University of Sussex, Institute of Development Studies, Civil Society and Governance programme.

Kirsch, J. D., Hume, K. M. and Jalandoni, N. T. (1999). *Giving and Volunteering in the United States: Findings from a National Survey.* Washington, DC: Independent sector.

NCVO (2001), "The Tide has Turned," *NCVO Research Quarterly,* Issue 13, 2001.

Salamon, L. M., Anheier, H. K., List, R., Toepler, S., Sokolowsky, S.W. and Associates (1999). *Global civil Society: Dimensions of the Nonprofit Sector.* Baltimore: The Johns Hopkins University, Institute for Policy Studies.

Shye, S., Lazar, A., Duchin R. and Gidron B. (2000). *Philanthropy in Israel—Patterns of Giving and Volunteering in the Israeli Public.* Beersheba: Ben Gurion University, Israeli Center for Third Sector Research.

CHAPTER 3

Ajzenstadt, M. and Z. Rosenhek (2000). "Privatization and New Modes of State Intervention: The Long-Term Care Program in Israel," *Journal of Social Policy*, 29(2), 247–262.

Bar-Mor, H. (1997) "Israel," in L. Salamon .(ed.). *International Guide on Nonprofit Law.* New York: Wiley, pp. 166–181.

DeHartog, A. (1998) "State Support for Public Institutions—the Burgeoning of Special Funds," *Mishpatim* [Law] 29(1), 75–107 (Hebrew).

DeHartog, A. (1999). *State Support for Public Institutions—Legislation versus Reality* (Jerusalem: Floresheimer Institute for Political Research) (Hebrew).

Doron, A. (1989). "The Privatization of Welfare Services: A New Battle for the Image of Israeli Society," *Bitahon Sotziali* [Social Security] 34, 18–34 (Hebrew).

Doron, A. (1999). "Welfare Policy in Israel—Developments in the 80s and 90s," in D. Nachmias and G. Menahem (eds.), *Public Policy in Israel* (Jerusalem: The Israel Institute for Democracy) 437–474 (Hebrew).

Gal, J. (1994). "The Commercialization and Privatization of the Welfare State—Implications for Israel," in *Chevra ve-Revaha* [Society and Welfare] 15, 7–24 (Hebrew).

Gidron, B., H. Katz, and M. Bar (2000). *The Third Sector in Israel: The Roles of the Sector.* Beer-Sheva: Ben Gurion University of the Negev, The Israeli Center for Third sector Research.

Gliksberg, D. (1995). *The Taxation of Nonprofit Institutions* (Hebrew).

Katan, Y. and A. Loewenstein (1999). *A Decade since the Enactment of the Long-Term Care Insurance Law—Implications and Lessons* (Jerusalem: The Center for Social Policy Research in Israel) (Hebrew).

Salamon, L. and H. Anheier (1999). *Global Civil Society.* Johns Hopkins University.

Shmid, H. and A. Borowsky (2000). "Selected Issues in the Delivery of Services to the Elderly," *Bitachon Sotziali (Social Security)*, 57, 59–81 (Hebrew).

Stessman Y., (2000). "NII Activity in Developing Services," in *NII Annual Survey 2000* (Jerusalem: National Insurance Institute) 219–234 (Hebrew).

Telias, M., Y. Katan, and B. Gidron (2000). *Government and Local Authority Policy toward the Third Sector in Israel* (Be'er Sheva: The Israeli Center for Third Sector Research) (Hebrew).

Tzahor, E. (1996). "The Reform in the Law of Amutot," *In the Third Sector*, May 2–4.

Yishai, Y. (1987). *Interest Groups in Israel* (Tel Aviv: 'Am 'Oved) (Hebrew).

Yishai, Y. (1998). "Civil Society in Transition: Interest Politics in Israel," *ANNALS*, AAPSS 555, 147–162.

CHAPTER 4

Adler, Ch. and N. Balas (2000). "Teach the Youngster according to his Style," in *Pluralism in Israel: From the Melting Pot to a "Jerusalem Mix"*, Jerusalem, The Center for Social Policy Studies, 133–152 (Hebrew).

Andrews, F. F. (1931). *The Holy Land under the Mandate*, Boston, Houghton Mifflin, Vol. 1.

Anheier, H. K. and W. Seibel (2001). *The Nonprofit Sector in Germany*, Manchester, Manchester University Press.

Atzmon, Y. (1990) "Women in Israeli Politics," *State, Government, and International Relations*, 33, 5–19 (Hebrew).

Avissar, A. (1970) "Jewish Institutions in Hebron," in A. Avissar (ed.) *The Book of Hebron*, Jerusalem, Keter, 176–212 (in Hebrew).

Barbetta, G. P. (1997). *The Nonprofit Sector in Italy*, Manchester, Manchester University Press.

Bar-Eli, A. (1999). "Statism and the Labor Movement in the Early 1950s: Structural Assumptions," in M. Bar-On (ed.) *The Challenge of Sovereignty: Art and Thought During the First Decade of the State*, Jerusalem, Yad Ben-Zvi, 23–44 (in Hebrew).

Bar-Mor, H. (1997). "Israel," in L. Salomon (ed.) *International Guide on Nonprofit Law*, New York, Wiley, 166–181.

Ben-Meir, D. (1988). *Voluntary Work in Israel in Theory and in Practice*, Jerusalem, Keter (Hebrew).

Ben-Porat, A. (1999). *Where Have all the Bourgeoisie Gone?* Jerusalem, Magness (Hebrew).

Bergman, Y. (1944). *The Tzedaka in Israel*, Jerusalem, Tarshish (Hebrew).

Berkowitz, M. (1996). "Toward an Understanding of Fundraising, Philanthropy and Charity in Western Zionism, 1897–1933," *Voluntas*, 7, 241–258.

Bogen, B. (1917). *Jewish Philanthropy* New York Macmillan.

Central Bureau of Statistics (1998). *A Survey of Revenues and Expenditures of Nonprofit Organizations, 1980–1996*, Jerusalem, Central Bureau of Statistics (Hebrew).

Divshoni, G. (1928). "Tzedaka Institutions in Eretz Yisrael," *Ha'Aretz Daily*, June 27 (Hebrew).

Don-Yehiya, E. (1995). "Political Religion in a New State: Ben-Gurion's *Mamlachtiyut*," in I. S. Troen, and N. Lucas (eds.) *Israel: The First Decade of Independence*, Albany, SUNY Press, 171–192.

Doron, A. (1999). "Welfare Policy in Israel: Developments during the 1980s and 1990s," in D. Nachmias and G. Menachem (eds.) *Public Policy in Israel*, Jerusalem, The Israeli Institute for Democracy, 437–474 (Hebrew).

Dowty, A. (1995). "Israel's First Decade: Building a Civic State," in I. S. Troen, and N. Lucas (eds.) *Israel: The First Decade of Independence*, Albany, SUNY Press, 31–50.

Eisenstadt, S. N. (1956). "The Social Conditions of the Development of Voluntary Associations: A case Study of Israel," *Scripta Hierosolomytana*, 3, 104–125.

Eisenstadt, S. N. (1989). *Ongoing Changes within Israeli Society*, Jerusalem, Magness (Hebrew).

Elazar, D. (1994). *Covenant and Polity in Biblical Israel: Biblical Foundations and Jewish Expressions*, Transaction Publishers.

Elazar, D. (Ed.) (1997). *Kinship and Consent: The Jewish Political Tradition and Its Contemporary Uses*, Transaction Publishers.

Eliav, M. (1978). *The Settlement of Eretz Yisrael in the 19th Century (1777–1881)*, Jerusalem, Keter (Hebrew).

Elitzur, A. (1947). *Twenty-Five Years of Keren Hayessod*, Jerusalem, The Keren Hayessod Central Office (Hebrew).

Elkayam, M. (1990). *Jaffa-Neve Tzedek: The Beginnings of Tel-Aviv*, Tel-Aviv, Ministry of Defense Publishing House (Hebrew).

Fogel-Bijaoui, S. (1992). "Women's Organizations in Israel," *International Problems*, 52, 65–76 (Hebrew).

Friedman, M. (1995). "The structural Foundation for Religio-Political Accommodation in Israel: Fallacy and Reality," in I. S. Troen, and N. Lucas (eds.) *Israel: The First Decade of Independence*, Albany, SUNY Press, 51–81.

Frisch, E. (1924). *Historical Survey of Jewish Philanthropy from Earliest Times to the Nineteenth Century*, New York: The Macmillan Company.

Galnoor, Y. (1982). "The Israeli Democracy and Citizen Participation," *Molad*, 41, 71–87 (Hebrew).

Gat, B. Z. (1974). *The Jewish Community in Eretz Yisrael, 1840–1881*, Jerusalem, Yad Ben Zvi (Hebrew).

Gidron, B. (1992). "A Resurgent Third Sector and its Relationship to Government in Israel," in B. Gidron, R. Kramer and L. Salamon (eds.), *Government and the Third Sector—Emerging Relationships in Welfare States*, San Francisco: Jossey-Bass Publishers, 176–195.

Gidron, B. (1997). "The Evolution of Israel's Third Sector: The Role of Predominant Ideology," *Voluntas* 8, 11–38.

Gidron, B. and D. Bargal, (1986). "Self-Help Awareness in Israel: An Expression of Structural Changes and Expanding Citizen Participation," *Journal of Voluntary Action Research*, 15, 47–56.

Greenberg, Y. (1991). "Mapam's Attitudes towards the Histadrut," in A. Margalit (ed.) *The United Left: The Social Path of the Mapam during the Initial Phase of Statehood, 1948–1954*, Giv'at Haviva, Yad Ya'ari, 223–276 (Hebrew).

Grinberg, L. L. (1991). *Split Corporatism in Israel*, Albany, SUNY Press.

Harman, Z. (1970). "Non-Governmental Initiative," in Jarus, A., Marcus, J., Oren, J. and Rapaport, C. (Eds.) *Children and Families in Israel*. The Henrietta Szold Institute. New York, Gordon and Breach, 542–553.

Hermann, T. (1995). "New Challenges to New Authority: Israeli Grassroots Activism in the 1950s," in I. S. Troen and N. Lucas (eds.) *Israel: The First Decade of Independence*, Albany, SUNY Press, 105–122.

Hermann, T. (1996). "Do They Have a Chance? Protest and Political Structure of Opportunities in Israel," *Israel Studies*, 1(1), 144–170.

Horowitz, D. and M. Lissak (1977). *From a Yishuv (The Jewish Community during the Pre-State Era) to a State*, Tel-Aviv, Am Oved (in Hebrew).

In the Circle of Mutual Aid (*Bemaagal Ha'ezra Hahadadit*) (1946). *A Decade of "Mish'an": 1935–1945*, Haifa, Haifa Labor Council (in Hebrew).

Jaffe, E. (1992). "Sociological and Religious Origins of the Non-Profit Sector in Israel," *International Sociology*, 8, 159–176.

Jaffe, E. (1993). "The Role of Nonprofit Organizations among the *Haredi* (Ultra-Orthodox) Jewish Community in Israel," *Journal of Social Work and Policy in Israel*, 7–8, 45–55.

Kamen, C. (1987). "After the Catastrophe: The Arabs in Israel, 1948–51. Part I," *Middle Eastern Studies*, 23, 453–495.

Karagila, Z. (1981). "Primary Sources on the Halukkah in Eretz Yisrael," *Katedra*, 20, 56–76 (Hebrew).

Katan, Y. (1997). "The Involvement of NGOs in Personal Welfare Services," in Y. Katan (ed.) *Personal Welfare Services: Trends and Changes*, Center for Social Policy Studies and Ramot, Tel-Aviv University Publishing House, 137–160 (Hebrew).

Katan, Y. (2000). "Your Own City's Poor Should be Preferred," in *Pluralism in Israel: From the Melting Pot to a "Jerusalem Mix"*, Jerusalem, The Center for Social Policy Studies, 153–164 (Hebrew).

Katz, Y. (1958). *Tradition and Crisis: The Jewish Society at the End of the Middle Ages*, Jerusalem, The Bialik Institute (Hebrew).

Kendall, J. and M. Knapp (1996). *The Nonprofit Sector in the UK*, Manchester, Manchester University Press.

Kimmerling, B. (1995). *Between State and Society: The Sociology of Politics*, Tel-Aviv, Open University (Hebrew).

Kramer, R. (1976). *The Voluntary Service Agency in Israel*, Institute of International Studies, University of California, Berkeley.

Landau, D. (1993). *Piety and Power*, New York, Hill and Wang.

Lehman-Wilzig, S. N. (1990). *Stiff-Necked People, Bottle-Necked System: The Evolution and Roots of Israeli Public Protest, 1949–1986*, Bloomington, Indiana University Press.

Lehman-Wilzig, S. N. (1992). *Wildlife: Grassroots Revolts in Israel in the Post-Socialist Era*, Albany, SUNY Press.

Levin, M. (1973). *Balm in Gilead—The Story of Hadassah* New York: Schocken Books.

Lissak, M. (1988). "Ben Gurion's Perception of Institution Building," in S. Avineri (ed.) *David Ben Gurion: A Profile of a Workers' Movement Leader*, Tel Aviv, Am Oved, 108–117 (Hebrew).

Lissak, M. (1998). "Decline of the Political Parties and Flourish of Sectorialism," in D. Koren (ed.) *The End of Political Parties: The Israeli Democracy in Crisis*, Tel Aviv, Ha'Kibutz Ha'Meuchad, 129–140 (Hebrew).

Lissak, M. (1999). *The Mass Immigration of the 1950's: The Failure of the Melting Pot*, Jerusalem, The Bialik Institute (Hebrew).

Loewenberg, F. (1991). "Voluntary Organizations in Developing Countries and Colonial Societies: The Social Service Department of the Palestine Jewish Community in the 1930s," *Nonprofit and Voluntary Sector Quarterly*, 20, 415–428.

Loewenberg, F. M. (1997). "What Does Judaism Say about Voluntarism," *Journal of Social Work and Policy in Israel*, 9–10, 77–87.

Lustick, I. (1980). *Arabs in the Jewish State—Israel's Control of a National Minority*, Austin: University of Texas Press.

Mashka, S. (1940). *Workers' Expenditures on Taxes, Donations, and Other Non-Consumption Items*, Central Committee of the Histadrut, Department for Information and Statistics, Report No. 1 (Hebrew).

Ministry of Social Welfare (1966). *Developments in Family, Youth and Child Welfare and in the Planning, Organization and Administration of Social Services (1964/65)*. Report submitted to the Economic and Social Council of the United Nations, Jerusalem, October.

Nachmias, D. and A. Sand (1999). "Governance and Public Policy," in D. Nachmias and G. Menachem (eds.) *Public Policy in Israel*, Jerusalem, The Israeli Institute for Democracy, 11–34 (Hebrew).

Ofer, D. (1995). "Defining Relationships: The Joint Distribution Committee and Israel, 1948–1950," in I. S. Troen and N. Lucas (eds.) *Israel: The First Decade of Independence*, Albany, SUNY Press, 713–731.

Pevsner, Y. (ed.) (1926). *All of Eretz Yisrael*, Tel-Aviv, Commerce and Industry (Hebrew).

Pond, Y. (1999). *Divisiveness or Participation: Agudat Yisrael vis-à-vis Zionism and the State of Israel*, Jerusalem, Magness (Hebrew).

Rahat, M. (1998). *Shas: The Spirit and the Power*, Tel-Aviv, Alpha (Hebrew).

Reiter, Y. (1997). *Islamic Institutions in Jerusalem*, London: Kluwer Law International.

Report by Welfare Minister Dr. Yossef Burg on Activities by the Ministry of Welfare (1965), Jerusalem, Information Center (Hebrew).

Roniger, L. (1994). "Cultural Prisms, Western Individualism and the Israeli Case," *Ethnos*, 59(1–2) 37–55.

Rosenhek, Z. (1998). "Policy Paradigms and the Dynamics of the Welfare State: The Israeli Welfare State and the Zionist Colonial Project," *International Journal of Sociology and Social Policy*, 18, 157–202.

Roter, R., N. Shamai and F. Wood (1985). "The Non-Profit Sector and Volunteering," in Y. Kop (ed.), *Israel's Outlays for Human Services—1984*, Jerusalem: The Center for Social Policy Studies in Israel.

Salamon, Y. (1985). "Social and Economic Aspects of the Ashkenazi Community in Eretz Yisrael at the End of the 19th Century," in N. Gross (ed.) *The Economic Life of Jews*, Jerusalem, Zalman Shazar Center for the Advancement of Research in Jewish History, pp. 333–346 (Hebrew).

Salzberger, L. and J. Rosenfeld (1974). "The Anatomy of 267 Social Welfare Agencies in Jerusalem: Findings from a Census," *Social Service Review*, 48, 255–267.

Segev, T. (1999). *The Days of the Anemones (Red Berets): Eretz Yisrael during the Mandate*, Jerusalem, Keter (Hebrew).

Silber, I. and Z. Rosenhek, (1999). *The Historical Development of the Israeli Third Sector*, Beer Sheva, Ben Gurion University, The Israeli Center for Third Sector Research.

Stock, E. (1995). "Philanthropy and Politics: Modes of Interaction between Israel and the Diaspora," in Troen, I. S. and N. Lucas (eds.) *Israel: The First Decade of Independence*, Albany, SUNY Press, 699–711.

Tzahor, Z. (1994). *Vision and Reality: Ben Gurion between Ideology and Politics*, Tel-Aviv, Sifriyat Poalim (Hebrew).

Yanai, N. (1987). "Ben Gurion's Perception of Statism," *Katedra*, 45, September, 169–189 (Hebrew).

Yanai, N. (1994). "Ben Gurion's Perception of Citizenship," *Iyunim Bi'Tkumat Israel*, 4, 494–504 (Hebrew).

Yatziv, G. (1999). *The Sectoral Society*, Tel-Aviv The Bialik Institute (Hebrew).

Yefet, Ch. (1957). *Welfare Services in Israel*, Jerusalem, The Social Services Authority (Hebrew).

Yishai, Y. (1990). "State and Welfare Groups: Competition or Cooperation? Some Observations on the Israeli Scene," *Nonprofit and Voluntary Sector Quarterly*, 19, 215–235.

Yishai, Y. (1991). *Land of Paradoxes: Interest Politics in Israel*, Albany, SUNY Press.

Yishai, Y. (1998). "Civil Society in Transition: Interest politics in Israel," *Annals of the American Academy of Political and Social Science*, 555, 147–162.

Yishay, Y. (1998). "Political Parties or Social Movements: Integration or Separation?" in D. Koren (ed.) *The End of Political Parties: The Israeli Democracy in Crisis*, Tel Aviv, Ha'Kibutz Ha'Meuchad, 155–166 (Hebrew).

Zeidan, E. and A. Ghanem (2000). *Patterns of Giving and Volunteering in the Arab-Palestinian Society in Israel*, Beer-Sheva, The Israeli Center for Third Sector Research.

CHAPTER 5

Ajzenstadt, M. (1996). "Issues on privatization of social services in Israel: Home Care services, correction and prevention of violence," in Y. Katan (ed.). *Personal Welfare Services—Trends and Changes*. Jerusalem: Israeli Center for Research of Social Policy, pp. 189–210 (Hebrew).

Ajzenstadt, M. and Z. Rosenhek (2000). "Privatization and New Modes of State Intervention: The Long-Term Care Program in Israel," *Journal of Social Policy*, 29(2), 247–262.

Alboim-Dror, R. (1998). "Roots of the Israeli education system," in A. Peled (ed.). *The Israeli Education System Jubilee*. Jerusalem: The Ministry of Education, Culture and Sports, pp. 21–37 (Hebrew).

Bar-Siman-Tov, R. and S. Langerman (1988). *Complementary Curriculum in Elementary Schools with Parents Funding*. Jerusalem: The Henrietta Szold Institute (Hebrew).

Cnaan, S. and N. Dror (1997). "A Partnership: A Case Study." Paper presented at Van Leer Forum conference *Modes of Foundation Operation in Israel*, June, Jerusalem: Van Leer Jerusalem Institute.

Cohen, A. and Cohen, E. (1996). *Gray Education in Israel*. Jerusalem: Institute for Research of Education Systems (Hebrew).

Doron, A. (1989). "Privatization of Welfare Services: A New Arena for the Struggle to Preserve the Integrity of the Israeli Society," *Social Security*, 34, 18–34 (Hebrew).

Doron, A. (1999). "Israeli Welfare Policy—Developments in the 1980s and 1990s," in Nachmias D. and G. Menahem (eds.). *Public Policy in Israel*. Jerusalem: The Israeli Institute for Democracy. 437–474 (Hebrew).

Doron, A. and Kramer, R. M. (1992). *The Israeli Welfare State*. Tel-Aviv: Am-Oved (Hebrew).

Dror, I. (1998). "Fifty Years of Education in the Israeli State—Historical Perspectives: Eras and Dilemmas," in Peled, A. (ed.). *The Israeli Education System Jubilee*. Jerusalem: The Ministry of Education, Culture and Sports, pp. 39–66 (Hebrew).

Esping-Andersen, G. (1990). *The Three Worlds of Welfare Capitalism*. Cambridge: Polity Press.

Friedman, M. (1991). *The Haredi Society—Sources, Directions and Processes*. Jerusalem: Jerusalem Institute for Israel Research (Hebrew).

Gal, J. (1994). "Commercialization and Privatization of the Welfare State—Implications for Israel," *Society and Welfare*, 16, 7–24 (Hebrew).

Gaziel, H. (1996). *Politics and Policy making in Israel's Education System*. Brighton: Sussex Academic Press.

Gaziel. H. (1998). "Education Policy in Israel: Structures and Processes," in A. Peled (ed.). *The Israeli Education System Jubilee*. Jerusalem: The Ministry of Education, Culture and Sports, pp. 84–67 (Hebrew).

Gera, R. and B. Morgenstein. (2000). *Receivers of Home Care allowance 1999*. Jerusalem: The national Insurance Institute.

Gidron, B. (1997). "The Evolution of Israel's Third Sector: The Role of Predominant Ideology," *Voluntas*, 8(1), 11 –38.

Gidron , B. and H. Katz. (1998). *The Third Sector in Israel: Borders, Characteristics and Processes*. Beer Sheve, Ben Gurion University, The Israeli Center for Third Sector Research.

Gidron, B. and H. Katz (1999). *The Third Sector in Israel—Economic Data*. Beer Sheva. Ben-Gurion University of the Negev (Hebrew).

Gidron, B., H. Katz and M. Bar (2000). *The Israeli Third Sector 2000: The Roles of the Sector*. Beer Sheva: Israeli Center for Third Sector Research.

Gross R., B. Rosen and A. Shirom (1999). "The Israeli Health System in the Wake of the National Health Insurance Bill," *Social Security* 54, 11–34 (Hebrew).

Harrison, J. (1993). "The Growth of Private Education in Israel: Causes and Consequences," in A. Yogev and J. Dronkers. (Eds.). *International Perspectives on Education and Society*, Vol. 3. Middlesex: JAI Press, pp. 193–226.

Higher Education Budget Proposal, 1998. Ministry of Finance, Jerusalem (Hebrew).

Higher Education Budget Proposal, 2001. Ministry of Finance, Jerusalem (Hebrew).

Inbar, D. (1989). "A Back Door Process of School Privatization: the Case of Israel," in W. Lowe Boyd and J. G. Cibulka. (Eds.). *Private Schools and Public Policy: International Perspectives*. London: Falmer, pp. 269–284.

Katan, J. (1988). "Voluntary Organizations—Substitute or Partner for Governmental Welfare Activities," *Social Security*, 32, 57–73 (Hebrew).

Katan, J. (1996). "Involvement of Non-Governmental Organizations in Personal Welfare Services," in J. Katan (ed.) *Personal Welfare Services—Directions and Change*. Jerusalem: Center for Social Policy Research in Israel, 137–159 (Hebrew).

Katan, J. and A. Loewenstein (1999). *Ten Years to the Home Care Law—Implications and Lessons*. Jerusalem: Center for Social Policy Research in Israel (Hebrew).

Kramer, R. (1988). "The Ever-Changing Role of Voluntary Agencies in the Welfare State," *Society and Welfare*, 9, 121–127 (Hebrew).

Kramer, R. M. (1981). *Voluntary Agencies in the Welfare State*. Berkeley: University of California Press.

Ministry of Health. (2000). *Health Status in Israel 1999*. Tel Hashomer: Ministry of Health.

Ministry of Health Budget Proposal, 1998. Jerusalem (Hebrew).

Ministry of Health Budget Proposal, 2001. Jerusalem (Hebrew).

Ministry of Education and Culture, Budget Proposal, 1998. Jerusalem (Hebrew).

Ministry of Labor and Social Welfare, Budget Proposal, 1998. Jerusalem (Hebrew).

Ministry of Labor and Social Welfare, Budget Proposal, 2001. Jerusalem (Hebrew).

Ministry of Labor and Social Welfare, (2001). *Committee Report on Developing Local Associations for Children at Risk within the "Kadima" Master Plan on Children and Youth at Risk and Family Violence*. Jerusalem: Ministry of Labor and Social Welfare, Department of Social and Personal Services, Services for Children, Youth and Community (Hebrew).

Ministry of Labor and Social Welfare, (2001). *Summary of Development Programs—2000*. Jerusalem: The Ministry of Labor and Social Welfare, The Head Engineer Unit.

Neipris, J. (1984). *Social Welfare and Social Services in Israel*. Jerusalem: Publications of Councils of Schools for Social Work in Israel (Hebrew).

Salamon, L. (1995). *Partners in Public Service*. Baltimore: Johns Hopkins University Press.

Schwartz, S. (1995). Who Guarantees the Yishuv's Health? *Social Security*, 43, 5–23 (Hebrew)

Schwartz, S. (2000). *Medical Fund, Histadrut and Government, 1947–1960*. Beer-Sheva, The Ben-Gurion Heritage Center (Hebrew).

Sebba, L. and V. Shiffer (1998). "Education: The case of Ultra-Orthodox Community in Israel," in G. Dougles and L. Sebba. (Eds.). *Children Rights and Traditional Values*. Ashgate: Dartmouth, pp. 160–193.

Segen, N., R. Alon, G. Bar-Eli, G. Gur, N. Shtrasser and I. Weizman (1996). "Privatization and Service Purchasing by the Ministry of Education and Culture," in A. Meir (ed.). *Lines on the Horizon*. Jerusalem: Ministry of Education and Culture, pp. 37–56 (Hebrew).

Shapiro, R. (1989). "Social-Educational Uniqueness: Specialized Schools—Background, Development and Problems," in Ministry of Education and Culture. Planning Education Policy: *Position Paper and Decisions of the Pedagogical Secretariat Permanent Committee*. Jerusalem: Ministry of Education and Culture, pp. 135–174 (Hebrew).

Sheleg, Y. (2000). *The New Religious: Contemporary View of the Religious Society in Israel*. Jerusalem: Keter (Hebrew).

Shiffer, V. (1998). *The Haredi Education in Israel: Allocation, Regulation and Control*. Jerusalem: Floresheimer Institute for Policy Studies (Hebrew).

Shirom, A. (1999). "Formation and Development of Incorporation Policy for Public Hospitals in Israel," in D. Nachmias and G. Menahem (eds.). *Public Policy in Israel*. Jerusalem: The Israeli Institute for Democracy, pp. 327–379 (Hebrew).

State Comptroller, *Annual Report no. 46, 1996*, Jerusalem (Hebrew).

State Comptroller, *Annual Report no. 49, 1998*, Jerusalem (Hebrew).

State Comptroller, *Annual Report no. 47, 1997*, Jerusalem (Hebrew).

State Comptroller, *Annual Report no. 50b, 2000*, Jerusalem (Hebrew).

State Comptroller, *Annual Report no. 51b, 2001*, Jerusalem (Hebrew).

Telias, M., Katan, J. and Gidron, B. (2000). *Local and Central Government Policy Toward The Third Sector in Israel*. Beer Sheva: The Israeli Center for Third Sector Research (Hebrew).

Yishai, Y. (1990). "State and Welfare Groups: Competition or Cooperation? Some Observations on the Israeli Scene," *Non-Profit and Voluntary Sector Quarterly*, 19(3), 215 –235.

Yogev, A. (1999). "Putting the Chaos in Order? Education Policy in Israel in the Post-Modern Era," in D. Nachmias and G. Menachem (eds.). *Public Policy in Israel*. Jerusalem: The Israeli Institute for Democracy, pp. 291–325 (Hebrew).

Young, D. (2000). "Alternative Models of Government-Nonprofit Sector Relations: Theoretical and International Perspectives," *Nonprofit and Voluntary Sector Quarterly*, 29(1), 149–172.

CHAPTER 6

Aharoni, Y. (1998). "The Changing Political Economy of Israel," *ANNALS*, AAPSS, 555, 127–146.

Anheier, H. K. (2000). *The CIVICUS Civil Society Diamond*. London: London School of Economics, Centre for Civil Society.

Arian, A. (1998). *The Second Republic: Politics in Israel*. Chatham, N. J: Chatham House.

Avineri, S. (1996). "The State of Israel between Solidarity and Pluralism," in M. Lissak and B. Knei-Paz (eds.) *Israel Toward the Year 2000—Society, Politics, and Culture*. Jerusalem: Magnes, pp. 394–388 (Hebrew).

Bar, M. (1999). *Organizations of the handicapped or handicapped organizations? The activity of interest groups in the welfare sphere in the process of determining policy regarding regulations on handicapped children*. Masters Thesis, School of Social Work, The Hebrew University of Jerusalem (Hebrew).

Barber, B. R. (1999). "Clansmen, Consumers, and Citizens: Three Takes on Civil Society," in R. K. Fullinwider (Ed.) *Civil Society, Democracy and Civic Renewal*. New York: Rowman and Littlefield, pp. 9–30.

Ben-Aryeh, A. (1999). *Involvement of Members of the 13th Knesset in Welfare issues*. Doctoral Dissertation. Jerusalem: the Hebrew University of Jerusalem (Hebrew).

Ben-Eliezer, A. (1999). "Is a civil society taking shape in Israel? Politics and the Identity of the New Associations," *Israeli Sociology* (1), 51–97 (Hebrew).

Bernstein, D. (1979). "The Black Panthers: Conflicts and Protest in Israeli Society," *Megamot 25*, 65–80 (Hebrew).

Berry, J.M. (1977). *Lobbying for the People*. Princeton: Princeton University Press.

Boris, E. T and Mosher-Williams, R. (1999). "Nonprofit Advocacy Organizations: Assessing the Definitions, Classifications and Data," *Nonprofit and Voluntary Sector Quarterly*, 27(4), 488–506.

Boris, E. T. (1999). "Nonprofit Organizations in a Democracy: Varied Roles and Responsibilities," in E.T. Boris and C.E. Steuerle, *Nonprofit and Government*. Washington: The Urban Institute Press, pp. 3–30.

Cohen, J. and J. Rogers (1993). "Associations and Democracy," *Social Philosophy and Policy* 10(2), 282–312.

Cohen, J. L. (1995). "Interpreting the Notion of Civil Society," in M. Walzer (Ed.) *Toward a Global Civil Society* Oxford: Berghahn.

Cohen, J. L. (1999a). "American Civil Society Talk," in R. K. Fullinwider (Ed.) *Civil Society, Democracy and Civic Renewal*. New York: Rowman and Littlefield, pp. 55–85.

Cohen, J. L. (1999b). "Trust, Voluntary Association and Workable Democracy: The Contemporary American Discourse of Civil Society," in M. E. Warren (Ed.) *Democracy and Trust*. Cambridge: Cambridge University Press, pp. 208–248.

Dahrendorf, R. (1997). *After 1989: Morals, Revolution and Civil Society*. London: Macmillan.

Deri, D. (1992). *Protest, Politics and Policy Innovations: The Struggle of the Homeless* Jerusalem: Jerusalem Institute for Israel Studies (Hebrew).

Edwards, B. and M.W. Foley (1998). "Civil Society and Social Capital beyond Putnam," *American Behavioral Scientist*, 42(1), 124–139.

Eran, Y. (1992). *Voluntary organizations in the welfare system*. Tel-Aviv: Ramot (Hebrew).

Fogel-Bijaoui, S. (1992). "Women's Organizations in Israel—A Snapshot," *International Problems*, 59 (3–4), 65–77 (Hebrew).

Fogel-Bijaoui, S. (1998). "Women and Citizenship in Israel: Analysis of Silencing," *Politika*, 1, 47–71 (Hebrew).

Gal-Noor, Y. (1996). "The Crisis in Israel's Political System: The Parties as a Central Factor," in M. Lissak and B. Knei-Paz (eds.) *Israel Toward the Year 2000—Society, Politics, and Culture*. Jerusalem: Magnes, pp. 144–174 (Hebrew).

Gidron, B. (1997). "Evolution of Israel's Third Sector: The Role of Predominant Ideology," *Voluntas* 8(1), 11–38.

Gidron, B., H. Katz, and M. Bar. *The Third Sector in Israel 2000: The Roles of the Sector*. Beersheva: Ben-Gurion University, the Israeli Center for Third Sector Research.

Helman, S. and T. Rappaport (1997). "They're Ashkenazi Women, Single, Whores of Arabs, Who Don't Believe in God and Don't Love Eretz Israel: 'Women in Black' and the Challenge of the Social Order," *Teoria ve'Bikoret*, 10,175–192 (Hebrew).

Herman, T. (1996). "Do They Have a Chance? Protest and Political Structure of Opportunities," *Israel Studies*, 1(1), 144–170.

Herman, T. (1995). *From the Bottom up: Social Movements and Political Protest* Vol. 1. Tel-Aviv: Open University (Hebrew).

Horowitz, T. and Leshem, A. (1998). "Immigrants from the Former Soviet Union in the Cultural Space in Israel," in M. Sikron and A. Leshem (Eds.). *Portrait of Immigration (Aliya): Absorption Processes of Immigrants from the Former Soviet Union, 1990–1995*. Jerusalem: Magnes, 291–333 (Hebrew).

Horowitz, D. and M. Lissak (1989). *Trouble in Utopia: The Overburdened Polity of Israel.* Albany: State University of New York Press.

James, E. (1997). "Whither the Third Sector? Yesterday, Today and Tomorrow," *Voluntas*, 8(1), 1–10.

Jenkins, J. C. (1987). "Nonprofit Organization and Policy Advocacy," in W.W. Powell (Ed). *The Nonprofit Sector: A Research Handbook.* New Haven: Yale University Press, 296–318.

Kadman, Y. (1992). "The Law for Preventing Abuse of Minors and Dependents—A Turning-Point in Israeli Society's Attitude to Child Abuse," *Bitachon Sociali* 38, 135–146 (Hebrew).

Kimmerling, B. (1995). *Between State and Society: The Sociology of Politics.* Tel-Aviv: Open University (Hebrew).

Knei-Paz, B. (1996). "Israel towards the Year 2000: A Changing World," in M. Lissak and B. Knei-Paz (eds.) *Israel Toward the Year 2000—Society, Politics, and Culture.* Jerusalem: Magnes, pp. 408–427 (Hebrew).

Kramer, R. M. (1981). *Voluntary Agencies in the Welfare State.* Berkeley: University of California Press.

Kramer, R. (1988). "The Changing Role of Voluntary Agencies in the Welfare State," *Hevra u'Revacha*, 9, 121–127 (Hebrew).

Lehman-Wilzig, S. (1992). *Public Protest in Israel 1949–1992.* Ramat-Gan: Bar-Ilan (Hebrew).

Lehman-Wilzig, S. (1999). "Israeli Democracy: How Democratic? How Liberal?" in R. Cohen-Almagor (Ed.), *Basic Issues in Israeli Democracy.* Tel-Aviv: Sifriat Poalim, pp. 265–284 (Hebrew).

Lissak, M. (1998). "The Decline of the Political Parties and the Resurgence of Sectorialism," in D. Koren (ed.) *The Decline of Political Parties: The Israeli Democracy in Distress* Tel Aviv, Hakibutz Hame'uchad, pp. 129–140 (Hebrew).

Lyons, M. (1996). *Nonprofit Sector or Civil Society: are they Competing Paradigms?* Paper presented at the biennial Conference of Australian and New Zealand Third Sector Research, Wellington.

Nachmias, D. and A.Sand (1999). "Governance and Public Policy," in D. Nachmias and G. Menachem, (Eds.). *Public Policy in Israel* Jerusalem: the Israeli Institute for Democracy, 11–34 (Hebrew).

Putnam, R. D. (1993). *Making Democracy Work.* Princeton: Princeton University Press.

Putnam, R. D. (2000). *Bowling Alone: The Collapse and Revival of American Community.* New York: Simon and Schuster.

Ramon. M. (1997). *Guide to the Self-Help Organizations in Israel.* Tel-Aviv: the Israeli Center for Self-Help (Hebrew).

Reid, E. J. (1999). "Nonprofit Advocacy and Political Participation," in E.T. Boris and C. E. Steuerle *Nonprofit and Government.* Washington: The Urban Institute Press.

Salamon, L. M. (1995). *Partners in Public Service: Government-Nonprofit Relations in the Modern Welfare State.* Baltimore: Johns Hopkins University Press.

Smooha, S. (1999). "Changes in Israeli Society—Fifty Years On," *Alpayim*, 17, 239–261 (Hebrew).

Sasson-Levy, A. (1995). *Awareness of Revolutionaries—Identity of Conformists: The Protest Movement The 21st century* Jerusalem: The Shein Center for Social Science Research, Hebrew University of Jerusalem (Hebrew).

Scoff, R. and D. R. Stevenson (1998). *The National Taxonomy of Exempt Entities Manual.* Washington: Urban Institute.

Shye, S., A.Lazar, R.Duchin, and B.Gidron (1999). *Philanthropy in Israel: Patterns of Giving and Volunteering by the Israeli Public* Beersheva: Ben-Gurion University, The Israeli Center for Third Sector Research.

Smith, S. R. and M.Lipsky (1993.) *Nonprofits for Hire.* Cambridge: Harvard University Press.

Trentman, F. (2000). *Paradoxes of Civil Society: New Perspectives on Modern German and British History.* New York: Berghahn.

Walzer, M. (1995). "The Concept of Civil Society," in M. Walzer (Ed.) *Toward a Global Civil Society.* Oxford: Berghahn.

Wolfsfeld, G. (1988). *The Politics of Provocation: Participation and Protest in Israel.* New York: State University of New York Press.

Ya'ar-Yuchtman, E. (1998). "Political Parties and the Public's Trust," in D. Koren (ed.) *The Decline of Political Parties: The Israeli Democracy in Distress* Tel Aviv, Hakibutz Hame'uchad, pp. 224–242 (Hebrew).

Yishai, Y. (1999). "Democracy for the People? Determining Welfare Policy in Israel," *Bitachon Sociali*, 56, 126–137 (Hebrew).

Yishai, Y. (2001). "Civil Society: A Divisive or Unifying Factor?" Paper presented at the *Conference on the Civil Society in Israel*. The Israeli Center for Third Sector Research, Ben-Gurion University, March.

Yishai, Y. (1998). *Civil Society in Israel Towards the 21st Century—Between Society and State*. Jerusalem: Paul Baerwald School of Social Work, the Hebrew University of Jerusalem (Hebrew).

Zalmanovich, Y. (1998). "Transitions in Israel's Policymaking Network," *ANNALS*, AAPSS 555, 193–208.

Zeidan, E. and A. Ghanem, (2000). *Giving and Volunteering in Palestinian-Arab Society in Israel*. Beersheva: The Israeli Center for Third Sector Research, Ben-Gurion University of the Negev.

CHAPTER 7

Akzin, B. (1955). *The Role of Parties in Israeli Democracy*. Gainesville, FL.

Arian, A. (1972). *The Elections in Israel, 1969*. Jerusalem: Academic Press.

Ben-Eliezer, A. (1999). "Is a Civil Society Taking Shape in Israel? Politics and the Identity of the New Associations." *Israeli Sociology* (1), 51–97 (Hebrew).

Doron, A. and R. M. Kramer (1992). *The Israeli Welfare State*. Tel-Aviv: Am-Oved (Hebrew).

Elazar, D. (1986). *Israel: Building a New Society*, Bloomington: Indiana University Press.

Esping-Andersen, G. (1990). *The Three Worlds of Welfare Capitalism*. Cambridge: Polity Press.

Foley, M. W. and B. Edwards (1996). "The Paradox of Civil Society," *Journal of Democracy* 7(3), 38–52.

Galnoor, I. (1982). "The Israeli Democracy and Social Participation," *Molad*, 41, 71–87 (Hebrew).

Hansmann, H. (1987). "Economic Theories of Nonprofit Organizations", in W. W. Powell (Ed.) *The Nonprofit Sector: A Research Handbook*. New Haven: Yale University Press, 27–42.

James, E. (1987). "The Nonprofit Sector in Comparative Perspective," in W. W. Powell (Ed.) *The Nonprofit Sector: A Research Handbook*. New Haven: Yale University Press, 397–415.

Kramer, R. (1976). *The Voluntary Service Agency in Israel*. Berkeley: Institute of International Studies, University of California.

Putnam, R. D. (1993). *Making Democracy Work*. Princeton: Princeton University Press.

Putnam, R. D. (2000). *Bowling Alone: The Collapse and Revival of American Community*. New York: Simon and Schuster.

Smith, D. H. (2000). *Grassroots Associations*. Sage Publications.

Salamon, L. and H. K. Anheier (1998). "Social Origins of Civil Society: Explaining the Nonprofit Sector Cross-Nationally," *Voluntas*, 9(3), 213–248.

Weisbrod, B. A. (1977). *The Voluntary Nonprofit Sector*. Lexington: Lexington Books.

Yishai, Y. (1987). *Interest Groups in Israel*, Tel Aviv, Am Oved (Hebrew).

Yishai, Y. (1990). "State and Welfare Groups: Competition or Cooperation? Some Observations on the Israeli Scene," *Non-Profit and Voluntary Sector Quarterly*, 19(3), 215 –235.

Yishai, Y. (1998). *Civil Society in Israel towards the 21st Century – Between Society and State*. Jerusalem: Paul Baerwald School of Social Work, the Hebrew University of Jerusalem (Hebrew).

Yishai, Y. (1999). "Democracy for the People? Determining Welfare Policy in Israel." *Bitachon Sociali*, 56, 126–137 (Hebrew).

Glossary

Agudat Yisrael.   A political party. Founded in 1912 and represents the interests of the "ultra-Orthodox" population (mostly Ashkenazi) in Israeli politics since 1948. It is steered by a council of religious sages. Controls the orthodox independent educational system.

Amuta/Amutot.   The Israeli term for a non-profit organization/association. The term comes for the word *Amit* (friend/colleague) denoting a friendly association.

Ashkenazi.   The term used for Jews who derive from Europe (excluding most countries in the Mediterranean Basin) and who generally follow the customs originating in medieval German Judaism.

Basic Law.   Israel has no constitution. Instead, it has a number of foundational laws, intended to eventually form a constitution.

British mandate.   After the Ottoman (Turkish) Empire was defeated in WWI, the British controlled Palestine. In July 1922, the League of Nations entrusted Great Britain with the "Mandate for Palestine", until its termination by the UN resolution of the Partition of Palestine (1947), which led to the withdrawal of the British forces the following year and the establishment of the state of Israel.

David Ben Gurion.   (1886–1973) Founder of the Histadrut and founder and leader of Mapai political party. First prime minister of Israel who deeply influenced the way the country was governed during the first two decades of independence.

Eretz Yisrael.   The Land of Israel, the Hebrew term for the geographic entity known since Roman times as Palestine.

Haredi.   Ultra-Orthodox Jews in Israel.

Ha-Vaad Ha-Leumi (The National Committee).   The governing body, organized by the Jewish Agency of the Jewish community during the British Mandate. All Zionist factions were represented in it.

Histadrut.   The Federation of Jewish Labor Unions, founded in 1920. It comprised of various labor and professional associations. It owned services such as the Klalit Health Fund, Mish'an—homes for the elderly and, Amal vocational education schools, as well as businesses such as Bank Hapoalim—the workers' bank; Shikun Ovdim and Solel Bone—building and contracting companies, and a military organization (Haganah).

Intifada.   a Palestinian popular uprising. The first one was between December 1987 and September 1993, and the second started in September 2000.

Keren Hayesod.   Jewish Foundation Fund (JFF)—The financial arm of the World Zionist Organization founded in 1920. Collected donations from Jewish communities in the US and worldwide.

Knesset.   The Israeli parliament, the 120 Knesset members (MKs) are elected every 4 years.

Kolelim.   A Jewish rabbinic academy of continuing and adult learning.

Kupat/Kupot Holim.   Health funds—health insurance and service organizations similar to US HMOs; sometimes referred to as "sick funds" which is a translation of the concept from German (Krankenkasse).

Mapai.   Mifleget Poalei Eretz Yisrael—Land of Israel Worker's Party, established 1930, a Zionist-socialist party. Served as the dominant political party in the pre-state and early years since independence. Mapai led every coalition and was the Prime Minister's party from 1948 until it merged with another socialist party into the Labor alignment in 1968.

Mapam.   (United Workers' Party) A socialist-Zionist party, left of Mapai; was the second largest political party in the early years of the State.

Mizrahi.   Religious Zionist movement founded in 1902 to encourage Zionism among religious Jews and promote religious and cultural ideas among its constituents

Mizrahi (adjective).   Jews stemming from countries in the Middle East and North Africa; non-Ashkenazi

"National Institutions".   A general term for the pre-state governing institutions in Palestine representing the Jewish Community and working on its behalf, including the JFF, the Jewish Agency, The Jewish National Fund, etc.

National Insurance Institute (NII).   Israel's social security agency, the principal vehicle for transfer payments, both on a universal and on an entitlement basis. Established 1953. Since 1995 also collects the national health tax and transfers it to the health funds.

Shas.   A Mizrahi orthodox religious party, with its own council of religious sages. It entered Israeli politics in 1984, and gradually increased in political clout. In the 1999 election it won 17 Knesset seats and was the third largest party in the parliament. Has its own educational system—Ma'ayan Ha-Hinuch Ha-Torani, and several educational and welfare networks.

The American Jewish Joint Distribution Committee ("The Joint", JDC). Established 1914. Its mission is to serve the needs of Jews throughout the world, through financing and provision of social services.

The Jewish Agency.   Established 1929 as the formal representative of the Jewish community vis-à-vis the British mandatory government. It gradually acquired the attributes of a proto-government for the Jewish community.

Waqf.   Muslim Charitable religious endowment of funds or real estate.

World Zionist Organization.   The central organization of the world Zionist movement, founded by Theodor Herzl at the First Zionist Congress in Basle in 1897.

Yeshiva/yeshivot.   A Jewish rabbinic academy of higher learning.

Yishuv.   The Jewish community of Palestine. The pre-Zionist community is generally designated the "Old Yishuv," and the community evolving since the 1880's the "New Yishuv."

Index